ALONE AND WITH OTHERS

Murray Melbin

Alone and With Others

A GRAMMAR OF

INTERPERSONAL BEHAVIOR

HARPER & ROW, PUBLISHERS

NEW YORK, EVANSTON, SAN FRANCISCO, LONDON

1817

FIRST EDITION

STANDARD BOOK NUMBER: 06-012927-1

LIBRARY OF CONGRESS CATALOG CARD NUMBER: 73-83613

In memory of my mother   Anna Boiucaner Melbin

Contents

⸙

Tables, Figures, and Matrices

Thanks

" . . . the habit of communicating our ideas, our observations, and our way of thinking to each other, has established between us a sort of community of opinions in which it is often difficult for every one to know his own."—Lavoisier

Mohammed T. Tayyabkhan, Leonard S. Cottrell, Jr., Virginia Hilu, Alan J. Horowitz, Jonathan Jenness, Lawrence B. Katz, J. Rolf Kjolseth, Nina Frank Melbin, Gerald M. Platt, David Sirota, William F. Soskin, Julia C. Spring, Alfred H. Stanton, Edward A. Tiryakian, Robert N. Wilson, and my students at Harvard and at Boston University.

Russell Sage Foundation for a postdoctoral residency fellowship, National Science Foundation for grant G10919, National Institute of Mental Health for grant M-5702(A), and the Grant Foundation for two summer fellowships at the University of Colorado.

I also thank this book for the zest of writing it. Its content is far from what I planned. Composing its pages was a discovery, and only then I realized I was writing *this* book.

ALONE AND WITH OTHERS

1

Introduction

Mr. Juggins, the hero of Stephen Leacock's allegory on infinite regression, once interfered on a camping trip to help someone nail a board onto a tree for a shelf.

"Stop a minute," he said, "you need to saw the end of the board off before you put it up." Then Juggins looked around for a saw, and when he got it he had hardly made more than a stroke or two with it before he stopped. "This saw," he said, "needs to be filed up a bit." So he went and hunted up a file to sharpen the saw, but found that before he could use the file he needed to put a proper handle on it, and to make a handle he went to look for a sapling in the bush, but to cut the sapling he found that he needed to sharpen up the axe. To do this, of course, he had to fix the grindstone so as to make it run properly. . . . This was quite impossible without a better set of tools. Juggins went to the village to get the tools required, and, of course, he never came back. He was rediscovered—weeks later—in the city, getting prices on wholesale tool machinery.*

A thorough study of interpersonal behavior can be equally retroactive. Review the assumptions needed to understand the action of one person toward another, and you will find that they interlock. A modest resolution of one ends in the midst of several others. Each assumption, once uncovered, hints at more basic ones. There is danger of being drawn into an epistemological vortex toward Mr. Juggins's fate, who

passed back through childhood into infancy, and presently just as his annuity runs to a point and vanishes, he will back up clear through the Curtain of Existence and die—or be born. . . .

* References begin on page 317.

1

One reason that interpersonal behavior is hard to study and systematically understand is that the venture involves direct attention to ourselves and to others like us. We are limited by people's rights to privacy. When access for study is granted, spells of self-consciousness interfere with what would happen naturally. There are also attributes of social conduct itself that add to the difficulty. Behavior is transient. Until recently we did not have the means of catching and fixing a specimen of it for leisurely study. Even now we can only snare and hold on to those dimensions of interpersonal behavior that are seen and heard. There is more involved in human interaction. Interpersonal acts are also brief. Some stream by so rapidly that we dwell more upon them in retrospect rather than perceive them fully in their moment. It is an awesome quality of an act that its spark, having been momentarily struck, may go out quickly and leave people fumbling for a long time with its consequences and probing the past for clues to its cause.

The greatest difficulty in studying behavior is that it is complicated. Although a realm of apparent familiarity, the interpersonal act has resisted adequate definition. Its vast scope and variety as well as its complexity has made it intractable to study. Of course, there has been much research on the topic. This includes anthropological explorations, field surveys, observations of small groups, and laboratory experiments. Sometimes the nature of behavior is taken for granted, and it is studied for its causes or for its effects or for its relevance to human personality or to large-scale social systems. Some students address themselves to measuring social interaction itself. Others go beyond this, formulating issues that a theory of behavior must resolve, and ask "What is the act as people understand it?"

This book is the result of one such venture. I will deal with several topics concerning social conduct: the description of acts, their interpretation, and their causes. These do not exhaust the variety of topics. Yet they are some of the most vital ones. I settled on them after reviewing many ideas that have accumulated about the subject matter. The science of interpersonal behavior is in an early stage of inquiry. It is a time for disciplined innocence in research. In my attempt to describe and interpret how people act with one another in everyday matters, I found I could not rely on some of the traditional beliefs about social interaction. I will devote a portion of these introductory remarks to assumptions I could not accept and have found hindering. They are popular fallacies. Others may not believe that they are fallacies, but a review of the literature of this field will readily confirm that they are popular.

Popular Fallacies

A direct connection is often assumed between an interpersonal act and some other process—either its cause, its effect, its function, or its meaning. This happens because social conduct is often studied indirectly or with great attention to its significance for other matters. Some writers seem to forget that they are not describing interpersonal behavior when they treat attitudes, needs, norms, or values. The topic in those instances has been turned inside out. Behavior is camouflaged by the entrails of motives and the tissues of social rules. My criticism is directed equally to reliance on systems of personality and on systems of society. It is not feasible to use just one set of terms and concepts to refer both to aspects of personality structure or social structure and to overt actions.

Categories employed to describe an act sometimes baldly posit an identity between the event and its cause. For example, the distinction between *voluntary* and *involuntary* behavior is a supposition about cause. Labeling behavior *expressive* or *instrumental* assumes one can guess the goals of action from the action. To call an act *compulsive* or *impulsive* does not tell what a person does. It implies what the labeler would have us believe gave rise to whatever it was that he does. By the same token, one cannot rely on such shadow indicators as values or norms or ideologies as representatives of behavior. Behavior results from many influences. It is not easy to unravel the act pattern and discern what ideology prompted it. It is also hard to decide with confidence what are the dominant values of a social group. A careful inquiry uncovers contradictions and lack of consensus. Dominant values do influence behavior just as behavior influences ideas and values, but the two are not so nearly congruent that the study of one will do for the study of both.

The elementary rules of scientific procedure include a taboo about marrying answers to questions in research. It follows that if one aims to discover the conditions under which certain categories of action occur, then the classification of those acts must be free of assumed causal conditions. Similarly, tying an act to its consequences by definition precludes the open-minded study of possible consequences. Yet some writers refer directly to the rewards of certain actions for an individual or to solidarity-enhancing functions of certain actions for a group. Descriptive categories of behavior that embody such assumptions smuggle in answers to the questions that should be asked about the effects of acts. If behavior may have one of several effects, and if behavior is tied to one of the outcomes by definition, the issue of its effects may no longer be studied impartially. So, independent definitions and measurements are precious. If not, the categories will saddle one's research with handicaps to insight. The researcher may become insensitive to certain events, seeing what he is well prepared to see and being unable to recognize or interpret unexpected outcomes. We know how easily one can assemble data to suit a favored outlook. We know how readily someone with a hypothesis seeks confirming evidence and recognizes its confirmations while remaining oblivious to contradicting events.

The intellectual origin of seeking to interpret an event according to its consequence for an organism or a social system that produced it is Darwin's brilliant hypothesis of natural selection according to fitness as the basis of the origin of species. Is not some useful function therefore implied by every persisting pattern, including behavior? The answer is no, because of two relevant qualifiers of the hypothesis of evolution. One is that *harmful or neutral* genes may be preserved in the gene pool of a species as long as the overall adaptation remains advantageous. The other is that behavior is often the first step for initiating a modification of the species, but the act is not initially caused by the gene with which it may prove to be compatible. A mutation may occur that has no effect as long as the creatures carrying it do not engage in behavior that brings home its benefits. When such acts occur, a selective advantage may then be conferred upon that subgroup. It begins to result in relatively more prolific reproduction, greater representation of that mutant type in the population, and finally the establishment of that gene in the pool of the species.

Similar qualifications apply to understanding the causes and consequences of interpersonal behavior:

1. An act does not uniquely indicate its cause. There may be several possible independent reasons for the event. Goffman gives the example of persons with handicaps who try to conceal them. A near-blind person who bumps into furniture or trips over objects as he tries to act as if he can see may be judged clumsy; a deaf person who does not respond to remarks made to him may be judged inattentive. Neither clumsiness or inattentiveness is the cause of these acts.

2. An act does not uniquely indicate its consequences. What are the

outcomes of gestures of goodwill and gestures of anger? Pleasure and pain are not distinct consequences of pleasantness and nastiness. The friendly attentions of a man to a woman could cause pain and unease. The lady's husband may be pained. The man's wife may be uneasy. If neither is married but the man is drunk, the recipient of flattery may be disquieted. Often the practice of venting feelings points to relationships with built-in safety valves rather than to occasions of interpersonal discord. Much irritation is expressed in a marriage. Such blowing off steam may avoid the more severe consequences that could follow if catharsis were blocked. Observers of the military scene recognize a similar function in much of soldiers' griping. Also, the same declaration that raises the morale of one faction in an argument may simultaneously prompt despair or hostility in other hearers. One can no more assume that an act has an inevitable outcome than one can say that hens lay omelettes.

3. The meaning of an act is not inherent in it. For example, pleasure and pain may be conveyed by conduct that is neutral in its overt form. A supervisor who matter-of-factly orders a subordinate to carry out a certain task may please the latter immensely if the task is important, thereby connoting trust or esteem for his ability. A petty bureaucrat in the payroll office of a company may destroy the serenity of whoever comes into contact with him by impersonally requesting adherence to every rule in his officialdom—returning forms not completely filled out, deducting taxes even when a cash advance is made, creating a delay by phoning to verify an authorization, waiting for a signed receipt before dispensing the money. Another man may convey an emotional message by not speaking to an acquaintance when passing or by avoiding contact when the two are at the same meeting. Thus *absence* of overt expression can be expressive. It makes methodological sense to separate the description of an act from its potential interpretations.

This separation of cause, consequence, and meaning from the event itself has useful implications in the study of behavior. It permits the possibility of multiple causes, of alternative causes, of multiple meaning, of alternative meaning, of multiple effects, and of alternative effects. It permits justice to be done to the wide variety of tactics humans employ to help or to hurt one another. It allows for the broad range of meanings that are conveyed in social communication.

A related, venerable assumption that still appears in writings on interpersonal behavior is that overt expressions of feeling reflect people's inner states directly. Darwin conducted research on this proposition too, under-taking "to determine which movements and features of the body commonly characterized certain states of the mind." This project followed from his thesis that the several races of man were descended from a single parent stock. Hence—their constitutions being the same—the actions of people in many lands should show universal patterns. He gathered much evidence about behavior throughout the world and was forced to recognize from his catalog of descriptions and anecdotal reports that there was considerable diversity in the moods signified by the same forms. A blush might reflect shyness or rage; a wrinkled brow might be a sign of ill temper or of deep thought. He concluded that the human constitution and its nervous system are influential in shaping many expressions but that they are not a pure and simple source of them.

In the first half of this century, a similar doctrine was endorsed in social-psychological study. Called isomorphism, it assumed an identity point-for-point between a person's internal state and his behavior. There is no room in such a tight linkage for a mock scream meant as a joke or for a smile on the face of a person who is emotionally upset. People often disguise inner sadness with happy visages. Almost anyone—not only the emotionally ill—may feign euphoria when severely troubled. A cordial smile may represent pleasure or mask simmering hostility. Even animals dissemble. A bird will fake a broken wing, staggering and dragging it along the ground to lure a predator away from a nest filled with young. Knowing that others interpret overt behavior to represent motives, people often act deliberately to convey certain impressions and studiously monitor the cues they provide for this end.

Asch rejected the pure position of isomorphism and suggested that persons who stand on common ground psychologically would recognize each other's internal states from the overt cues, while an outsider might not. A glum look, for example, might signify a private joke between two friends. An onlooker relying on no more than he could observe would not think so. Inasmuch as the scientific study of interpersonal behavior will bring researchers to places where they are not fully informed about rela-tions among persons, it is possible to agree on what a person did while disagreeing over what his action meant. The primary task in the study of conduct is description without interpretation.

It is curious to realize now uncharted is the immediate realm in which two or more people interact with one another. The presuppositions about the direct links between acts and their causes and consequences and meanings are entrenched and respectable, and many of them are uncritically used though they are not supported by more careful analysis. History makes it clear that the length of time an idea has persisted and has been accepted is inadequate evidence for its scientific utility.

In this book I have submitted several long-unquestioned doctrines to review as well as attended to current controversies. If I found a notion obscure or internally difficult, I tried to avoid that notion as a basis for description or explanation. Sometimes I have suggested an alternative formula. Sometimes I have identified the problem without resolving it. The most difficult part was to master questions to be asked. It is more important and often harder to identify a useful question about one's subject matter than to find an answer for it.

An Approach to the Study of Acts

Where should one start the study of interpersonal behavior? What is an interpersonal act? How does it begin? When does it end? How can one act be distinguished from another? What gives it its meaning? How is it known and understood by persons exposed to it? What *are* the acts of a given social relationship? What kinds? How many? Which are the most frequent?

These topics guide my inquiry and discussion. In Part One I offer some basic definitions and assumptions. In Part Two I describe a research program to assemble facts about social conduct. Such facts become the basis for testing assumptions and for learning more about the subject matter. Accordingly, in Part Three I apply the ideas to the data of a case study. The findings permit me to clarify earlier propositions and prompt some revisions. In Part Four I treat some related topics in behavior, such as its multiple causes and the problem of cross-cultural comparisons.

My essay is an overture to a particular line of study. Description of interpersonal behavior is its first goal. We know that neither personality structures nor societies literally interact. Individuals do. The moment of that interpersonal meeting brings the several systems together. So action, rather than needs, values, attitudes, or norms, deserves primary regard. In this early exploration I keep in touch with observations and trace the noticeable processes that compose interpersonal acts.

Another basic rule in understanding a social relationship is to get facts about all that goes on. In gathering information no portion of behavior should be ignored. One may wonder why not focus on important events alone, for which the remainder of social conduct is interstitial. In a letter to me about my work, a colleague asked why I found it necessary to develop a general classification of interpersonal behaviors before determining which of them are in fact related to certain interests. My reply was that I sought a method that was not tailored to a given hypothesis about cause or effect. I did not know at first which aspects of behavior were significant or central. Of course it helps to focus on important acts. But which are the important ones? We do not know in advance. To be selective early in research risks ignoring what may later prove to be important. What is crucial may be so subtle or so common that it is easily overlooked. For example, human oxygen intake is terribly important. Yet it is both omnipresent and un-noticed. Behavior may deliver its precious cargo unobtrusively too.

Truly we do not know the facts. We do not know comprehensively what mothers do, what managers do, what friends do with one another. Most research on interpersonal behavior has been focused on the fascinating or controversial episodes. Too little effort has been made *to learn about the set from which this dramatic conduct comes.* When knowledge of that set is vague, we cannot say whether a striking incident is rare or habitual or whether it is exceeded in its wonder or importance by other practices. Contradictions between research findings are also easy to incur and pre-serve when the background population is unknown. On the other hand, if we clearly define the sets of acts from which findings are drawn, we may discover that incompatible findings refer to two different—albeit closely related—aggregates and are therefore not true contradictions. The student who curbs his prejudice and addresses himself to whatever has been assembled in a systematic survey will learn from the trivial as well as the dramatic. He will come across neglected but significant classes of behavior.

The facts themselves when soundly arranged may make heretofore puzzling questions irrelevant and point in new directions to vital issues. Such a program is not based on a cult of aimlessness or on unswerving faith in serendipity. It is an attempt to preserve neutrality concerning ques-tions about the meanings of different acts, their causes and their effects. The data collected without bias become a store of information to be drawn on for diverse purposes. Actions considered irrelevant to one issue would still be available for use at another time for other questions, some of them unforeseen by the data collector. Barker and Wright argue this too:

Some will say that theoretically neutral data do not exist, that data are good or bad only in relation to the questions asked by a particular investigator and that without specific theoretical guides data collection becomes blind.

With this we do not entirely agree. Data have other values than their relevance to a single theory or problem . . . the directly perceived action is the starting place of much theory construction, and is the final testing ground of important phases of theoretical systems. While it may readily be granted that science should leave the surface of behavior and achieve a more basic and inclusive reality, this deeper understanding must, nevertheless, begin and end at the surface.

I will try to develop a single method to describe and measure interpersonal behavior wherever it is found. It should be applicable to studying any social situation. It should not be fitted closely to concerns about leadership or problem-solving or love or social change. A measurement that stands by itself can serve a spectrum of theoretical and practical interests rather than be ruled by the notions of one. In such an approach a ready place will be found for many of the variables and issues currently of interest to social scientists.

In trying to establish such a measure, I have been led to conclude that a person's overt conduct can be summarized by the same formula whether he acts in private or in the company of his fellows. A single descriptive scheme can be used for the behavior of a person alone and for the aggregate of individuals interacting in a group, hence the title of this book.

Earlier I said that one should clearly separate descriptions of an act from assumptions about the forces that influence it. I will try to minimize interpretations in my procedures for data collection and systematic description (Part Two). But to some extent an effective description carries in its makeup some potential explanation. Attention to observable conditions under which acts occur becomes one vantage for explaining behavior. Although such accounts are modest compared to those that imply causes or consequences in their descriptive categories, these sketches avoid premature commitment. They are not presumptive but empirical.

What needs to be explained? I distinguish between the instigation of an act and its specific form. An act may be thought of as the result of factors that spur it and factors that shape it. The former refers to precipitators, goads, and implies the question "How come anything happens at all?" I pass over that question in this essay. I am not concerned with behavioral arousal. I assume that where there is life there is energy expended. A living person is always behaving. Instead I seek to explain how conduct is channeled in some ways rather than in others.

The third main topic, along with description and explanation, is the interpretation of behavior. People encounter one another. Through some extraordinary procedure they convey messages. These messages are perceived and understood. We might say that meaningful communication takes place. Usually we cannot tell whether the message received was the one intended. Nor does one person's understanding signify that others share it. It may not matter, for there are many misses and mysteries present in encounters, and yet social life goes on. Inasmuch as descriptions of conduct may carry some of its meanings, I will try to show how to identify these meanings.

A Grammar for Behavior

Grammar traditionally refers to verbal speech or its written form. It is variously defined as a study of the architecture of language, the way in which sentences are constructed, or a set of rules capable of generating sentences correctly. In connection with semantics, grammar sometimes identifies the study of the relation between language form and proper meaning. A grammar is also a treatment of the elements of any subject. These connotations are significant in developing a grammar for behavior.

Just as speech is "a structured scheme of oral communication," behavior repertoires are structured systems of gestural communication, verbal and other, used by persons in social relationships. Because it has properties that repeat themselves and can be recognized, behavior is an objective phenomenon. It has form. It has discoverable rules of organization. It has meanings embodied in its form. The rules of organizing behavior into acts are behavior's syntax. The meaningful embodiment is its semantic structure. Therefore, behavior can be treated descriptively and analyzed for these aspects. The similarities and the aims—describing structure, deriving meaning, and predicting the course of interpersonal behavior—make the term *grammar* appropriate for this essay. But although I have benefited from some understanding and application of principles of dealing with grammars of language, I do not always use those ideas in the same way. I do not use the entire set of them, nor do I rely solely on principles from those systems.

The similarity between language grammars and behavior grammars is partly given by the structure of interpersonal conduct. An act of one person stimulates one or more sense receptors of at least one other. There is even the case of an act that provides zero change in stimulation, as I will show. Elements of behavior are used alone or compounded in use. Simple and compound acts, sets of reactions commonly used in given social situations, and their differential frequencies of occurrence in social relationships are all part of the morphology of action.

Another similarity is based on subsuming speech and other types of conduct under a general theory of communication. The mathematical study of communication refers as much to what messages can be produced as to which are produced. In speech, for example, the message uttered has been selected from a set of possible alternatives. In the same way, to understand the workings of a behavioral system, one must deal with known possibilities as well as with actual events. What does occur is part of the larger set of possible happenings just as what is said is part of a larger set of possible utterances. The format of behavioral description should encompass both the actual and the possible.

I will explore this area for a semantic component of action too. Knowledge of both the actual and the possible can be the foundation of a technique for deriving connotations of conduct and for meaningful assays of social relationships.

Thus I use the idea of a grammar to give perspective to interpersonal behavior. It covers the structure of acts, some rules by which acts unfold, and the way in which the significance of acts may be found. Many solutions to these issues in turn engender questions that call for more research. For the sake of continuity, I will direct attention to some promising trails.

PART ONE

Basic Ideas

2

Sensations

Having distinguished an act from assumptions about its causes and effects, an act's description should begin with its observables. An act has properties of its own. All interpretations of behavior, whether the sophisticated diagnoses of a clinician or the snap judgments of a layman, begin with and are based upon categorizing its outward cues. These cues are noticeable muscle movements, patterns of sound, and touch and pressure and smell and heat and taste. An individual learns through his receptors that an act has occurred. Therefore, it is proper to take sensory access as the initial condition of social opportunities. An interpersonal situation occurs any time two or more persons have sensory access to one another.

All interpersonal acts, all the gestures by which messages may be conveyed, depend on being gathered in by receptors. Sensory access is required, and interpersonal behavior is *overt action between two or more people in sensory access*. Interpersonal acts take place only under such a condition. All parties must have access to one another directly and simultaneously, though not necessarily through the same modes. Telephone conversations are included here, but written correspondence—because of the intermediaries required—is not. Similarly, voting in an election is not interpersonal if the secret ballot is used, whereas the conduct of a town meeting is. Dissemination of news by way of radio and television is not interpersonal because the sensory access is unidirectional.

Suppose an observer notes that two individuals have mutual access to each other. Is he justified in assuming that they are aware of it? The observer must suppose that a living person is responding to his environment, including the people in it, if he is not sensorily impaired. This is a plausible assumption, for even the criterion of awareness may be misleading. Studies of subliminal perception have shown that people respond to stimuli that they are not conscious of perceiving. (Abrahamson) Therefore, if a man is observed to have sensory access to another, we must describe the man's conduct as interpersonal. It does not matter whether or not he knows the others to whom he responds. The event is still observable. All of us on some occasions are unaware of others to whom we have access; for example, we might not know that they are within earshot. Yet even without realizing this, we reach their receptors.

Humans employ seven main reception channels interpersonally: vision, hearing, smell, touch, pressure, temperature, and taste. The various channels differ in their effectiveness over physical distance. They can be ranked according to the distance over which they permit access to a person. The most distantly effective mode is vision, followed by hearing and then probably smell, touch, temperature, pressure, and taste.

It is possible for the effectiveness of sensory modes over distance to undergo some reordering of rank in different environments. Sometimes hearing is more distantly effective than vision. Persons in the forest or jungle can converse over greater lengths than they can see one another. It is common to lose sight of one's fellows in a line of march, the man in front disappearing among the foliage no more than six feet ahead. Shooting tragedies on hunting trips sometimes occur because men succumb to this limitation and fire at sounds without confirming the nature of their target by sight. Breezes may make olfactory senses more distantly effective than they are normally. Stiff winds at other angles can make them less effective than touch or pressure.

The degree to which receptors are stimulated in receiving behavior information from others is called *sensory utilization*. Since the stimulation of particular receptors depends upon the nature of the act, use of these routes is also a part of meaningful communication. Messages can be measured objectively and interpreted more precisely by noting the sensory channels utilized.

Sensory Distance and Social Distance

Even when all the channels are at the disposal of persons who are interacting, there is an orderly progression in the frequency of their use and in the combinations that are utilized for messages. The more distantly effective the mode, the more universal and more frequent its use. Vision is man's most used mode. It happens that about two-thirds of all the nerve fibers leading from sense organs to the central nervous system come from the eyes. The proximal receptors are used less often and less generally. We see many more people than we touch; we touch many more people than we taste. Thus there is a hierarchy in the use of sensory channels in interaction. The pattern of use is a clue to the nature of relationships between individuals.

Beginning with the most distantly effective and universally used channels, here is an outline of the progression to social intimacy:

1. A person's vision makes him accessible to others at a great physical distance. Socially he is also the most generally accessible by this channel. The sight mode is used for the most superficial contacts between people. In public places people are in visual range of one another, and interaction based on seeing can occur between people who do not know each other personally. Social distance is greatest among those who do not proceed beyond this mode in their encounters. In subways, buses, or other public transportation where people face one another while traveling, individuals seek out and stare at a neutral region, avoiding eye contacts with strangers.

Under some conditions strangers passing one another on the street may nod and smile. People who perceive that they share some common interest, common social status, or common property often nod or wave in passing one another. Mothers with baby carriages in the park do it. Owners of certain automobiles do it. On the East Coast of the United States, surfboarders who notice surfboards tied to the tops of other automobiles do it. At a lake where I spent several summers, people acted as if they were acquaintances by waving as they traveled past each other in their boats.

2. A person is next most accessible as he comes within earshot. Social contacts via spoken sound are more focused and more personal than by visual contact. The combination of visual and auditory access to another person is typical of a broad range of casual contacts (for example, persons on the street who ask others for directions) and of formal relationships (for example, job applicants who interact with members of a personnel office).

Although it should be casual, there are situations in which the transition from visual to auditory communication is experienced with some trepidation. In a restaurant some diners try to catch their waiter's eye rather than call to him, and will forego the mustard or delay eating if they. do not have a fork, because use of the auditory channel would establish contact with other diners toward whom the call was not directed. Uneasiness descends upon some young men who gaze at and even smile at girls at social dances but cannot bring themselves to speak to them. Adding auditory contact to visual contact is a great advance in the potential for a relationship. That is the serial order followed. A boy trying to meet a girl begins by talking to her rather than pinching her, almost all of the time.

3. Smell is next in order of distal effectiveness. Humans smell much more actively and widely than most people realize. We are usually unaware of it because variety in the strengths of odors is restricted by dietary habits and hygienic practices. Members of the same culture usually eat similar foods and follow similar habits of cleanliness and adapt to the narrowed range of odors that results. This decrement in olfactory sensitivity is over-looked until one meets someone who has a distinctly deviant odor. In our culture the most common source of deviant odors, that of perfumes used by women, is an approved one, indicating that we have not indiscriminately turned up our noses at this form of sensory communication. We seem to be entering that stage of a historical cycle in which men use fragrant shaving lotions and colognes. There is selectivity among occasions at which per-fumes and lotions are used. They are employed more often for evening social situations than for work. This use corresponds to the implied increase in intimacy of interpersonal contacts at times of recreation.

4. Only nearby persons are available for touching or physical pressure. In our culture the freest use of touching is the handshake upon being introduced. It is a ritualized signal of the promise of intimacy. It connotes a pledge of trust, closeness, potential friendship, and alliance. If the occa-sion is a reunion, the handshake is interpreted as a gesture reasserting an intimacy that was suspended while the people were out of touch.

There is often a truncated and casual brushing of hands at the consum-mation of a retail transaction in which money and goods are exchanged, but more elaborate kinds of touching bespeak familiarity. These include putting an arm around the shoulders, locking arms while walking, linking hands while singing at a campfire. Adults tousle children's hair, boys pull girls' pigtails, girls comb each other's hair in mutual grooming rituals. A boy and a girl on a date may begin by holding hands, then clasp one another about the waist and hold one another in some forms of social dancing.

5. The use of pressure is a deepening of the intimacy keynoted by touch.

Lovers move from caresses to squeezing and embracing. People who get to know each other well are frequently punching, pinching, and slapping one another on the back. Use of pressure affirms a greater degree of intimacy in a relationship. The boss pats a worker on the back. The teacher rests his hands on a student's shoulders as he walks around the classroom. A wife caressingly strokes her husband's shoulders as she passes him. At the start of a game basketball players huddle together and clasp hands to affirm team integrity. Members of football teams pummel one another when their team scores points. The member who gets cuffed the most is the player who contributed most directly to the scoring.

Touching and pressure contacts are tied to aggression and destructive assaults too. (I do not distinguish between receptors for pressure and for pain because it is hard for an observer to tell whether one or both are being affected.) Instances of hostility such as twisting limbs, wrestling, and punching fit here. These instances do not deny the principle of the sensory order of relationships between people. Enemies, like friends, have a much less casual and more pertinent relationship than do acquaintances or persons who do not know one another. Physical aggression accentuates a particularly close relationship between combatants, in which the actions of one have a powerful influence on the actions of the other. Often combat is the climax of an ongoing relationship. Men who fight, even if they did not know each other well beforehand, commit themselves to an intimately focused relationship and spend much effort to affect one another.

6. Near-maximum proximity is required for the temperature of the other person to be sensed. People who freely get physically close enough to do so are called warm friends.

7. Taste experiences are reserved for only the closest interpersonal interactions, as between parent and child or between lovers. While war heroes and ambassadors may be publicly embraced cheek to cheek or lip to cheek, these events are essentially instances of touching—slightly more personal forms of the handshake. A kiss on the lips is different. Taste is usually reserved for forms of sexual stimulation, including kissing, biting, and sucking.

This review points up the ties between biological structure, physical space, and social relationships. When someone says, "He is close to him," the closeness is more than figurative. There is a strong correlation between physical nearness and social closeness. The key to these degrees of intimacy can be objectively translated by the frequency and number of sense receptors used in interaction. The more channels used, more often, for longer time periods, and more intensely (for example, decibels, pounds of pressure), the more ardently involved are the participants with one another. This involvement is accompanied by more complex implications of their conduct and more profound consequences. An intimate relationship does not imply that all behavior in it is characterized by full use of the range of access, but that there is relatively greater use over a period of time than is manifest in more distant relationships over the same time period. A simple but generally recognized form of the principle that sensory distance influences social distance is that people in sustained proximity tend to establish closer relationships. Sensory-access populations become mating populations, as when a boy marries the girl next door or the girl who sits near him in the classroom. Festinger, Schachter, and Back showed that friendships among persons in a housing project developed according to the frequency with which they met one another on the stairways. By the same principle, it is unpleasant and uncomfortable to have someone physically close if he is not liked or if one does not want to be influenced by him. Strangers in a crowded elevator hold themselves in and immobilize themselves to limit touching.

Cultural practices also inhibit utilization of sensory channels. Public buildings contain separate dressing rooms and toilet facilities for men and women. Great effort is also expended, especially in the United States, to disguise body and mouth and room odors by using special-formula soaps, mouth rinses, deodorants, and room sprays. This may be a reflection of the level of intimacy to which people are prone in this society. Sensory constraints apply to levels of intimacy in many cultures. Lowie listed numerous examples to taboos that prohibit the use of a particular channel between persons, often kinsmen by marriage. The taboos are expressed as follows: "must not look in the face of," "must not speak directly to," or "must not touch." For example, in some cultures one is not supposed to look at one's mother-in-law and must take a circuitous route to avoid meeting her. Rules of sensory avoidance are also invoked for particular ceremonies. The tradition of the bridegroom forbidden to view his bride until a certain stage of the wedding ritual is a custom from which the relic of a flimsy veil still persists in contemporary weddings in the United States. Hand gestures occur in distinctly different ranges in different cultures. In our country the Italian and Jewish immigrants who maintain their subcultures employ more and different hand gestures than their assimilated brethren. (Efron and Foley) Touch is also based on a group of signals that are potentially encodable. Touch involves a range of taps, pokes, pettings, punches, and strokes that are difficult to systematize because they are part of more intimate relationships not commonly studied directly by researchers. Further variation and constraint in sensory stimulation is to be found among different social classes of a society. We have learned that child-rearing practices in the United States differ in different social classes. Working-class parents are more likely to use physical punishment as a means of control, whereas upper-middle class parents are more likely to rely on verbalized threats of withdrawal of love and are less often likely to lay hands on their children for purposes of control.

Because of these variations, I do not insist upon an absolute principle of sensory and social distance to which all cultures and societies conform. The principle is geared to baselines for given social groups. Applied within a given culture, class, or social group, this proposition should hold: the closer the social relationship, the more often will proximally effective receptors be utilized.

The opposite pattern applies as well. As people withdraw from social relationships, they sever sensory contacts. Arguments are accompanied by a cessation of customary contacts, including not speaking, averting one's eyes, turning away, refusing to shake hands. A spat between lovers is often accompanied by a refusal to kiss. Reconciliations are often accompanied by handshakes or kissing. The desire for privacy, regardless of spatial arrangements, is universally fulfilled by creating barriers to sensory access.

Sensory Utilization as a Means of Control

In the mathematical study of communication, the quantity of regulation that can be achieved over a behaving system is limited to the quantity of information that can be transmitted to it over available channels. This idea is applicable to social behavior. The ability to influence others depends on the extent to which one can reach them through their receptors. Increased access increases the chances of influence. So control is dependent on proximity.

This was demonstrated dramatically in Milgram's experimental study of obedience. Subjects participating one at a time were called upon to administer increasingly severe electric shocks to another person. They were given a plausible reason for doing so—having been told that they were participating in a scientific experiment on the use of punishment to enhance learning. The subject did not know that his victim was a paid professional actor who actually was not being shocked but who was cued to express protests of rising intensity as the subject persisted in the series of trials. The faked shock instrument panel included a directly wired link between levers at graded shock levels and an automatic recording device, so that an objective record was made of what the subject did at the apparatus. In different trials of this experiment, Milgram varied the degree of sensory access between the subject and the victim—who appealed to the subject to stop the (faked) shocks on the ground that they were painful—and between the subject and the experimenter, who urged that the subject continue the shocks for the sake of research. The subjects experienced intense emotion over the conflicting demands made upon them by the entreaties of the victim to stop and by the commands of the experimenter to continue. Many of them gnawed their lips, sweated, trembled, groaned, and broke into nervous laughter. Even while they expressed disapproval about hurting another human being, many subjects went on with the experiment when told to do so. While this phenomenon and other aspects of the findings are not wholly explainable by referring to conditions of sensory utilization, some telling correlations are nevertheless apparent.

In general the influence of the experimenter or of the victim upon the subject was directly related to one or the other's greater physical proximity to the subject and the consequent access to more receptors. In one condition the experimenter was in the same room with the subject. When the subject expressed doubt about continuing and the experimenter said he should go on, only a few of the subjects flouted authority and broke off before the end of the projected series of trials. In another condition the experimenter was out of the room and gave orders by telephone. Here about three times as many of the subjects discontinued the experiment and discontinued sooner than in the preceding condition. They also disobeyed by lying. They pulled low voltage levers while assuring the experimenter that they were raising the shock voltage. This fact was revealed later by checking the entries on the automatic recording device. This shows, incidentally, that inner sadism did not play a major part in the overall findings. For here the subjects willingly undermined the ostensible purpose of the experiment if they could escape from the experimenter's influence and deliver weaker shocks.

The proximity of the apparent victim was also varied. Here, too, the nearer the victim was to the subject, the greater his influence upon the subject. When the protesting victim was close by and the subject had to touch the victim (through a protective sheet of material) and press his hand onto an electric grid in order for the shock to be delivered, two-thirds of the subjects disobeyed and stopped the trials. In contrast, when the victim was out of sight behind a partition and was heard only when pounding on the wall or voicing protests but was not seen or touched, only one-third of the subjects disobeyed before the experiment was to end. Milgram systematically questioned the subjects after their participation. He reports that the increased proximity to the victim did not alter the subject's attribution of a given level of pain to the other. That is, subjects reported that they did not become more aware of the victim's suffering in one condition than in any other. Thus their disobedience was not due to consideration of greater hurt being inflicted.

Milgram interprets the relative influences according to physical proximity. He says that "As the victim is brought closer, the subject finds it harder to administer shocks to him. When the victim's position is held constant relative to the subject, and the authority (experimenter) is made more remote, the subject finds it easier to break off the experiment. The effect is substantial in both cases but manipulation of the experimenter's position yielded the more powerful results. Obedience to destructive commands is highly dependent on the proximal relations between the authority and subject." I would reinterpret proximity in terms of opportunities to utilize more sensory channels in interpersonal communication. While this interpretation does not entirely account for the findings, it did turn out that the subject was influenced more by the person who made his claim through more sense modes and more proximal ones.

In this spirit a teacher scolding a pupil may insist, "Look at me when I'm talking to you!" A mother may shake her child as she scolds him. In a pleasanter vein, when a man wants to influence a woman or if she wants to put him into a romantic mood, he or she sets the stage by arranging candlelight dinners that diminish surrounding distraction, by playing mood music on the phonograph, and by wearing perfume or cologne. Skin contact is made early and frequently by someone interested in seduction.

When structural interference prevents one or more modalities from being utilized, the potential control over the other person decreases. Getting out of sensory reach or appearing to be so becomes a deliberate technique employed by those who seek to avoid influence. Sometimes on the street one looks the other way to prevent catching the eye of another with whom one would rather not interact. Merton points out that full visibility in a work situation is psychologically taxing on subordinates and that supervisors often relax their surveillance, permitting some leeway in adherence to company regulations. Husbands do not hear when wives mention that they need new winter coats. A girl who does not want to be bothered by a persistent but unwelcome suitor may not answer her phone. If she lives alone, this course entails the risk of preventing contact with other men in whom she may be interested. If she lives with her family or has roommates, she may have someone else screen the calls, forbidding auditory access to specific persons. Men who refrain from developing more intimate relations with others greet them from too far a distance to make handshaking feasible. The remark "Keep your distance!" is meant specifically to prevent touch contact and is meant generally as an admonition against possible interaction and influence.

Finally there is that most conventional of all interpersonal controls, spoken communication. It is based on restricting vocal signals to small portions of their possible range. Voice signals are encodable as phonetic symbols. Although man is capable of vocalizing a large variety of noises, from the myriad combinations of coughs, plosives, clicks, and vowels he has settled on very few sounds—less than one hundred—to use regularly for speech in any known tongue. All human groups rely on between twenty-five to eighty-five distinguishable sounds for their languages. According to various authorities, English is restricted to from thirty-two to forty-five phonemes, so at least forty other phonemes live outside our culture's linguistic fences. The relevant sounds of everyday contacts also include idiomatic sighs, grunts, and snorts. Members of a given language group become so habituated to its sounds that they are often unable to distinguish phonemes that are not part of that language but that are in full-fledged use in another tongue.

Sensory Impairment

Anything that interferes with the receptivity of a sense mode blocks the possibility for communication involving that channel. It therefore interferes with the occurrence of interpersonal situations that depend upon access to that channel.

Many types of sensory curtailment happen not because of physical defects but as correlates of a social condition. Included here is the isolation from others that occurs when a child is punished by being sent to his room; when infants in orphanage cribs are ignored as long as they are quiet; when mental patients or prison inmates are locked in solitary confinement; when explorers, hermits, or castaways cut themselves off from others; and when pilots fly airplanes alone at high altitudes during periods of radio silence. Debilitating effects upon these individuals, who are deprived of ordinary sensory exchanges with other persons, have been recorded in numerous anecdotal reports and case studies.

Ruth First was imprisoned in the Union of South Africa and placed in solitary confinement for nearly four months as a result of her political activities in opposition to apartheid. She reports that with the passage of days she began to lose her ability to concentrate and noted a diminishing of her inventive and imaginative powers. Richard E. Byrd, one of the first men to spend time at the South Pole, lived by himself for several months during one expedition. His isolation was self-imposed, he could establish contact via radio with his companions at another Antarctic base if he chose to. He testified that he kept a fairly complete diary while he occupied the base alone. But in his entry for April 1, he comments that he was surprised and puzzled to find that not more of the emotions and circumstances he experienced were actually committed to paper. The entry for April 21 reports that he does not awaken in full possession of his faculties and feels he is groping around lost and bewildered. On May 12 he correctly diagnoses his problem: "The silence of this place . . . seems to merge in and become part of the indescribable *evenness*. . . ."

A more definitive set of findings has been obtained from experiments designed to study the effects of curbing almost all forms of sensory input. In these experiments, carried out using volunteers, each subject is not only removed from contact with others but also from much of the ordinary sensorimotor contact he has with himself. A subject is typically asked to lie quietly on a bed in a small cubicle. His eyes are shielded by translucent goggles that diffuse available light so that no patterns are discernible. His ears are cupped in sponge rubber pads. His fingers and arms are swathed in gloves and tubelike encasements that prevent bending the wrists and elbows. (Bexton, Heron, Scott) In another form of this experiment, the subject is suspended blindfolded in a tank of water that is kept at body temperature.

While termed *sensory deprivation,* these conditions are more accurately described as *reduced variation in sensory input.* That is, the subject may see light in his field of vision, but it is unvaried. A hissing monotone that obscures distinguishable sounds may be piped in through his earphones. Either description is acceptable because awareness of sensation is due to changes in the level of stimulation. Unvaried input therefore deprives the person of the conditions for differentiating and is equivalent to no stimulation. *Restricted variety* more accurately describes these circumstances.

Although there were differences among individuals, the general findings of these experiments were that restricted variety in stimulation results in marked changes in cognitive and emotional activity. There is a severe decrement in intellectual ability, a confusion in thinking, a lassitude in trying to solve problems by reasoning, an inability to maintain attention or concentrate on a topic. Heron reports that ". . . the subjects at first spent some time in organized thought, reviewing their work, making attempts to solve personal problems, and so on. As time wore on, however, this type of activity became harder because of difficulty in concentrating, and the subjects preferred 'just to let their minds drift.' Finally, blank periods during which they could think of nothing would frequently occur." When tested during this period, the subjects were notably inefficient in solving simple problems of mental arithmetic or anagrams. With the decrease in thinking came rising emotional tension, complaints of discomfort (although they were snugly padded), irritability, restlessness, and anxiousness bordering on panic. These studies show that a person cannot behave coherently and comfortably without varied sensations. When his sensory input becomes uniform, he becomes cognitively dull and emotionally aroused. Since the subjects were allowed to terminate the experiments upon request, and many of them did so before fulfilling the extreme lengths to which the experimenters were prepared to go, these findings refer to only the incipient phases of what could have turned into thoughtless, raging disturbances.

Sensory Overload

The consequences of severe restriction can be better understood by noting what happens to individuals when they are bombarded with interpersonal stimulation.

Before discussing the conditions of sensory overload, I should note that people do not discriminate as widely as one might imagine, knowing the physiological capacities of their several receptors. Receptor capacities are finite. Each is by itself able to make out a range of excitation, but each has a modest upper limit. For example, a human has a capacity to distinguish somewhere from three to sixteen light brightnesses visually or sound intensities aurally, with the average number of distinctions being seven. Of course, this example refers to but one dimension in each modality. In addition to loudness in the auditory channel, one also distinguishes variations in pitch. But the result is not a sheer exponential multiplication of sensitivity to stimuli. One reason is that the receptors do not work independently. They interact with one another, and some dominate others. People do not understand speech as efficiently if they cannot see the speaker's lips. This is apparently true even for the normal listener, who remains unaware that he is lip reading. (Broadbent) Vision is also dominant over touch. When vision and touch provide contradictory information, as when an object looks smaller but feels larger (which can be achieved with certain paraphernalia in a laboratory), the individual rescales his touch perception so that it becomes consistent with his visual perception. (Rock and Harris) Pressure also impairs tactile thresholds. Hearing constricts the range of visual acuity; that is, one sees less sensitively if there is sound stimulation at the same time. Much use of one channel therefore curtails the capacity of another; although man is a multichannel receiver, his capacity to receive is not the simple product of those channels.

A second reason for sensory ability below the biological maximums is the human disposition toward negative sensory adaptation resulting in lowered responsiveness. This accounts, for example, for regular dwellers becoming unaware of certain odors in their household whereas a newcomer notices them immediately. Adjustment to a shift in stimulus levels occurs sluggishly. Compare, for example, the difference in adapting to darkness as night slowly falls versus adjusting to darkness after switching off the lights at night. The interaction among sense modes plus this habituation during use restricts the range of sensory ability.

Now consider what might happen at the upper end of the range, when individuals are flooded with stimulation. This flooding occurs when people come physically close to many other persons with whom they are not psychologically or socially intimate. It can happen when people pack into sports stadiums, theaters, elevators, public transportation terminals and vehicles, cocktail parties, street crowds, public auctions, religious assemblies, and so on.

In discussing people in the mass, I refer here to only a portion of the phenomena customarily labeled collective behavior. In these instances each person's access to others is increased. Each has more receptors effectively receiving stimulation from others. Each is able to smell and touch and press against others and to become aware of the warmth of bodies around him as well as to receive the sights and murmurings of the throng. Each individual may contribute to the stimulation that inundates him, and each contribution is multiplied in the mass. Many individuals shouting at once can produce a roar.

In dense groups these multitudinous signals result in a high absolute level of stimulation for all participants. It can reach a level of flooding that washes out the ability of an individual to discriminate. Just as details of a landscape are effaced under a very bright sun—or as blasting loudspeakers obliterate a melody—excessive stimulation upon individuals in crowds is received by them in more homogenized form. The magnitudes of impinging stimuli limit their ordinary abilities to differentiate the input.

This condition is similar in potency to the condition of sensory deprivation because restricted variety in input and impaired ability to differentiate are related. Absence of variety prevents the opportunity to distinguish. Inability to differentiate prevents the experience of variety. A scarcity or an excess of stimulation affects one's receptors similarly. Excess or scarcity has similar impact on behavior too. The conduct of people in dense crowds, like that of individuals whose sensory input is curbed, also exhibits unreason and irritability.

As in the case of sensory deprivation, most of the time people are exposed only to the incipient conditions of sensory overload. Yet crowd experiences provide common examples of thought dispelled and emotion aroused.

When a person walks into a large sports stadium or a concert hall and confronts the spectacle, his first sight of the massed array of people has a dizzying and overpowering effect. His usual awareness of solid personal boundaries gives way temporarily, and he feels himself flowing outward and merging with the mass. In a crowded room, as at a reception, intelligent conversation disintegrates. If one is pressed too closely on all sides, he either depresses his external sensitivity with alcoholic drinks or begins to feel a sense of intolerable oppression that builds into a desperate concern about liberty. When someone escapes from such mob scenes, he explains it by remarking "It was so crowded in there that I couldn't hear myself think." When there is no retreat from extreme closeness with others, thoughtfulness declines and is replaced by volatility. The more packed are elevators or buses or trains, the more one's awareness of the surround intrudes and forces suspension of private musings.

Popular tradition asserts that individuals become suggestible blockheads when acting in crowds. It has been said that a crowd sweeps away each member's sense of responsibility, reveals his stupidity, and ignites his primitive instincts for violence. LeBon wrote that a man who joins a crowd "descends several rungs in the ladder of civilization. Isolated, he may be a cultivated individual; in a crowd, he is a barbarian. . . ." These condemnations are inaccurate. Crowds manifest many types of irrational behavior. These include such nondestructive forms as people's performances at religious gatherings, audience applause, spectators' frenzied cheering, and the adoration of a charismatic figure by a multitude, as well as rioting and panic. Crowds sometimes act nobly and generously. Moreover, individuals operate effectively in the mass if their behavior is well coordinated. Inasmuch as crowds accomplish what they set out to do, they are effective agencies and not stupid. We usually confuse our disapproval of what they accomplish with our judgment of how they accomplish it. And individuals also commit evil and cruelty when acting alone.

Let us put aside particular outcomes and analyze the deterioration of reason, intensification of emotion, and rapid spread of control over individuals that occur in crowds. Since the crowd is composed of individuals, how can the result of unified action be explained? It is a mistake to presume that all people present are initially joined together in a common purpose or share the same impulse. People gather. They mill about close to one another. They unsuspectingly become sensorily attuned to the throng of which they are a part. With many receptors accessible in proximity, there is greater opportunity for interpersonal engagement. Each utilization of an additional channel is the crossing of a threshold, a step in the establishment of more social influence. Individuals begin to fall under one another's spell before there is any focused goal, and the aggregate subtly acquires a collective coordination. The mass begins to dominate each individual because environmental information affects conduct. In this way the submission of individuals *precedes* the moment that may call for ethical judgment or thoughtful assessment.

That is why the performance of immoral or stupid or courageous acts later comes so easily. The individual is primarily persuaded to perform an act rather than to seek a goal. In panics, for example, people are ready to flee due to the actions of others about them before they have a clear idea of what the threat might be. A leading movement at the edge of a crowd quickly rouses the rest of it. A small number of persons who suddenly rise up in front bring the rest of an audience to its feet. In a uniformly disinterested audience, the cadence of applause often takes control of each person, and—excluding the theaters and music halls of large cities where performing stars may have installed claques—the audience concludes its applause almost as one. Finally, because each person makes a contribution to the mass effect, members of crowds overwhelm themselves. Simmel observed that "the individual, by being carried away, carries away."

There are, of course, differences in individual susceptibility to crowd influence. But the aggregate acquires a collective coordination that cannot be countered individually. The cautioner is easily shouted down, and if he is drowned out, he cannot exert influence on the group.

This formulation covers many of the vaguer terms, such as contagion, imitation, facilitation, primitive sympathy, and suggestion, that have been used to account for the dramatic spread of influence in a crowd. It also fits the common assertion that crowds have to be a certain size to produce impetuous conduct. The process can be traced as follows: the size of the crowd leads to density, to proximity, to greater sensory access, to greater environmental control, to sensory overload, to restricted variety of input, to diminished differentiation, to deterioration of intellect, to emotionalism, and finally to an unthinking mob that can be led.

I have dealt only with the mechanism by which deterioration of reason, intensification of emotion, and rapid spread of control are imposed upon individuals in the crowd. Obviously it is not sufficient to account for the specific consequences—often wasteful, cruel, and tragic—that follow. Those cannot be explained by a single cause. Nor does the process inevitably unfold from its beginnings. But the inability to differentiate variety is the key, and the potential is given by the flood of stimulation in dense groups. The mechanism described here partakes of many events involving people in the mass. The striking characteristics of aroused crowd behavior are similar to the behavioral characteristics of individuals whose variety of sensory input is restricted by deprivation. They are actions of disturbed, highly emotional creatures with deteriorated intellectual capacities.

A Case of Inability to Differentiate

While I have declared that the individual in a crowd is primarily persuaded to perform an act rather than to seek a goal, it is also useful to study the intentions and beliefs of its members, especially those who are its evident leaders. I will show by an example how these intentions and beliefs can influence events that unfold.

In the civil disturbances in the United States during the summer of 1967, members of the Negro community engaged in unlawful acts of arson and looting, and members of both white and black communities engaged in acts of racial violence. Do these instances confirm the process stemming from restriction in the variety of sensory input?

The events of the summer of 1967 made up one chapter in a long history of interracial tensions that includes a buildup of grievances coupled with a slow and arduous movement in the direction of racial equality. The outbreaks had causes that accumulated before the summer. They were not spontaneous outbursts without past history. Usually the incident that directly triggered the lawlessness and violence was a relatively trivial one when gauged against the context of grievances formed by events during the years or even the weeks prior to the disturbance.

In many neighborhoods vandalism and the breaking of windows were followed by the looting of stores. This looting was opportunistic but also deliberate and not a matter of large, wild mobs assaulting store fronts. Sometimes it was downright leisurely. The *Report of the National Advisory Commission on Civil Disorders* includes the following comment: "Numerous eyewitnesses interviewed by Commission investigators tell of the carefree mood with which people ran in and out of stores, looting and laughing, and joking with the police officers. Stores with 'Soul Brothers' signs appeared no more immune than others. Looters paid no attention to residents who shouted at them and called their actions senseless. An epidemic of excitement had swept over persons on the street." Although exciting, this looting was blatantly calculated and not mob impetuousness. The Report notes that in Detroit there may have been criminal elements organized spontaneously to take advantage of the cover of the civil disorder and that some autos were observed returning again and again to haul away goods from stores methodically looted.

However, there were several groups of people who showed the types of irrationalism, panic, and violence that are typically associated with aroused mobs. Their behavior appeared to be tinged with an inability to differentiate sensations or information. Some groups that succumbed to these conditions were the citizens on the scenes at which the disorders began. Density of people was a common factor in the flare-ups. The Report also notes that in all twenty-four major disturbances investigated "the initial disturbance area consisted of streets with relatively high concentrations of pedestrian and automobile traffic at the time . . . In most instances, the temperature during the day on which violence first erupted was quite high. This contributed to the size of the crowds on the street, particularly in areas of congested housing."

Other groups that showed panic and irrational violence were some units of the National Guard and, to a lesser but still significant extent, some local police units. Their behavior was also associated with restriction in sensory variety and with a narrowed base of information about what was going on.

With reference to the first factor, the periods of violence generally subsided during the daytime and flared up rapidly again at night. With reference to the second factor, rumors that organized groups of blacks were preparing to strike were not checked out as a matter of course but were accepted by these National Guard and police units as the impending situation.

With those rumors in mind some National Guard units shot out the street lights in the neighborhoods they entered so as to avoid being visible targets. Then in the dark, they used their guns in response to sounds of firecrackers or to the sounds of their comrades' shots as well as in response to the occasional shots from bona fide snipers. Often when they heard noises or saw a flash of light, they began firing in the direction of the stimulus. It has been determined that several times two National Guard units stationed in proximity to each other were actually firing at each other, each prompted by the other's volleys. The Newark Director of Police told the investigating commission, ". . . in the Springfield Avenue area it was so bad that, in my opinion, Guardsmen were firing upon police and police were firing back at them . . . I really don't believe there was as much sniping as we thought. . . ." The Report continues in another section: "According to the best information available to the Commission, most reported sniping incidents were demonstrated to be gunfire by either police or National Guardsmen." A newspaper editor later confessed regret that his paper had alluded to snipers' nests which, when checked out, "were the constituted authorities shooting at each other, most of them."

A dramatic turnabout and improvement in one section of Detroit occurred one night when army paratroopers under the command of Colonel A. R. Bolling arrived in the area. The place was so dark and still that the colonel at first thought he had come to the wrong location. But upon investigating, the colonel found National Guard troops crouching behind the walls of a building. They claimed that they were pinned down by sniper fire. Colonel Bolling ordered all light in the building turned on and instructed his paratroopers to show themselves conspicuously. Across the street, nearly every window in an apartment house had been shot out, and its walls were pockmarked with bullet holes. The paratroopers made efforts to establish contact with the terrorized citizenry of the area, and within hours after their arrival the area they occupied was the quietest in the city. They were forbidden to fire en masse. Whereas hundreds of mostly false reports of snipers were fed into police headquarters, the Army recorded only ten. Elsewhere in the city guardsmen persisted in shooting out the lights and keeping themselves in obscurity.

Ability to differentiate sensations and ideas is the circumstance under which reason thrives. Too little stimulation or information starves reason. Too much stimulation or information makes it buckle. At either extreme thought loses its way, and an urge wells up to dispense with analysis and get into action.

Sensation and Idealism

My discussion, which began as an analysis of sensations as they present themselves in the immediate interpersonal situation, terminates with a broader lesson. To be sure, there is more to social encounters than spoken conversation, and in Part Three I will test the idea of a positive connection between sensory utilization and social intimacy. Beyond this, however, I have dwelt on the reconciliation between two themes of human experience—sensing and thinking.

Years ago the senses were believed to be the pure sources of knowledge. Were they not the only means of contact we had with the outside world? The doctrine of sensationism, that all perception is the experience of the receptors as immediately given, was the culmination of efforts to reduce thought and even motives to sensory elements. Sensations, declared Locke, were the first source of ideas. Condillac went further, claiming that sensations alone were sufficient clues to mental life and that pleasantness and unpleasantness were inherent in the sensory experience itself. There was even a notion that a pleasant or unpleasant sensation directly constituted a will or motivation to prolong or to terminate the sensory experience. This doctrine was rejected in due time because of new insights about the nature of human experience and behavior. It was replaced by a doctrine of idealism, based on the belief that reason and will were organizing factors that went beyond sensory experience. Man's conduct was credited with freedom from his immediate environment. With the discovery of the unconscious life as well as the attention to innate drives, sensory stimulation receded as a topic of concern. The early part of this century saw students of human behavior enumerating instincts rather than receptors. "Sense perception," wrote Whitehead, "despite its prominence in consciousness, belongs to the superficialities of experience." Emphasis had shifted from outright sensationism purporting to explain behavior to reason as its explanation, to a viewpoint of impulsive irrationalism still purporting to explain behavior.

With the start of the second half of the twentieth century, the role of sensation in thought as well as in interpersonal behavior has again received attention. We have evidence that humans are dependent upon their sensory milieu for mental functioning. Because of this evidence we are brought to recognize the intellectual implications of direct interpersonal experience and the relation between sense and reason. There is a strong parallel between the effectiveness of thought and understanding based on sensory deprivation and overload and that based on a paucity or a multitude of ideas. Extremes hamper the ability to differentiate. Hindrance can come from deprivation or from overload, and extremes can refer to sense impressions or to ideas. All these forms result in cognitive disablement. On the other hand, the ability to act in the light of reason depends on moderation, whether we speak of crude sensory inputs or the amount of ideas to which people are exposed.

Considering the possible range of information and alternative viewpoints bearing on a problem, people suffer both from information that is too meager and from a superabundance of information. Information overload, a deluge of new knowledge and opinions and pronouncements, scatters attention and diffuses recognition. The inflow cannot be sorted fast enough. Critical filters become clogged. People can neither distinguish the important from the trivial nor juggle the alternatives without dropping many of them. Similarly, a dearth of variety in ideas impairs thoughtfulness. We know that curtailing considerations, excluding alternatives, and suppressing dissent accompany intolerance, unreasonableness, and the either-or logic of extremism.

I have referred to the behavior of some National Guard units and some police during the disorders of the summer of 1967. There were, of course, other factors involved in their conduct. The guardsmen in particular were inexperienced and afraid, and in some cases they treated their assignment as a military action. But the instances of troops firing at troops were affected by restriction in variety of sensory input combined with distortions conveyed by rumors. If not verified, rumors slanted in one way undermine reasonable analysis. A plethora of contradictory rumors, as a form of information overload, can have the same effect.

The individual was once credited with reason and with being superior to the mob. The sensory deprivation studies tell us that this is a fallacy. Crowds are no more irresponsible and unreasonable than the sensorily isolated individual, for without varied stimulation in his environment the individual becomes a highly emotional creature with defective intellectual capacities. By reinterpreting sensory deprivation as restricted variety of input, we notice its similarity to the homogenizing consequences of the sensory flooding that occurs in crowds.

In this chapter I have talked of how sensations bear upon human relationships, thinking, and action. Social conduct has additional components, and I will proceed in this recital from its sensory to its nonobservable aspects. In the next chapter I will treat the nature of mind as it underlies and participates in communication and interpersonal acts.

3

Mind

⁓

The fullest and most sustained sensory access one has is in the most intimate of all social relationships—that of a person with himself. One uses this access in the presence of others as well as in their absence. I will first list some examples that occur more often when a person is alone.

Alone

When not in the presence of other persons, an individual makes use of access to himself and is stimulated by himself. Some of this he cannot help. His nose, for example, is a part of every scene. Other usage entails some form of overt action for its accomplishment.

In front of a mirror, the increase in personal visual contact is so great that one may—if he has the time—begin exploring. He will look at himself unshaved and begin to make motions with his jaw that turn into grimaces. Soon he becomes absorbed in carrying on a gyrating conversation with the face in the mirror, inspecting it from several angles, getting as close as possible in order to see the pores in the skin. Women engage in full-dress interactions with themselves in front of full-length mirrors. Teen-agers have the highest rate of sensory exploration, which increases at the onset of puberty, but they do not give up the practice as adults.

When a baby is awake and alone he is often heard babbling to himself. A child playing by himself will talk to himself. An adult working by himself will whistle or sing or hum, particularly if he is in a quiet environment. A person will sing in the shower or while driving alone for a long distance in an automobile, repeating a melody many times in different octaves, tremolo, with gusto, and otherwise, listening to the range and timbre of his own voice. When singing in the car, one often stops while passing another vehicle and then begins again.

People also feel themselves, pinch themselves, stroke themselves, and finger their hair. A person sometimes tries to feel what his arm is like, where the bones are and what a bone feels like under skin. The head, crotch, back, and chin are sites of scratching and rubbing. One traces the contours of his ear with his fingers, feels his biceps or his thighs, nibbles at his fingers or his arm or his shoulder to feel the skin there. He explores his mouth and lips with his tongue. He masturbates while reading alone or lying in the protective concealment of his bed. He sniffs at his armpits and smells a hard-to-reach part of his body by rubbing or wiping his fingers there and then bringing them to his nose. He tries to find out how warm a certain part of his body is by pressing his cheek or the back of his hand against the surface. He tastes himself, licking sweat, biting his forearm muscles, biting his lip. He also attends to kinaesthetic sensations by deliberately flexing muscles, such as the calves of his legs.

Why do we sing in the shower or when alone on a long trip in an automobile? Because the activity itself contributes to sensory variation in a rather homogeneous auditory environment. The closed sedan or the closed bathroom is private and intimate. These snug cubicles seem to be ideal places for reviewing the resonances of one's voice. But it is not only a matter of being alone. These cubicles are limiting environs that exclude varied stimulation. The auditory input from the steady hiss of the shower or from the steady drone of the engine becomes too steady. It approaches the situation of that channel described in the experimental treatment to achieve sensory deprivation. This homogeneity becomes uncomfortable. In the shower, moreover, the enclosed space—perhaps with steam swirling up and diffusing the light—may impose a loss of visual variety. Unable to stand the monotony, we produce our own variety. In this case there is no constraint to bursting into song and to trying whatever sounds give satisfaction. The song counteracts the neutralizing noise created by water drumming about the ears or by the wind whistling hoarsely and steadily past the partly-rolled-down window of the car, which noises effectively filter out variations in sound. We like the sound of our voices at these times because of the relief they provide. Sensory homogeneity is not limited to the experimental laboratory, and it is unbearable wherever it is found.

Individuals who are alone and fall into daydreaming sometimes fancy that parts of their own body are those of another person. One shakes one's hand while imagining it is someone else's, rubs a cheek against the soft skin of the inside upper arm that stands for another's cheek. Children are observed creating imaginary playmates.

Helen Keller was born a healthy, bright child and was beginning to learn to talk when she was severely struck by a disease at the age of nineteen months. Although she survived, she lost her sight and hearing forever. For the next four years she had only the crudest interaction with her family and a few other people and showed only the barest progress in socialization to the human community. Then a remarkable woman named Anne Mansfield Sullivan succeeded in teaching her to communicate with others by making tactile signals in the palms of their hands. In one of her letters to a friend Miss Sullivan wrote, "She begins to spell the minute she wakes up in the morning, and continues all day long. If I refuse to talk to her, she spells into her own hand, and apparently carries on the liveliest conversation with herself." In this way Helen solved the problem of interacting with herself when alone, in spite of impaired sensory channels. So an individual who is alone can engage in acts that have the properties of dealing with others. If the social environment is bare, one creates a little society through parts of one's own body. If a person is an environment to himself, even the hermit is not truly without company.

One implication of this circumstance is that, when difficulties or other strains develop in one's life, one may interact with oneself if there is no one else to whom one can go for solace. People look in mirrors more, talk to themselves more, and pay more attention to what they are like. A person will hold a discourse with himself, confirming his feelings and resolves, rehearsing planned future actions. These activities help reiterate the boundaries of one's self-image and reestablish a sense of coherence. On an occasion of adult tragedy for me, I went to a mirror to watch myself weep. The first impact I received confirmed my wretchedness. I was shocked at the condition of the person I viewed. Yet although despairing and frightened, I actually got some reassurance from not being alone, by being able to see myself and to taste the tears rolling down my cheeks. Children, too, sometimes seem to be listening to their own wailing. While alone at his station at the South Pole, Byrd became very sick after a freak turn of events resulted in his nearly being overcome by fumes. Faced with the possibility of dying, he reports in an entry on June 2 that "something persuaded me to take down the shaving mirror from its nail near the shelf. The face that looked back at me was that of an old and feeble man . . . Something broke inside me then. What was to be gained by struggling?"

The history of his subsequent success tells us that he was able to respond constructively to his own appeal.

Sensorimotor Feedback

It is not haphazard to interact with oneself in a way that preserves or reestablishes effectiveness in a course of action. Research has found this interaction to be a component of all behavior, from neutral episodes to crises. It generally happens without the person's being aware of its pervasive role in his conduct. It is a feedback from one's physical actions to one's sensory channels or, proprioceptively, to the central nervous system.

Feedback is the information received by an acting entity about its own behavior. More generally, feedback is a behaving system's output that has become input to that system. Its relevance to human conduct was first demonstrated in experiments on hearing.

Lee used a special tape recording setup to study speech and hearing disorders and discovered that it could artificially create stuttering in speakers. Ordinarily in the use of a tape recorder, the same magnetic device is employed first to record sounds and later to play them back. Lee inserted an extra device in his apparatus to make the recording and reproduction functions more independent. When a subject talked into a microphone, his voice was recorded on a tape passing through the first device on its way to the second. The tape continued moving and passed through the second device, which was switched to reproduce sounds, and the speaker's voice was played back to him via a headset. With the volume in these earphones turned up high enough to dominate over the sounds ordinarily received through bone conduction, the subject had to rely on this electronic feedback arrangement in order to hear his own voice. By spacing the recording and the reproducing devices so that a fraction of a second elapsed while a given portion of the tape traveled from the first to the second device, Lee imposed a condition of *delayed auditory feedback* for the subject. When subjects read a moderately difficult text aloud into the recording microphone with the playback to the headset turned on, they kept halting. They slowed their speaking pace, raised their voices, repeated syllables, and lengthened sounds as if they were beset with a speech disorder.

Other researchers repeated this study and verified that almost all subjects show one or more of these changes: slowing the speaking rate, speaking louder, and repeating or lengthening sounds (especially continuant sounds like vowels). It has been suggested that the dimensions of some rooms and halls are such that the time taken for sounds to echo from the walls is longer than the ordinary range of the habituated feedback interval and that this may account for the hesitation and stuttering of some speakers at public gatherings. Delays in auditory feedback have been tried for nonverbal motor tasks, such as whistling, playing musical instruments, and handclapping. All these activities were disturbed by the delay. Chase and his colleagues found that with a quarter of a second delay in connection with keytapping tasks, subjects tended to tap the key harder, hold it down longer, and increase the pauses between the taps, and some subjects tapped four times instead of three as instructed.

Then Smith and his colleagues reported findings of a study of *delayed visual feedback* that they achieved using television equipment. Their subjects were asked to perform various paper and pencil tasks. Some subjects undertook them in the customary way, watching their hands at work. Other subjects were prevented from seeing their hands directly by an opaque screen placed under their chins, but they could watch their hands at work via a television system set up to monitor their hand movements. Still another group of subjects was treated like the second group except that—by means of videotape recording—a split-second delay was imposed between the camera and the appearance of the picture on the screen. Subjects in this last group differed markedly from the other two in performance. As in the auditory feedback delay, subjects became confused and irritated. Their work was laborious and frustrating, their movements erratic and jerky and oscillating. When writing words they duplicated letters or inserted ones that did not belong. It was a graphic stammer, analogous to the speech heard in the delayed auditory feedback conditions. The performance of the delayed visual feedback group on a simple tracing task was ludicrous; it took ten times longer than for members of the other two groups, with much redundant motion, and the results were scrawls of overlapping lines that looked like doodles of a plate of spaghetti rather than any recognizable tracing figure.

If the delayed auditory feedback studies show how crucial timed sensory input is to speech, the delayed visual feedback studies not only extend this principle to sight but further imply that it may be an essential feature of all sensory modes. We know too that kinaesthetic feedback from the condition of the musculature is relied on for the effective actions that we neither hear nor see. An individual, therefore, is not simply sensorily dependent upon his larger environment. He is dependent on that part of the environment he himself produced a moment earlier. Here is a spiral character to behavior. One's sensory equipment receives stimulation from one's own motor activity, and then one monitors oneself as part of continuing the action. He has to hear himself speak one syllable before he can effectively say the next. He has to see his hand trace part of a line before he can extend the line further. As he begins producing sounds or movements, the information collected by this scanning helps him continue whatever he began. It is possible for people to accommodate to delayed feedback and to reinstate the course of speech or action. This becomes harder when the delay is linked to one sensory mode and not to others, so that the feedback is mismatched and the musculature is subjected to conflicting timing requirements.

We get an inkling about the nature of the interpersonal act from these findings. It is a multistage episode, each phase of which is partly controlled by information received from the preceding, completed portion of the pattern. Feedback itself is not necessarily helpful. It is merely a process that tells a person what he is doing. It may result in his stabilizing or changing his pattern of conduct. Since a person monitors his own behavior, he may become extremely self-conscious. If he judges himself harshly, the feedback may be the source of his undoing. It can lead to inhibited behavior in the presence of others.

The delayed feedback studies show that any act implies at least one alternative—that the particular act might not have taken place. This may appear to be a purely logical statement and not part of experience. But the above-mentioned studies reveal that only specific information is withheld under conditions of feedback delay. The process itself is not suspended. Some other information—in the case of auditory delay it is the preceding syllable that is heard rather than the one most recently uttered—is fed back as input. This alternative is of the same class as the data that would have been judged correct or relevant. The datum is in this case another vowel or consonant. Therefore, there is always a set of possible alternatives that could be fed back to the acting individual from his own behavior. A subset of these will result in the behavior pattern continuing along one course, while feedback of the remainder will result in an alteration of the behavior pattern as it unfolds. Feedback reveals a component of the structure of the act. Each of the phases subsequent to the act's beginning is logically *a set of at least two alternatives*. Whatever behavior takes place can be identified as a particular event that is one of a set of what could possibly occur. More than two alternatives can be part of the set from which one takes place.

For example, instead of simple auditory delay in which a spoken phoneme is heard tardily, one may have coughed.

Although the process was given its name by radio engineers, and although its practical implications were systematically revealed by mathematicians using cybernetic theory, the feedback mechanism was recognized decades earlier by George Herbert Mead. He said, "We must be constantly responding to the gesture we make if we are to carry on successful vocal conversation. . . . A person who is saying something is saying to himself what he says to others; otherwise he does not know what he is talking about . . . the individual organism enters in some sense into its own environmental field; its own body becomes a part of the set of environmental stimuli to which it responds or reacts." Mead thus pointed to human feedback—one's own body as the producer of signals to which one responds. The principle that people rely on feedback to perform coherent action has several implications. One pertains to the experience I reported in the preceding chapter. People are dependent on their environment, including being sensorily dependent upon their own motor activity in that environment. Second, since one course of action unfolds smoothly whereas other patterns such as those that occur under conditions of delayed feedback are emotionally disturbing and result in signs of a breakdown or blockage of action, it is fair to deduce that at least some courses of action are purposeful. The individual is apparently out to reach a goal and uses feedback to check on where he is according to his plan and adjusts his conduct accordingly. His goal, purpose, plan, or intent is not observable, and we cannot study it directly. Nor can we be so rash as to construe the particular goal from the outcome of the act. Many outcomes are unanticipated. Intentions do not ensure fulfillment. Yet we must adopt the premise implied by the feedback studies that behavior is often purposeful. Third, an observable feature is that, even when not according to plan, conduct unfolds sequentially. Fourth, as a logical lesson of the feedback findings, alternative actions are possible at any point in the sequence of behavior.

Muscular Readiness, Response, and Perception of Behavior

These qualities—feedback dependence, goal guidance, sequential unfolding, and course alternativeness—are part of experience with behavior and must constitute elements of people's knowledge of the structure of action whether or not they are aware of it. Yet because of a further implication of feedback, exposure to an event does not necessarily result in everyone's perceiving the same thing and understanding it in the same way. This is due to the constant flow of information about one's own activity. It happens partly through sensorimotor feedback and partly through messages from the musculature conveyed internally. For example, if one speaks aloud, he not only hears himself but also is aware of muscle tensions and skeletal displacements kinaesthetically. These tell him that he is moving his jaw, contracting his tongue, expelling air from his chest, and gesturing with his hand.

Even under passive conditions the musculature contributes to experience. Jacobson measured action potentials in the musculature under conditions of relaxing, paying attention, trying to recall, and imagining overt acts. He found that more muscular tension accompanied increased cognitive activity. Sensory tuning in often requires motor adjustments. In seeing, the eye's muscles act to center the object on the retina and continue to position the eye in order to maintain centering. The head is rotated so that it can face in the direction of seeing or oriented so that an ear is presented to the source of sound. One often has to shift position, lean forward, and reach out in order to touch. Yet even these receptive adjustments are more energetic than a general state of bodily tone that is ever-present. We may call sitting quietly a kind of behavior for it too entails a certain amount of muscular contraction. When movement is not overt, the location of effectors and skeletal posture are noted kinaesthetically. The transition from the normal tension level of a person ready to respond to his environment to an overt response is a progression of muscular states with each succeeding phase involving increasing tension. Freeman used the term *background energy* to refer to the generalized tonic condition of the musculature, a mild tension to muscles persisting even when one is relaxed. This condition is present even in sleep. Somewhat stronger tension levels are associated with the *arousal* condition, in which the body is ready to react. Even stronger and more selectively focused potentials are detectable in the condition of *attention,* in which the body is prepared to react in a certain way. Attention is partly an overt action. Changes in blood circulation and breathing often accompany it, body posture is oriented, and the musculature enters a phase of incipient contraction close to the threshold of noticeable movement. It is pertinent to speak of attention as incipient action. We can notice a state of fear in someone, a readiness to flee. We can notice a skeptical orientation on the face of a boss prior to hearing the excuse from a tardy employee who has often been late. The culmination of this increased tensing is gross overt movement.

Since behavior is fed back to him through sensory channels and proprio-ceptors, an individual always receives information about his own activity and bodily state as part of his total awareness. Therefore, *he always notes himself as a part of anything perceived*. He cannot avoid it. It is impossible for him to observe someone else's conduct without including components of his own somatic and physiological states in the evidence.

We gain some insight into how a person perceives the conduct of others from the fact that his bodily condition will be a part of that information. He sometimes ascribes to himself attributes of the people with whom he interacts. After having heard a suggestion proposed by another in a fast-moving discussion, he may conclude that it was his own idea. He is also disposed to attribute properties of himself to other people. After having gotten a receptive ear from another, he may conclude that the other is a good conversationalist. If he likes another person upon first meeting, he is likely to anticipate that they share the same values and have more in common than the other's conduct yet confirms.

Phenomena like these have made us skeptical about the human ability to perceive realistically. However, appreciating that feedback mechanisms result in simultaneous perception of one's own behavior and that of others, one can make a different interpretation of the nature of his reality. Accord-ing to this role of personal components in perceiving, each person notes things as they are, not with distortion. Since each contributes to the infor-mation he is about to receive, each will perceive differently to the degree that his physical state diverges from that of another. Different perceptions of reality reflect the truth of individual leitmotifs.

These perceptual blendings involve all experience with human and non-human objects, but the potentials for confusion between self and object are understandably greatest when one is perceiving something that is similar in size, attributes, and complexity to oneself, namely another person. Sensori-motor feedback befuddles information about external reality because per-sonal contributions to that information are similar to information from others. The other person will inevitably be regarded with self as part of the tableau.

One also makes mistakes in self-perception for the same reason. Since self-perception goes on in the company of others, one may perceive oneself according to categories that are established with components of another's behavior in them.

The individual is sometimes able to distinguish himself wholly from others because he interacts with himself when alone. But because he is unquestionably present when he interacts with others, others are never wholly distinguished from himself. He sometimes notices he behaves separately from them, but he cannot ever notice that they act separately from him.

His capacity to distinguish between his own and another's behavior differs for each sensory channel. The more proximal modes are less discriminating. It is possible to segregate that portion of another's behavior that is received visually by merely closing one's eyes while continuing to act. One might try mechanically to block access from another to one's ears by holding one's hands over them while continuing to speak, but it is harder to achieve perfect segregation. With touch, pressure, and temperature, one cannot effectively sort out self from other. These sensations always are blends of input from other and from self.

The Reality of Some Metaphors

Consider the attribution of sensory qualities to something to which sensation does not seem to apply. Such descriptions are commonly called metaphors because they appear to have no concrete fit to the objects described. A metaphor is an expression applied to something to which it does not literally pertain. The name of one thing may be extended to another because the latter bears one salient resemblance to the first although it is otherwise unlike. A man described as a "snake in the grass" is tagged to depict his concealed potential for attack but not to figure his serpentine appearance or the way he locomotes. Metaphors using the vocabulary of sensation are believed to be counterfeits of reality because there are no apparent likenesses between the attributed sensations and their referents. Even the figurative meanings seem obscure.

Human descriptions, however, do not merely describe objects. They describe composite relations between objects and their perceivers. The attribute referred to in the metaphor may therefore be in the perceiver rather than in the object. Taking this composite into account, the metaphor may turn out to have literal application.

There are metaphors, for example, based on the lore that the heart is the habitat of emotional experience. Happy or excited persons are described as lighthearted, or high, while sad or depressed persons are portrayed as heavyhearted, or low. A group of English words that includes grief, aggrieved, grievous, grave, aggravated and others comes from the single Latin root *ad gravis,* which means to add weight. It happens that the mass of blood in the human body can be shifted from one region to another. If unpleasantness or discouragement is experienced, glandular secretions of nor-epinephrine as well as impulses from the nervous system result in a constriction of the capillaries near the skin surface and a dilation of blood vessels in the viscera. There is consequently a decrease in blood flow to the limbs and musculature and an increased concentration of blood collecting in the vessels surrounding the inner organs. Under these conditions the internal large blood vessels actually carry a larger proportion of the body's weight in blood. The opposite moves take place when a person is emotionally excited. Blood pressure rises and the skin surface becomes flushed.

The individual who kinaesthetically notes the added weight of the blood collected in his visceral regions can provide an accurate description of the physical correlates of his psychological state. When he describes himself as downhearted, it is because his heart is actually in a lower position within his body cavity. When someone reports he is heavyhearted, his heart feels as if it weighs more. When someone says "I had that sinking feeling in the pit of my stomach," he reports changes he has felt kinaesthetically in his chest and abdomen—his heart organ being dragged down—as a result of the redistribution of blood. The same would apply to relief. When a greater portion of the blood moves to the somatic musculature, the person reports his experience as "my heart leaped."

The metaphor "he acted coldly" is sometimes used to tag an unpleasant encounter with another person. Here too the description may be literal. The person recruits the proper sensory term from the language of his body. When he feels unpleasant or depressed, there is less blood at the skin surface. There is therefore a lowered or lowering temperature at the skin surface. The human body has temperature receptors lodged among the blood vessels in the skin. The individual is therefore able to sense the decrease in warmth that follows the withdrawal of blood from that region. Nor-epinephrine, the secretion that induces constriction of blood vessels at the skin surface, also curbs the body's oxidation process, resulting in a drop in basal heat production. The individual, perceiving actions of another person that depress him, also receives feedback from himself that he is chilled. Since he is unable to sort out the sources of these inputs, he attributes the two correlated inputs to the same source: namely, the other person. He describes the other as cold. As beauty is in the eye of the beholder, coldness is in the skin of the sensor.

This feedback setup is the equipment underlying the process of projection. Freud described projection as treating inner stimuli as if they were acting not from within but from without. The phenomena of projection, of empathy, and of vicarious experience are all based on the mechanism of blending input from self with that of other. In projection the input is attributed to the other. In empathy it is supposed to be shared. In vicarious experience it is treated as belonging to oneself.

To summarize, a person gives off stimuli in the course of activity, then monitors them and includes them in his perceptions. His categories of emotions or of qualities thus represent an accurate reading of his body's concrete states. If he senses such feelings in the presence of another, he may attribute his own mood or quality to the other person. He then deals with the other according to how he copes with the stimuli he produces. In this respect it can be said factually that there are multiple realities. It is not that some outside reality is inaccessible to each individual but that each individual is out there too.

No Mind-Body Dualism

A persistent problem—the dualism posed by Descartes concerning mind and body—can now be repudiated. Descartes distinguished between substances extended in space and time and those not extended. The body was extended and took up both space and time, whereas the mind was a thinking and unextended thing, and these two were "entirely and absolutely distinct." "By the body I understand . . . something which can be confined to a certain place, and which can fill a given space in such a way that every other body will be excluded from it. . . . Nothing at all belonged to the nature or essence of body, except that it was a thing with length, breadth, and depth, admitting of various shapes and various motions. . . ." The other entity ". . . was a substance the whole essence or nature of which is to think, and that for its existence there is no need of any place, nor does it depend on any material thing. . . ." This latter entity was mind. Descartes and many others, even in this century, also believed that the mind inhabited the body. What were the bases for these beliefs? The mind was revealed to us by the behavior attributed to it. It was credited with thinking, which is variously defined by such terms as understands, conceives, affirms, denies, doubts, knows, reasons, judges, and chooses. Mind does not exist without these actions occurring, said Descartes. Moreover, he endowed the mind only with ideas that were not abstracted from sensation nor dependent on it. For him mind and body are separate, and so sensations and ideas are disparate in origin and function. The crucial mental process he credited to mind is the ability to generate sentences, to produce language. Mind is able to use speech or other signs to express thoughts on record for the benefit of others, to arrange speech in various ways, and to arrange different words together in forming statements. Chomsky, a contemporary champion of the Cartesian view, has also declared that language "has no existence apart from its mental representation. Whatever properties it has must be those that are given to it by the . . . mental processes of the organism."

We now have evidence that clearly brands the mind-body distinction as false. It shows that mind occupies space and time, that it is not distinct from body, and that it is not altogether located in the head nor even wholly confined within the body. First, central nervous system functioning is regulated by inputs from the musculature and the receptors. For example, although the brain cortex is known to be active itself, neural firing patterns of the cortex are kept in phase with sensory inputs. The firing patterns of its cells become haphazard when external stimulation is cut off. Second, the findings of the sensory deprivation studies and of the delayed feedback studies show that an abridgment of the normal amount of sensory variety or a delay in the feedback from motor action to sensation undermines mental coherence. Imagination and inventiveness begin to recede. Hebb reports that subjects show loss of ability to solve problems while in their sensorily uniform cubicles. They cannot concentrate. As for governing action, the evidence from delayed feedback studies shows clearly that coordinated conduct is not sufficiently achieved internally. It requires a properly timed return of information from the environment. So we are obliged to alter the traditional description of thought intervening between sensory input and motor output. Rather than being placed between the receptors and effectors, thought includes them as part of its functioning. Reasoning and decision-making processes do not occur at a time of suspended contacts with the body environment but during such contacts. Some of the coherence and continuity supplied to behavior depends on the interval between motor output and sensory input. From this we conclude that there is an essential channel of information transmission outside the body, between the musculature and the sensory apparatus. We must not be misled into ignoring this communication channel simply because it has no stable material structure. For effective thought to occur, there must be no obstruction in this channel just as there must be no obstructions in a route within the nervous system.

Here are two fully linked and interdependent circuits. One is within the central nervous system. The other is the set of looped channels through which communication flows to and from the effectors and receptors of the body. The latter includes some protracted routes from the central nervous system to the musculature and from there through the environment to sense organs and then back to the central nervous system.

What of producing language? Chomsky offered guidance in interpreting Descartes' reliance on language activity as an indicator of mind: humans ". . . speak in a way that is innovative, free from stimulus control, and also appropriate and coherent." Let us review these three criteria. We know that language use is not free from stimulus control. It is dependent on sensations. A person unable to receive sensations and timely feedback from his own activity—say because of inhibition due to drugs, because of restricted sensory variety, or because of delayed auditory feedback—falters and becomes incoherent. We are left then with the most important criterion, what Chomsky calls " 'the creative aspect of language use,' the distinctively human ability to express new thoughts and to understand entirely new expressions of thought." I know of no direct investigation of the relation between ability to generate new sentences and patterns of sensory input. But there is a telling finding from a study of a closely related type of linguistic creativity.

Among the battery of tests used in the earliest perceptual isolation studies were anagrams (in which the subject was asked to make a word from a group of jumbled letters) and word-making (in which the subject was charged with making as many new words as he could using the letters of a word supplied to him). These tests are closely related to the type of linguistic creativity Chomsky describes, for they parallel the creation of new sentences from a finite pool of words that were previously learned in different sentence contexts. The word-making test particularly resembles this procedure. It involves breaking up meaningful letter sequences and recombining them into other meaningful sequences. Heron reports that the experimental subjects did significantly worse on this test. They made more errors and more incorrect words than a comparison group who did not undergo the experience of sensory deprivation. They did poorly when tested while in the cubicle and again just upon emerging from isolation. In the word-making test the experimental subjects also made fewer words altogether (that is, correct plus incorrect words) than did the comparison group.

There is a definite conclusion to be reached because these criteria for a separate mind and body are not confirmed. If interference with spaces around a body causes thinking and problem solving and linguistic ability to deteriorate, then *thought and spatial extension have much in common.* If interference with that channel in space between mouth and ear, so that sentences produced by the mouth are delayed in their travel to the ear, causes speakers to hesitate and stumble over their words, then (as revealed by producing words and sentences) *thought and temporal extension have much in common.* If by impositions on space and time, coherence and speech and innovative language decline, then thought must depend vitally upon the activity of the body and its contribution via sensation and proprioception to the central nervous system. The body therefore participates in the mind process. The sensory deprivation and the delayed sensorimotor feedback studies demonstrated this with no destruction or damage to body structures. Perhaps the mind was thought to reside within the confines of the body because destruction of brain tissue resulted in permanent impairment of thought. The external sensorimotor feedback channel cannot properly be destroyed, and its crucial presence was overlooked. If a person is deprived of environment outside his skin without being otherwise harmed, his thought will no longer be intact. So mind occupies space and time.

We have found physical conditions under which the mind process falters. Can mind be something other than what has been tampered with? What is it that is still there when manifestations of it fade? Descartes' own strategy for making such decisions would be to ". . . proceed by setting aside all that in which the least doubt could be supposed to exist, just as if I had discovered that it was absolutely false. . . ." This rule will not allow that mind is something distinct from processes that—when altered—result in the departure of evidence for what mind is supposed to do. It will not do to protest that the activities of mind require sensory stimulation but that sensations are separate from the structure of mind just as an engine is still an engine when it does not have fuel in it to burn. The channels that are required for thinking, like the conduits for fuel, are part of the structure. A set of such channels is located outside the skin. Thinking is extended in space and time. It has the properties of motion and magnitude.

I do not say that the complete removal of mind has ever been scientifically demonstrated. Yet stopping short of what might be accomplished in this respect is based on humanitarian constraints and not on the perseverance of mind. The subjects are persons who intend to return to a normal life after their voluntary participation in these experiments.

Are we to assume, then, that all existence is material? The trouble with answering this question at face value is that matter is no longer understood to be what matter used to be. The atoms of Bohr are not the atoms of Democritus. The materialist faith of the philosophers and scientists of the eighteenth and nineteenth centuries stressed that observables are the foundation of theoretical principles and that knowledge is deducible from experience. That belief has been replaced by a more encompassing approach based on formal propositions that accommodate in their framework such intangibles as non-Euclidean spaces, frictionless tracks, perfectly rigid pillars, massless particles, the force of gravity, and imaginary numbers. The adequacy of describing any of these rests primarily on logical rather than empirical proof. We accept these things and talk about them within the same framework that we apply to the study of more familiar objects in order to avoid intolerable contradictions in the construction of knowledge. Therefore, the idea of material existence is a relic. It has been unintentionally preserved beyond the era of its relevance because the terminology and mathematics of modern science had their origins in the study of physical events.

Some Implications

I began with an extended review of sensory influences upon the individual acting alone. By linking the process to feedback through external as well as internal channels to the human body, I was led to some insights about how man acts and knows. We should be aware of the enlarged integrated character of an individual's activities. His behavior cannot be time-zoned into a pure sequence of the traditional components of sensation, thought, and action. Thought and reason depend on physical processes in time and space outside the body. The unitary man must be this larger whole, owning a portion of the environment as well as his body. Many have proclaimed the wholeness of man. Their position can now be buttressed by evidence for the participation of the sensory and motor functions in producing the phenomenon called mind.

An analysis of the old mind-body dualism showed it to be a faulty interpretation. This was demonstrated by applying the findings of the delayed feedback studies to Descartes' propositions and by deducing the consequences. Not even Descartes' own standard, that of doubting if there was no evidence to dispel that doubt, saves the mind-body distinction from being rejected. Being partially outside the body, mind simply encompasses more than it was believed to encompass.

The belief that an individual is bounded by his skin is familiar and widespread. He was thought of as an organism enclosed in it. If he was beset by circumstances outside his skin, they were considered impositions from the environment. This conventional dividing line between organism and environment is wrongly drawn. Skin does not demarcate the individual. Essential portions of him, even though they are not palpable, exist outside it.

We discard the old mind-body dualism because we have evidence to support a reconstruction of the whole man. Similarly, we may resurrect a once-rejected idea in which credence is renewed by current facts. I do not suggest embracing it again in all its detail, but it has some plausibility stemming from the newly understood structure of mind.

In the early part of this century it was popular to ascribe a *group mind* to people gathered together. Proponents of this concept saw that those individuals seemed to share feelings, consciousness, and even goals and referred to a nerve network that implied tangible connections through which ideas and passions of group members were rapidly disseminated and through which all were unified. The group mind notion was subsequently rejected because it required assuming a mental structure that sprang into existence upon the formation of a throng, one that transformed the throng into a superorganic entity capable of knowing itself. That seemed too much to assume. No one could locate the nerve network. Now, considering the part played by sensorimotor feedback, it can be said that people are in-fused with a special mentality when they are together.

When the individual is alone, all information about humans in his ex-ternal feedback loop is supplied by his own conduct. When he is with others, their sensorimotor feedback channels merge. All become coupled to one another by these external loops. Any overt gesture contributed by one is received by all. In the presence of others there can be no private external feedback.

A remarkable link is thereby forged in a social situation. Individual minds in sensory access are no longer separate thinking units but actually part of a network. Such mergers are created anew each time individuals come into contact and are dissolved when they part. The external channels that exist for each of them do not have rigid or narrow paths, so no violence or other alteration is done to bodily structures.

The mechanism of milling around, mentioned in Chapter 2, can now be identified more specifically. Milling dissolves the sense of separateness from others. It establishes a feeling of participating in a group. The individual becomes less clear about his own identity and more subject to control by others. Decisions for action acquire a groupwide status. LeBon said that a new entity is created by people in a crowd, an entity that has properties that are different from those of its individual constituents. All individuals, having been assembled in a group, feel, think, and act differently than they would were they alone. To designate the mental activity of a person in which information from the conduct of others mingles with his own feedback, we could use the term *interpersonal mind*. When two or more persons are in sensory contact, there is a partial replacement of individual mind by such a form.

This account is different from the older idea of group mind. It is not the creation of a third entity capable of knowing itself. It is not a nerve network uniting all individuals to one another. In a large crowd each person is not directly accessible to all others. Instead there is a series of overlapping feedback networks, each linking those proximal enough to have sensory access to one another. The minds so coupled are not congruent, for each person's inner workings are not directly affected. Yet some interpersonal influence is inevitable if interpersonal minds are operative. Students of behavior often describe the conditions under which group influence is resisted, or under which individuality is submerged, by referring to the content of the mind—the strength or weakness of its beliefs and values. This emphasis upon the so-called cognitive content of minds, while justified, is an incomplete description of interpersonal influence. For individuals sometimes disregard their beliefs and values. They become notably susceptible to being swayed by others in groups as a result of mergers in interpersonal existence, of being as one with others, of sharing intimately in their perceptions.

Because of this arrangement one cannot know other people without some impression of self as a portion of that knowledge. One never perceives behavior of another without incorporating into that perception some aspects of one's own state or conduct at the time. At first I suggested this idea as a clarification of the process of perception. Then by scrutiny of some popular metaphors, it was revealed as a basis for the existence of multiple realities and a difficulty in sorting them out, which sometimes leads to attributing erroneously a quality of oneself to another or to ascribing a quality of the other to oneself.

It would therefore be a blunder to break this living merger by assigning interpersonal actions to separate persons. Just as mind in the company of others is no longer individual, the structure of the interpersonal act—which depends so much upon mind—cannot be singular. Along with breaking down the traditional boundaries of the individual and outlining mind more suitably to include a part of his environment, we require a similarly revised demarcation of the interpersonal act.

4

Structure of an Act

c◊乙◊ɔ

Studying an interpersonal act requires not only an adequate description but also showing how it is known and understood by people in everyday life. Though an act is the elementary unit for counting and analysis, there is nothing elementary about its identification. Yet the insights, explanations, and understanding to be proposed rest on its conception and measurement.

The ideas in the two preceding chapters imply some features of the interpersonal act, and I will cite them here along with other properties of its structure based on empirical, theoretical, and logical considerations. Later in the chapter I will suggest how individuals develop conceptions of social behavior from daily experience. Despite the detail to be offered, I will need both an account in Part Two of how acts are measured and the interpretive example in Part Three to clarify the properties that are initially mentioned here.

Duration, Discontinuity, and Complexity

We commonly group things according to dimensions of interest though they differ on other dimensions. Elephants and eels differ in size, complexity, and length of life although they are both vertebrates. We enumerate individuals of different ages and sexes as units for the purpose of counting votes in elections, in demographic studies, and for calculating the rates of labor turnover. Ignoring secondary differences, we arrange for a clearer tally of the main objects of interest. Similarly, the duration of an act is a secondary attribute in understanding its structure. From their research on behavior, Barker and Wright learned that actions of older persons were more complex and took longer than actions of children. Although I will discuss a temporal aspect relevant to the study of behavior in Chapter 8, I will ignore time differences in outlining the unit of measurement. Unit acts vary in duration.

It is often assumed that behavior is continuous and that an observer who makes a record of it does violence to his subject by establishing junctures where events simply flow on. Part of the continuity of action, however, stems from the human ability to imagine sequences. With events stored in memory, perceiving an early phase of a familiar act will evoke anticipation of phases to come. The more a person learns about behavior, the more he may be disposed to extrapolate from action along its probable routes. There are sufficient cues for a person observing interpersonal conduct so that he can imaginatively impose continuity upon events that are phenomenally discrete. The continuity so established is an artifact of human thought.

By the same token, human thought can, for the purposes of studying interaction, conceive of and measure acts as discrete wholes. I do not say that human experience is a series of moments, springing into existence, vanishing instantly, and being created anew. There is much overlap among life's stream of events. There are also discontinuities within given dimensions of interpersonal experience. For example, many acts begin with the onset of sensory access or a change in access between individuals. Although the precise moment of access may be elusive, it is clear that such junctures occur. Persons sometimes have sensory access to one another and sometimes do not have such access. Ends of acts are difficult to identify, but some acts definitely end when sensory access ceases. We need only refer to a familiar instance, such as saying goodbye and departing after an encounter, to reject the assumption of a universally indivisible interaction flow. It can be said that acts have beginnings and ends and that their boundaries can be established without tearing vital connections.

Another type of variation that is secondary to the establishment of units is complexity. From daily experience it is clear that some actions are more elaborate and complicated than others. This has by no means been a standard assumption about unit acts. A classic error based on the opposite assumption—that all actions could be simplified enormously—was made during the first third of this century through the attempted fragmentation of industrial tasks. As a facet of an occupational career that came to be called Scientific Management, Frederick Taylor proposed that a job could be broken down into its basic elements and that the most efficient recombination of them could be figured out and taught to workers. This arrangement in turn would eliminate waste and increase industrial productivity, for men would have been converted into human machines in the best implications of the term *machines*. Some productive gains were won, usually on a short-run basis. But an upper limit—unnecessarily low—had been placed on human productivity. It went undiscovered in the formal records of industrial research until Elton Mayo and his colleagues demonstrated that for many of the tasks men are asked to do, the fragmentable model is actually inefficient. Today, most industrial engineers doubt that the supposed elementary parts of human work activity are independent of each other for practical purposes. Several writers (e.g., Bell) have pointed out that time-and-motion study is micromotion study and is divorced from the knowledge we have of humans and their natural activity rhythms.

In the brief history of the study of interaction, one of the most common practices in establishing act units has been to take apart the components of a complex sequence and to categorize the separate parts. But classifiers who break interaction into a stream of corpuscles and pigeonhole the individual bits lose the synthesizing character of act organization. What is then described often lacks the essential quality of wholeness that is found in social conduct. These researchers inadvertently settle a problem that still seems unresolved today. The issue can be exemplified by the case of the productive power of language. Speakers demonstrate the capacity to say things they have never said or things that have never been heard before. Yet their comments are understandable to other speakers of the language. Recognizing this directly or not, the student of interaction who approaches the study of social conduct by attending to speech alone proceeds to fragment the sentence in his coding of it. To do so is to have implicit confidence that either no organizing principle is destroyed by this fragmentation or that the rule is known so that the sentence can be reproduced readily. All the organizing principles for assembling components into sentences are not yet known. (Chomsky) Thus the fragmenters who descend the ladder to a lower level of study and categorization of speech elements may unwittingly remove the rungs as they go. Similarly, researchers who dismantle the act so that they may deal with its parts have not shown that they can return to the level of the whole again and reassemble, from their classification, the types of acts apparent in everyday experience.

I will assume that acts have a character of wholeness. I believe there are organizing principles for meaningful acts that differ from the rules pertaining to their components, just as sentences have structural features unlike those found in phrases or words. Therefore, just as they are not all the briefest units discernible but have differing lengths of life, acts are not all equal in complexity.

Two Main Parts of the Unit Act

The idea of interpersonal mind implies that an act will include the behavior of at least two people. Behavior emanating from one person is input to himself and to others simultaneously. In addition, he experiences others through the same channels by which he experiences himself. No one can be aware of another's conduct without sensing oneself. This implies that from the earliest events of life, before benefiting from language and established categories for perceiving and distinguishing things, even before being able to operate with a fully matured nervous system, an individual experiences a blend of signals in social encounters. Maturation will not change this case. Nor will insight, for the mechanics of the process remains the same. This mingling must appear in the conception of the social act. Its boundaries cannot be drawn around an individual but must include at least two persons.

Though the overt behavior of all those engaged in interaction is of the same type and is describable in the same way, we are often interested in portraying such conduct for a particular individual or class of people. We may, for example, wish to describe the behavior of a reporter or of a legislator. The conduct of the person of interest will be termed the *reaction*. The actions of the other will be cited as the *situation*. Behavior is involved in both components. Any category of conduct may be part of the situation or the reaction or both. For example, a legislator may reply to a reporter's question with a question. Thus the behavioral distinction between situation and reaction is a convention. The matter of whose conduct will be called the reaction is a decision to be made according to one's explicit interest.

Components of the Situation

Each encounter between people centers on one of a set of circumstances, a situation, that frames the interaction of the moment. Individuals have the potential for interpersonal behavior as soon as they can receive someone else's actions as well as their own. An act begins with the onset of sensory access. This is a *contact opportunity*. People who are sensorily impaired will have fewer contact opportunities to the degree that such opportunities ordinarily depend on those blocked channels. Thus the myopic man has fewer visual encounters. It is not necessary to assume that individuals are aware of contact opportunities as long as access or lack of access can be noted objectively. For example, a person may act as if he has direct access to another when he does not, as when an excited viewer shouts at a political speaker he is watching on television.

Access is achieved by persons coming into proximity even though they are not actively seeking the opportunity, as when one person passes another on the street. Visual or auditory signals can be sensed by anyone within eyesight or earshot. Because of this access many unintended contact opportunities are utilized. Someone's actions may indirectly call attention to him and evoke a response, as when someone is heard crying nearby or when two children are seen fighting. One of the problems of blaring an automobile horn in order to attract one person's attention is that it may attract the attention of every passing motorist and every nearby pedestrian as well. Unintended or not, these are instances of interpersonal behavior.

An act may begin when someone speaks to another. An act may begin when the behavior of a third party is thrust into the midst of an ongoing situation, as when men working together are interrupted by a supervisor who delivers further instructions. Sometimes specific acts begin within the context of a larger ongoing interpersonal situation, as when a choirmaster raises his baton to signal the start of another song or when a quarterback begins to call out signals for his team's next play. This class of beginnings makes plain that the onset of sensory access is not enough to identify all beginnings of acts. Sometimes an act starts with a change of topic during continued contact. In Chapter 7 I will suggest a way to identify such beginnings.

Defining a situation is like writing an introduction to a stage play. It embraces the aggregate of circumstances surrounding a contact opportunity. It includes a setting and a scene and a cast of characters. These qualifying conditions make up the context. The context sets boundaries that include certain features of the environment and of the individuals in it. It teems with properties that can be identified and enumerated. Everything that precedes a reaction and can be noted and measured may be consigned here. They are distinguishing circumstances, qualifiers to behavior. The most common conditions are universal. These include specific times of the day or week and specific dates. Still others, less widespread but nevertheless parts of the contexts for numerous acts, are particular locales such as the home, the marketplace, and the halls of ministry. The identification of observable conditions alone can be virtually endless if one determines to make it so. The uniqueness ascribed to a particular event is due to the infinitesimal likelihood that its conditions will ever again be assembled in the identical constellation.

Many situational features remain constant throughout an event and are parts of classes of acts. For example, the status of each participant—such as the job he holds—may be identified as a property of the situation. Except for acts in which one or another individual says "You're fired" or "You're promoted" or "I quit," job status does not change in the course of the event. The room or locale in which interaction occurs does not vanish when a reaction gets under way. It is even present after the event to become part of another act.

Along with contact opportunity and context, the situation is also composed of the behavior of one or more persons. This behavior may persevere throughout the episode. For example, a person may continue to express unhappiness even as another tries to console him. In this instance the action may be mutually sustaining, with the latter's reassurance encouraging the other to reveal his worries more fully and that revelation evoking more reassurance. So situation and reaction occur almost together. The periods of their existence overlap. However, for the sake of convenience in discussion and analysis, the situation will always be taken as the initial phase of the act, as having a slight head start over the reaction.

In ongoing interaction, the reaction of one person adds to the situation for the other. Every denouement is an overture to a new act.

A Set of Alternative Reactions

The other main part of an interpersonal event is the *reaction*—the behavior of the individual whose conduct is of primary interest. To use the term *reaction* for whatever an individual does recognizes that life has gone on before the moment in question and that his overt conduct has emerged from those proceedings. This statement should not imply that the situation is always the specific stimulus to the reaction. The individual responds to something prior somewhere—perhaps in his memory—and the situation is the observable concurrent circumstance.

Inasmuch as the reaction comes slightly after the situation, it has the character of feedback to the event. The studies of breakdowns in behavior due to delayed feedback call attention to a fundamental attribute that is part of the structure of an act. Those findings tell us that any course of action is one of at least two alternatives. The other course may not be a coherent one, but it can occur and would be noticeably different from the first. Just as delayed feedback can be properly interpreted as another kind of feedback, a given reaction can be recognized as one of a set of possible alternative behaviors associated with a situation.

This principle has biological and social significance. Biologically it is a behavioral milestone along the phylogenetic scale. More than any other, the human animal has evolved to be less constrained by instinctual or environmental determinants. He shows great flexibility in conduct and is most likely to be so in that most creative of situations—interaction with other people. This is not to say that instinct and immediate environment fail to affect human behavior. They certainly do. But the script is not so definitively written. The one-to-one correspondence between a stimulus and a response for lower animals has been replaced for humans by multiple correspondences between situations and reactions. Indeed, the same reaction may occur in several different situations.

The set of different reactions for a given situation will be called *alternatives*. At a dinner table, for example, one person is talking, another looks and listens without eating, a third walks around the table and serves the diners, and a fourth eats heartily without looking at the speaker. All are in sensory access. The situation is actively dominated by the speaker in that he is providing more output that is sensory input to all. The reactions to him differ, and all can be noted and enumerated. A similar approach can be used in studying problem-solving conferences, jury deliberations, and other interpersonal assemblies of more than two people. In these instances, where several people are present and are reacting differently to a situation, the alternatives occur simultaneously. At times when only two people are in contact, alternative reactions will occur on repeated occasions of the same situation.

Since we can imagine alternative reactions, this act-structure has a place for possible events as well as for those that have been observed to happen. In this way knowledge of behavior is not merely based on observables but is also logical.

I can now distinguish among and define three forms of interpersonal behavior. The specific activity of two or more people in sensory access that occurs at a moment in time in a given place, with all its unique qualities and organization, is an *event*. The event classified into categories that express it as a reaction to a situation is an *act*. It is hard to describe an event without allocating its qualities to conventional word categories, and we usually talk of an event in terms of the linguistic class of acts subsuming it. Knowledge also exists or can be logically implied concerning alternative reactions for that situation. This aggregate, which may be partly non-empirical, is a conception that goes beyond reference to a given event to summarize cumulative experience and is the *whole act,* or act-whole. When my discussion applies both to acts and to whole acts with minimal ambiguity, I will use the shorter term for convenience.

The whole act is close to Mead's description of the game, in which the successful execution of a play depends on the distribution and performance of all members of the team. In the game each person takes a role and behaves by taking into consideration how his teammates will react. The circumstances to which they respond is the situation, and each of their different responses is an alternative reaction. The result is a well-coordinated episode in which the deployment and conduct of each participant requires the awareness of each other's conduct. The performance of each is understood in the light of the other alternatives. The reaction of one person might be hard to understand if taken alone. For example, why would an infielder in a baseball game run away from a ball hit toward him and end up covering a base? We comprehend this by noting that another player came over to grab the ball, a player who was farther from the base to be covered than the one who ran away from the ball and toward the base. In the same way, in a stage play the placement and conduct of one actor takes into account the alternative reactions of others on the scene.

The structure of the interpersonal act has a similar pattern. However, instead of referring only to simultaneous reactions of other people, it may refer to the alternative conduct of others in the same position and same social relationship *at other times.* Even when only two people meet one another repeatedly in the same situation, their reactions may differ on different occasions.

The dictum that the whole is greater than the sum of its parts is one of those imprecise sayings that may seem to apply to the act. It does fit if the action perceived is not solely implied by what is observable. An event is made up of myriad muscle contractions. Because the sensory modes of an observer are integrated in their use, the event is selected and organized. Additional shaping is given by basing the categorization on feedback from the observer's own incipient motor reactions. This condensing and forcing into a category results in much lost or discarded information. What remains represents more than itself. If perception is selective in this way, ignoring some sense data and condensing the remainder, then the act is also less than the sum of its parts. Yet the category of action evoked bestows additional information that was not transmitted in the event. One fills in knowledge of alternative reactions that took place in this situation at other times or imagines alternatives that could happen. Now the whole is more than the sum of its parts. The word *sum* is clearly inadequate here. An organization has been created.

Quantitative Properties

Day after day we give greetings and take departures. Sometimes we refuse solicitors; other times we make contributions. We carry out certain practices again and again. Other matters find us steadfastly disinterested. With the passage of time many acts repeat themselves. Noted, categorized, and tallied, these summaries reveal different frequencies for different reactions to the same situations. Every reaction can be assigned a numerical value on this basis. Assuming that events will occur in the future as they have in the past, the summaries of frequency enable us to calculate the relative probability of each reaction in a set.

A simple version of this scheme is used in work-sampling studies by efficiency engineers. Such studies are usually concerned with down-time that might occur because of a breakdown of a machine or because employees return late from a coffee break. Here only two categories are used, productive activity and down-time. Each is measured and expressed as a fraction of 1.000. The fraction is readily convertible into an amount that refers to the duration of the period under consideration.

The alternatives in a given set are seldom equiprobable. One or more of them occur often; some happen rarely. If a reaction never occurs in a given situation, its probability for that situation is zero.

Probabilities for a set of reactions are calculated according to the situation they follow. Some readers will recognize that this calculation measures a stochastic process, particularly the Markovian form. A Markov process is one in which the likelihoods of certain events depend on the events that immediately precede them. The description is stochastic because the probability of a given reaction can be different in different situations.

In the first paragraph of this section, I expressed an assumption needed to establish behavioral probabilities—that interpersonal acts would happen in the future as they have in the past. Naturally, behavior patterns can change. Whether the change is cyclical or evolutionary, it would still compel readjusting the probabilities of reactions following situations. I mention the matter of change here because the invention of Markovian expressions has spawned many useful variants. An early form of the Markov process calls for an assumption of unchanging probabilities. It clearly cannot apply here. The format for the whole act is found in the types sometimes called unstable Markov processes. Nevertheless, to describe behavior patterns for a single time period, I will tentatively assume stable probabilities.

The circumstances portrayed by these statistical forms are more familiar than the terms by which they are called. Consider the case of asking an employer for a raise in salary. In that situation there are several anticipated alternative reactions. The employer may consent, he may refuse, he may make a counter-offer concerning the enlargement of fringe benefits; he may perform some other reaction as well. Each of these is an event of ascertainable likelihood, and one of the reactions is usually judged to have a higher probability than the others in the situation. Employees embarking on this venture usually do so after having reached a conclusion about the relative likelihoods. Change a condition, perhaps the installation of a new boss, and those probabilities will undergo change.

The whole act can now be defined as *a set of probable alternative reactions to a situation.* The description of all whole acts can follow this format. It would specify: (a) the situational context, including the positions of the participants and the social relationships involved, (b) the conduct of one or more persons as the behavioral part of that situation, (c) the probability of that situation occurring out of all situations found in the social relationship, (d) the various reactions of one or more persons (in the position being studied) to that situation, and (e) the relative probabilities for the set of alternative reactions. The whole act is describable qualitatively and quantitatively. Neither distorts the information contributed by the other but rather enhances it. In Chapter 9 I will show that this format can be applied to an ensemble of act-wholes for a given social relationship.

Learning About Social Behavior

I have outlined the structure of interpersonal acts. Do people know behavior in the same way? The doctrine of psychological oneness among members of a society is prevalent in social theories. People in a group are said to share a common pool of beliefs and values; hence we may expect them to share knowledge of acts and to be able to reach mutual understanding. For several reasons this sharing, even among members of the same group, is not perfect. It is due to variations in social experience. Each person is to some rate his own composer of full-fledged acts because of differences in sensitivity and idiosyncratic exposure.

The individual establishes knowledge of acts in the way he learns from all experiences. Observed events are stored in memory. Interpersonal encounters repeat themselves. Although unique events can be recalled, the episode itself is remembered according to categories whose contents are summaries of many concrete occasions. Minor variations in performance are ignored. Each category encompasses a behavioral domain with its central themes set off from the cores of other acts. The individual picks up knowledge indirectly too, from anecdotes and parables, from books, and from television dramas.

With continued experience it dawns on the individual that events have alternative possibilities as they unfold. He observes that all those present in a situation do not give the same reaction to it. He also notes that an individual's conduct in the same interpersonal situation is not always the same at different times. He begins to group his knowledge of alternative courses of action into a set of reactions associated with each situation. Since the set is assembled from pooled experience, memory joins in constructing the idea of the whole act.

As the individual becomes aware of alternative reactions, his cumulative impressions tell him that the alternatives do not occur with equal frequency. He establishes rough estimates of their relative likelihoods. He concludes that some reactions are more probable than others, that some are common and others are rare. He stops at this ordinal arrangement of likelihoods and it affords some predictability of how others will react in given situations.

Although the organization of behavioral experience is a private matter, the categories of conduct are not so private. Perceiving and categorizing events are performed at the same time by all interacting participants. In the presence of others, his reaction is joined by their reactions. Accordingly, whether conscious or not, in the presence of others his classification will be affected by clues from their reactions as well as from his own. Even if the participants do not react in the same way, each person senses other reactions along with feedback from his own. This results, for an event, in the same set of elements being given to all. They are all there, they all share. Repeating the same action with different people at different times further trims it to a standardized category. Thus the biological equipment that engenders shared consciousness also fosters shared behavior categories.

Some acts become more universally defined because on different occasions individuals perform reciprocal portions. One time the individual asks a question of someone else and gets an answer. Another time another person asks a question, and the individual answers. The interrogative exchange has a plot of its own, and one comes to see that he may take one or another of the parts. Similar generalizing from reciprocal experience happens throughout the interpersonal realm. In time the individual assembles a large catalog of diverse social behavior.

How much of a sense of community does each man develop from his experience? How unified is his knowledge of social life around him and of his own place in it? Some forces work to consolidate this understanding. Other forces resist it. Shared knowledge is enhanced as the person stores indirect information from what he reads and learns through hearsay. But these sources are relied on more as he matures, not at first. An individual's cognizance is initially fragmentary. Categories of acts are established largely from experience on the scale of individuals in pairs or in primary groups (small numbers of persons in sustained sensory contact). From this coupling of minds comes coupled perceptions and similar act categories. Paired likeness of perceptions, more than community-wide consensus, is the ordinary stuff of social awareness. Small group experiences such as those of a family are also common. Shared categories become more widespread when people interact in large aggregates. Awareness of a common bond among participants at political rallies, among people singing together in church, and among comrades around a campfire stems from this melding of perceptions.

A person retains some of the ambiguity and contradictions he perceives. He is exposed to varied conduct as an active participant in various groups and acquires a ragged and multiple summary of the behavioral community. It is a fly's eye-view, compound but not integrated.

When an outline is made of the structure and properties of a basic unit of study, an ever-present concern is whether some features included as part of it should have been left out and reserved for questions concerning determinants of the unit's form or occurrence. Whatever is ascribed to the unit in excess of what is needed to define it is thereby made less accessible to explanation, for it appears as a property or dimension given in advance. Is the duration of an act, for example, merely a property of the unit, or is it determined by the forces affecting the frequency of the act's occurrence? Is the complexity of an act inversely related to the frequency with which it happens? Were these questions answered, still other issues could be raised about this basic unit.

It may seem that situation and reaction are merely new labels for the classic stimulus-response of behaviorism. Although somewhat alike, there are important differences. An interpersonal act refers to more than one individual. The situation is larger and more complex than a stimulus. It includes both context and conduct. At least part of it endures throughout the reaction and even after it. The situation is not necessarily the impetus to the reaction but refers to an observable interpersonal circumstance when an individual is behaving. The reaction is understood as part of a set of alternatives; it is not unique but has a probability relative to them. I will bring out other differences in Part Three when I present a case study.

5

Meaning

⚜

This account of behavior has progressed from sensations of it to the mind that experiences it to the structure of the act as established in the mind. Categories of observed conduct are used to build ideas of acts by being organized, summarized, and augmented by lessons and imagination. Given this knowledge of act-structure, can it be said that people share understandings, that they communicate and comprehend one another's messages?

The answer to this question is based on the nature of meaning. Meaning is a topic that benefits from discussion by example as well as from formal exposition. Accordingly, in this chapter I will outline properties of a kind of meaning that is related to the conception of whole acts. The operations for interpreting meaning—a procedure that social scientists may use which parallels what people do in daily life—will be described in Part Three when a case study is presented.

Types of Meaning

In the grammar of interpersonal behavior, an act's meaning rests on its structure. One might say that behavior semantics is dependent on behavioral syntax or simply that some of the act's content is carried in its form. The idea of meaning is not so easy to use today as it must have been in the past, when men subscribed to notions of a basically unchanging world, of clearcut boundaries between objects in that world—such as immutable species of living things—and even of conceptions of brain activity as linear transmission of neural impulses through chains of single cells. All these beliefs gave support to the idea of each phenomenon's having its unitary and intrinsic significance. One act with one meaning, inseparable, forever. This principle is no longer tenable in the face of such brilliant hypotheses as evolution and relativity. The notion of meaning itself has softened and become imprecise. People commonly hold several different perspectives on meaning. It is fair, therefore, to find a number of different interpretations for any given act, one derived from each of the perspectives.

The simplest definition of meaning is *nominal,* which is the category by which an act is called. It is a label, just as the label of a proper name stands for a certain person. It denotes an event or defines what something is. For example, if one scuba dives, it means he goes under water wearing a self-contained underwater breathing apparatus. The *signal* character of an act is its standing for something else besides its named content. For example, jumping up and yelping "Ouch!" means a painful surprise. Hat-tipping means respect. The *causal* meaning of conduct refers to the actor's purpose or motive or to the effective force leading to the act. For example, his coming home late means he has been detained at work. The parent who means to prevent an accident orders his child to get out of the roadway. The *consequential* meaning is an act's supposed effects. For example, a good player rejoins his team after his injury has healed, and it means three goals for his side. Consequential meaning is also implied if a leader's conduct is said to be inspiring to his followers or if an unpleasant rejoinder is said to give pain. There is also *moral* meaning, in which an appraisal is made of an act according to the values of the interpreter. Someone may say, "If he does that, it means that he's despicable."

In spite of this variety, meaning has resisted a definition that would be acceptable as both an idea and a method for comprehending social acts. None of the above-mentioned perspectives has led to a satisfactory way of interpreting behavior, one that resembles how understanding is conventionally established in everyday life. Even people who employ these outlooks in daily intercourse founder when using them. Some of the reasons for their difficulty stem from the amount of knowledge and assumptions required in interpretation, especially for causal, consequential, or moral meanings. Indeed, while the example of intention in admonishing a child playing in the street is straightforward, motives for actions are rarely unique. The same act may be prompted by different purposes. The same purpose may prompt different acts. Since it is necessary to know much about the individual's particular history and course of experience leading up to the event, and to understand the other, one cannot easily and consistently divine another's purpose in doing something. Nor can he rely directly on the other's testimony for understanding. People often speak to deceive themselves as well as others, especially on matters of intent.

Consequential meanings, drawing conclusions about the outcome or effect of an act, are burdened with similar handicaps. Such assumptions flirt with the errors of naive determinism and oversimplification. For acts do not have inevitable outcomes, nor are outcomes uniquely caused. To undertake this approach to interpreting meaning is to presume complete knowledge of all possible effects and their likelihoods. Recognizing this difficulty, the contemporary theory of decision-making has made a place for risk in the face of uncertainty about outcomes. This risk factor mirrors the puzzlement about utilitarianism in earlier days, in which the effects of an action could at best be given a probability and not a certainty. One can make a distinction between two questions in the theory of utilitarianism. One is whether a particular outcome of a course of action will occur at all. This outcome's probability can be determined if sufficient knowledge is available. The other matter is whether, if this outcome occurs, it will be beneficial. This too can be given a probability, but it depends on different knowledge; hence an outcome cannot be inevitably associated with its impact or benefit. The quality of a benefit or harm is not inherent in an outcome but is associated with it under certain contingencies.

Moral interpretations also require knowledge of the ethical standards of the person acting and insight about which principle—since several alternative ones are usually possible—the actor applied to the given event. The man on the street commonly applies his own standards to an event rather than striving to interpret it from the value-orientations of the other, and then he commonly remarks, "I can't understand why he would do a thing like that."

In spite of the obstacles to establishing meaning according to purpose or to outcome or to values, people employ all these perspectives in everyday encounters. They do not rely on one consistently or use them selectively but mix them unevenly. We can appreciate how interpretations easily fall prey to puzzlement. When the topic is the meaning of someone's conduct, it is striking how emphatic the disagreement can be and how quickly bafflement can overtake a conversation.

There is another kind of meaning. It is more than mere nominal designations or signs of acts, yet it is less ambitious than trying to fix the intentions of the actor or the consequences of his action. Nor is it a moral assay of conduct. This type is *connotation*. It is widely employed. Because it is based on actual social experience, connotation is an interpretive process that considers the structure of behavior. Langer gave connotation a structural definition, writing that

There is in fact no quality of meaning; its essence lies in the realm of logic, where one does not deal with qualities, but only with relations. . . . Meaning is not a quality but . . . a *pattern* viewed with reference to one special term round which it centers: this pattern emerges when we look at the given term *in its total relation to the other terms about it.*

Applied to acts, the meaning of an event comes through associating it with other alternatives in the act-whole. An act is known by the company it keeps.

This type of interpretation is so commonplace and pervasive that we are usually unaware of it. Yet we do it all the time. The experience of sensation, for example, is not merely of a stimulus impinging upon a receptor. It is discrimination between magnitudes of stimuli from one instant to the next. Understanding a quality of a person depends on knowing others to whom he can be compared. If someone says "A is a great teacher," one thinks of B and C who are also teachers. A similar relativity underlies our comprehension of speech. A word, though recognizable by itself, acquires a connotation depending on where it bobs up in a verbal stream and on other words that could have appeared but did not. Phrases are special combinations from a large set of alternatives. The intelligibility of a sentence depends upon these alternative possibilities even though they remain implicit. Meaning in behavior is similarly structured.

The connotation of an event will be derived from knowledge of other possibilities. Which others? Those that fit into the conception of the whole act. This form cradles the connotation. Its three parts can be identified as follows:

1. Preceding clues: earlier events in the sequence of interaction. If the act is that of hitting someone about the shoulders and head, it helps to know whether the person pummeled (a) insulted someone's sister or (b) scored the winning goal in the last second of a game. There is, of course, a large set of cultural understandings behind the use of preceding clues. I do not deny the existence of purpose or consequence to the act of hitting. However, in this case we need not infer intent or motive. We can establish correlations from observations of behavior as a basis for distinguishing the meanings of hitting someone.

2. Following clues: events that come later in the sequence of interaction. The behavioral component of a situation is a reaction to what went

on before. As reaction, it becomes in turn part of the situation for what will follow. To understand behavior as situation, one relies on a process already described in perceiving. An individual establishes perceptual categories in part according to his bodily reactions. They take place while sensations are being received. Similarly, we construct meaning for the behavior in a situation by noting reactions to it. G. H. Mead had this in mind, observing that "if one asked what the idea of a dog is . . . one would find a whole group of responses which are more or less connected together by definite paths so that when one uses the term 'dog' he does tend to call out this group of responses." Further in his discussion Mead remarked, "Just as in fencing the parry is an interpretation of the thrust, so, in the social act, the adjustive response of one organism to the gesture of another is the interpretation of that gesture by that organism—it is the meaning of that gesture."

3. Alternative clues: other reactions that occur in this situation on other occasions but that did not happen this time. Considering possible alternative reactions that flank the one which occurred represents the last step in the encirclement of an event by other conduct that contributes to its meaning. One reaction becomes an alternative to another by the device of mentally organizing experience with a given situation. Then, consciously or not, one becomes engrossed in this broader set of actions. We are usually aware of the set of alternatives following a situation. We refer to what might have happened, remarking, "He could have done so-and-so instead of what he did."

Here is an example that shows how these parts of act-structure contribute to understanding. Consider a sudden outburst of sobbing. What does it mean? It helps to know some preceding clues: a beauty contest was under way. The sobbing girl was one of the finalists. The winner has just been announced. In addition it helps to know an alternative reaction: another finalist, upon hearing the winner's name announced, flashed a wide smile to the assemblage and then congratulated the sobbing girl. If the meaning of this sobbing is still vague, it helps to know a following clue: a newsman reacts by thrusting a microphone within range and asks the girl in tears, "How do you feel about being the prettiest girl in the world?" Thus the meaning of the sudden outburst is given not only by the action itself but by the preceding, following, and alternative reactions. They demonstrate that connotative meaning is not inherent in an act but is conditional. Indeed, the alternatives could have been reversed. The winner could have smiled and kissed the sobbing loser. Sobbing would then connote something else. In the first case the sobbing means relief from tension, perhaps drenched with elation. It is the same meaning that applies when family members who have been apart under trying circumstances come together again. Astronaut John Glenn, returning home after his successful space flight, broke into tears upon being reunited with his wife.

The Reaction Zero

If alternative reactions add to understanding, we must pay attention to a stock form of behavior that is often overlooked. This form is based on assumptions put forth in Chapter 2, beginning with the idea that if a person is alive he is behaving. If an interpersonal situation can be identified for him, it is proper to cite his reaction.

We are not required to presume a causal relationship in identifying a situation and its reaction. The immediate impetus to overt conduct may come from inaccessible or hard-to-measure sources such as one's memory. An individual may react without any overt change in the behavior of others. For example, one of several people who are reading quietly says, "I think I'll go to sleep." The only noticeable change in his environment may be the time of day. We need not say that the situation brought on the reaction, only that the reaction took place in that situation. Having distinguished between the instigation of an act and its specific content, the student of interpersonal conduct must describe and explain *what* a person does when he behaves. Let us call whatever a person does in a situation his reaction. All observed behavior is therefore categorizable. It is not necessary that the conduct include overt behavioral change with respect to the surroundings in order to be tagged a reaction. In some situations little overt activity may take place. Because a reaction must be present if a situation has been identified, this type of behavior is a valid category of conduct, and some label like *Shows No Overt Change in Behavior* would acknowledge it.

There are good reasons for this circumstance to be designated a reaction if it applies to a contact opportunity. It is a logically possible action. To fully understand the workings of a behavior system, one must measure whatever happens. From personal experience we know that a person may not respond overtly though he could have done so. Social life is full of obstinate silences. Nor does such lack of overt change have to correspond with a person's internal states. The reaction may be covert. If there were no changes in movement by the individual compared to his movement or lack of it prior to the onset of a situation, then that is the reaction.

Shows No Overt Change in Behavior is a designation based on evidence available to the senses. It is a pattern of conduct that remains unaltered upon the onset of a contact opportunity. In the study of interpersonal acts, Shows No Overt Change in Behavior has the same status that air had before Torricelli's experimental demonstration that air exerted physical pressure. Air was there, but scientists of the day were not including it systematically in their considerations of the height that a liquid would rise in a tube.

Another reason for such a category in a descriptive scheme is that the initial classification of behavior is not the place to distinguish between interesting and uninteresting conduct. One may consider Shows No Overt Change in Behavior a trivial reaction—just as one looks through air to read these words—but it is not always trivial. The descriptive catalog should be capable of accepting all information about conduct, however unexciting, until improved theory and evidence resolve what sort of selectivity may be appropriate. Shows No Overt Change in Behavior is judged significant some of the time and not at other times. If one chooses to accept some of the instances as interesting, then he must accept the idea that it is categorically a proper reaction like any other.

Shows No Overt Change in Behavior applies to the case of one person's apparently not listening to another who is speaking to him. It applies to the instance of an individual's appearing to be unmoved following a dramatic announcement. It also applies to the occasion when a person perceives an embarrassing situation nearby and does not alter his conduct. That is, he acts as if nothing happened, avoiding confronting the other person by acknowledging awareness that would perhaps intensify the other's embarrassment. The absence of certain behavior may itself convey a message, as not greeting an acquaintance upon passing him on the street. Simmel wrote that "greeting somebody in the street proves no esteem whatever, but failure to do so conclusively proves the opposite . . . even the slightest omission can radically and definitely alter our relation to a person." In this way it may be said that nonoccurrence of certain alternatives gives significance to an event. Another implication is conveyed by the saying "Silence means consent." A supervisor may come upon some of his subordinates lounging or smoking against the rules but refrain from calling attention to the violations. It is a definite reaction to leave someone alone.

These examples again point to the merit of separating the initial classification of acts from studying them according to an issue of interest. The examples also show the merit of distinguishing between acts and consequences.

Inaction is a definite act in every person's repertoire. To varying degrees it is characteristic of every relationship. The portion of total behavior that is in this category may reveal other qualities of individuals and their interpersonal styles. This reaction category will not be found randomly distributed among persons in interaction. It is thus a matter of interest to learn the extent of its occurrence, the range of situations in which it appears, and the conditions under which it occurs with greater or lesser frequency.

A third reason for including the category is that the quantification of behavior has languished because of its impoverished notational systems. The idea of Shows No Overt Change in Behavior as one of the reaction alternatives affords a baseline against which enumerations of all actions can be made. A set of behavior categories without it is akin to an arithmetic without a zero.

Understanding Acts

As an individual learns about interpersonal behavior from experience and composes whole acts from aggregates of events, he is at the same time creating the mental structure of meaning.

Take note of a pertinent distinction between events and meaningful acts. The intrinsic properties of events include their patterns of physical gestures and the words used to refer to those movements. A gesture is any overt action, verbal or other. Gestures by themselves do not have meaningful wholeness, only mechanical wholeness. Word categories are mere labels or definitions. They do not yield connotative understanding, only nominal recognition. Let us accept as primitive components these physical movements and their names for the purpose of studying behavior. I will probe no further into their substructure. These primitive components permit a message to be conveyed, but this conveyance does not itself carry the interpretation. Instead, the event directs attention beyond the event—to the whole act as described in Chapter 4—for the location of meaning.

The whole act is a synthetic mental structure. Through repeated perception and habitual naming, social events become classified and stored in memory in a constellation. The particular organization exists only in the mind. Its parts—for example, alternative reactions—may never be perceived together in actual experience at a given time and place but are brought together in an abstracted arrangement of categorized episodes. Each episode, each act, can then be comprehended for a significance that is larger than itself because it will be understood according to other acts associated with it.

The transmission of meanings through behavior is a process of communication in which the event does not wholly contain the meaning but is a piece in a puzzle. The other pieces—knowledge of other events—are ready to interlock with one another in a number of ways. These bits of knowledge have universal joints, standard prongs and sockets. These connectors are distributed so that any piece selected as the key piece, when placed centrally, permits the other pieces to be fitted around it in a particular way. This brings to the foreground one meaningful message. The same pieces rearranged around another key event will make another message conspicuous. Still other bits of knowledge are available, about other acts, that can replace components as either central pieces or peripheral ones. These acts do not have to be altogether different from one another. Some are similar, differing only in intensity or a bit of detail, and they result in minor variations or shades of meaningful messages.

Such is the structure of connotation. The meaning of the single event is established as a person places a perceived act in the structure of his knowledge and fits other remembered acts together with it.

This type of understanding depends on experience. It is not intuitive but has to be learned. G. H. Mead declared that "the basis of meaning is thus objectively there in social conduct, or in nature in its relation to such conduct . . . the nature of meaning, as we have seen, is found to be implicit in the structure of the social act." Yet meaning goes beyond behavior. For the organization of memory is not matched by actual observed arrays of events. The current of meaning does not flow until at least a little system of parts is connected. The partially completed scheme waits, like a new road lacking a bridge or two, until enough units of experience are fitted into place. Then one recognizes the distribution of alternative reactions, and the act is illuminated.

The individual's capacity to understand conduct becomes universal from this moment on. He has a method for unifying social experience. Exposed to a new reaction to a situation, he treats it according to alternatives he knows. He is also able to deal with and interpret actions in combinations. I will recite some implications of this link between behavior and understanding to clarify the idea and the method of interpreting acts.

1. An event is discrete but its meaning is relational. Is there not a flaw in this relativistic principle? After all, each component is itself a category expressed in a given language, so it has cultural overtones. Are we not simply chasing the issue of meaning back to language with no gain in disclosure of understanding? No. Because the definition of words themselves reiterates this account of meaning. Words are understood according to words preceding and following them and according to words that could have been used in their stead. If a man says he likes a woman, we are aware that he did not say he loves her. We invoke the probable alternative in order to fix the connotation of the remark. Even though we regress to smaller and more elementary units in relying on language, we find that words are liable to similar aggregates and that the significance of words depends on these combinations.

2. In this type of meaning, events are combined in a set, and the combination gives meaning to each member. Thus the connotation of a reaction according to the dispersion of its alternatives applies simultaneously to each of the alternatives in a whole act, for they are all reactions. Each acquires significance by comparison with others.

3. Hartley wrote that "unless some differential effect in the behavior of the recipient occurs, communication has not taken place." This statement is fallacious for two reasons. One is that it cloaks a message in its consequences, thus forbidding appreciation of the act itself. Second, it implies that the reaction of Shows No Overt Change in Behavior is not a valid response to communication, which is like saying that zero is a meaningless number.

4. The distribution of reactions relative to one another among many whole acts further contributes to meaning. Some reactions that seem nominally similar do not occur in the same situations, and one or the other takes place in situations that could have elicited either. This complementary distribution implies that the two reactions share the same meaning and that one is a substitute for the other.

An opposite pattern is one in which two similar reactions consistently occur together in certain situations. This coupling implies that one alternative does not substitute for the other. In Chapter 10 I will elaborate these possibilities.

5. Meaning's fieldlike character depends on quantitative as well as qualitative aspects of action. What we call the obvious facts of daily life are both categorical impressions and awareness of frequencies. If alternative reactions are equally common in a set, the act is more difficult to understand. A girl cannot tell how much a boy likes her if he dates her friends equally often too. A reaction with 33⅓ percent probability has a clearer meaning if it is part of a set with two other reactions having 55⅔ percent and 11 percent likelihoods than if it is in a set with two others each having 33⅓ percent probabilities. Individual impressions of relative frequencies remain crude. Even so, these quantitative aspects further refine the interpretation of an event.

6. Since connotation depends on the particular members in the set, the same reactions as parts of different sets of alternatives will have different connotations. A single reaction that occurs in many situational sets may swarm with meanings. That acts are equivocal is no more mysterious than that words are equivocal. As a noun, for example, the word *check* stands for a pattern of alternately shaded squares or a certificate in lieu of cash. In the same way the act of sobbing can mean sorrow or joy or relief.

Just as it is possible to construct a dictionary by defining single words according to the nature and frequency of their association with other words as well as by their synonyms and antonyms, it is possible to construct a roster of meanings for reactions according to the nature and frequency of their association with other events. If one finds that the same act (or word) appears in several different sets of alternatives, it may be accorded several meanings. Meaning is therefore different for the same act in different cultures where the alternatives differ.

7. The typical study of interpersonal behavior is based on the assumption that each act has a single major meaning. The observer tries to discriminate the smallest portions of behavior. Upon chopping his observations into these segments, he would classify each segment only once for its significance. Perhaps the whole act's fortresslike complexity, impervious to gentle analytic probing, spurred that researcher to the strategy of reducing it to rubble and then of trying to rebuild something from the pieces. I rejected this fragmentation in discussing the nature of the unit act. To that view I now add an argument concerning meanings in units. More than one reaction may follow a given situation. Sometimes two or more reactions will be used in combination. Therefore, the number of component reactions in the act-whole is not necessarily the same as the number of meanings. These combinatorial possibilities permit more meanings to be generated than the

number of components used. There is no necessary one-to-one correspondence here. Whether a given reaction has one meaning or many must be decided by noting its dispersion among alternatives.

Whereas some situations are followed by only a few reactions, others show more diversity. Therefore, whole acts differ in the number of meanings they contain. I cited three plausible alternative reactions by a boss who is asked for a raise in salary. In comparison, a boss may show six or more alternative reactions to the situation of an employee's making a mistake at work. He may ignore it, call the man's attention to it, berate the man, dock his pay, try to instruct him in the correct procedure, or not tell the man but complain to others. Some of these reactions may be combined. The greater the number of alternatives, the more *complex* the whole act. The potential for act-complexity increases geometrically with the increase in the number of reactions, for it varies according to both the number of different alternatives in a set and the number used in combination.

8. From this multiplicity it can be recognized that meaning is not inherent in isolated acts. A unit of meaning does not exist in nature. The man on the street mistakenly assumes a straightforward connection between an event and its significance. He is often surprised to find that his neighbor—who also takes intrinsic meanings for granted—makes a different interpretation. A careful review of any meaning fixed to any act will uncover contingencies for sustaining the interpretation. Meaning is invariably conditional and depends on circumstances other than the event itself. Consider the act of telling an untruth. Providing another person with misleading information may be deemed artful strategy in a competitive game. It may also be taken as shrewdness in business, dishonesty in school, tactfulness in accepting gifts, and perjury on the witness stand. One cannot insist that these are part of the organic character of telling an untruth.

People speak of "art for art's sake" or "the meaning of work in itself." Such renderings of art and work are impossible to demonstrate. The significance of artistic creativity or work effort or any other type of conduct is given by its contexts and alternatives. It seems possible to glean a bit of significance from a gesture entirely out of context. But the organization of experience makes a gesture part of a set and makes that set in turn part of a larger set, and the gesture acquires its meaning by someone's being aware of its membership in these sets.

9. The genesis of connotation is not instantaneous. Social experience is required for this type of understanding. Repeated contacts are needed so that one may learn about the possibilities.

10. We cannot assume permanent meanings if they are implied by the sets of alternatives and their probabilities. Although the folk of one generation often fail to realize it, meanings are tentative. A mother making sure her child always wears galoshes in winter used to mean care; now this same act means overprotectiveness. Probabilities for reactions in a set may change. As one reaction begins happening with greater frequency, the probabilities of others will be altered. The significance of each of them may be modified accordingly (see item 5 above). As long as behavior patterns change, a lexicon of social conduct will remain on probation. In periods of rapidly changing social relationships, meanings are dispersed too.

11. An act does not acquire and carry all its meanings in any given era. New alternatives in future sets may engender novel interpretations of events. As long as men are active, they will revise and add to the meanings of their conduct through their conduct.

Understanding History

History is part of meaning because it is the primary way in which individuals establish knowledge of alternatives and probabilities. One cannot accomplish an effective interpretation of an act without referring to its history, that is, the knowledge of that situation with other alternatives, the knowledge of that reaction in other situations, and the alternatives that have come to be a party to it on other occasions. So the adult can glean more connotations from an event than can a child. There is a maxim that he who knows only his own generation remains a child. At the same time this knowledge of history—in the individual case we call it experience—can imply a burden for understanding a particular event. Sometimes we are handicapped and unable to appreciate an act because we are so imbued by the other meanings we accord it due to extensive knowledge.

An act once performed is relegated to the past and must be understood in retrospect. The charge is the same whether the event took place a moment ago or many years ago. Of course, there is less available to work with in the latter case. Personal testimony and one's own recollections are lacking, and we rely on memoirs and relics for clues. But the process is the same for understanding all events gone by. Having already been given in experience, the past is composed of a unique trajectory of events. In reviewing it for meaning, it is not enough to know what took place. We must treat the past as having a structure like the whole act; that is, we must realize that alternatives existed, each with its probability, even though it may not be easy to identify all the alternatives and determine their likelihoods.

Historians and logicians debating the nature of history sometimes touch this issue. Is history only a chronicling of events, or does it also presume to interpret the patterns revealed by the rendering of facts? Mommsen declared that history is nothing but the clear portrayal of actual happenings, based on carefully assembling testimony and weaving it into a narrative. He therefore warned that it is "a dangerous and harmful illusion for the professor of history to believe that historians can be trained at the university in the same way as philologists or mathematicians most assuredly can be." But history is not merely a faithful rendering of facts, for not every iota of experience is recounted. Alternative facts are therefore rejected. The more the historian seeks to develop a point of view for interpreting past events, the more he takes alternatives into consideration whether or not he makes them explicit. A pointed challenge that could be made to the scientific status of historicism is the frequent failure of historians systematically to treat the past as future in one stage of their analysis. By doing so they would cite the likelihoods of alternative events and enlarge the basis of their explanations by showing how the alternatives were excluded. Historical analysis rests on this technique of giving evidence or suggesting plausible alternative events as a way of deriving meaning from what did occur.

Ernest Nagel used an example of an event interpreted by the historian F. W. Maitland to show how the logic of historical inquiry is based on attention to alternatives and their probabilities. The event was the public phrasing of the title for Elizabeth, Queen of England, when she ascended the throne in 1558. She proclaimed herself "Elizabeth, by the Grace of God Queene of Englande Fraunce and Ireland defendour of the fayth. &c." Why did she offer an et cetera? In keeping with practices of nobility in those days, it was fitting in formal announcements to provide an unabbreviated pedigree and an unabridged claim to dominion. Maitland proposed that she deliberately took recourse to this appendage because of the grave and delicate dilemma over the relationship between the monarchy and the church. Her father, Henry VIII, had quarreled with Pope Clement VII about the rules concerning marriage and divorce that he found inconvenient and had as a consequence established the Church of England. When his daughter Mary became queen, she abrogated the statutes establishing ecclesiastical sovereignty of the British monarch and reaffirmed the supremacy of the Pope in Rome. When Elizabeth succeeded to the throne, she realized the perils of choosing between loyalty to Rome or breaking with Rome. She was uncertain of the alignments of political and military forces favoring one or the other alternative. Maitland concluded that Elizabeth gained time by this ambiguous formulation of her title. It enabled her to avoid a perilous commitment of the moment and was compatible with whatever decision she might eventually make. Nagel points out that there is in Maitland's analysis the suggestion that Elizabeth recognized at least these three alternatives and chose to temporize.

Plutarch, whose *Lives* has been criticized for some inaccuracies, employed another way of calling attention to alternatives in his analysis of events. He would select two individuals who shared certain outstanding attributes, say Lysander and Sylla, who were both great military leaders and who both later became heads of their states, and account for the different outcomes of the fortunes of their people by noting their selection of alternative policies for governing.

This model of analysis, presuming alternatives for which probabilities exist, is used both by experimental scientists in a future orientation and by historians in analyzing the past. The meanings of the findings of both types of research are given to us in terms of the possible alternatives that could have occurred but did not occur or that happened far less often than others.

Each person's biography is a lesson concerning the outcomes of selecting particular behavior routes among the alternatives available at a series of junctures. This pattern is made clear in the psychological analogue to historicism known as psychoanalysis. In several of its forms the patient is helped to become a historian, producing his own biography and reviewing obscure sections of it again and again. The therapist aids him in exploring past events, discussing their alternatives and possible consequences in order better to comprehend what happened and its meaning. This may include the suggestion of alternatives not consciously considered by the patient. The reconstruction of the patient's understanding of himself is achieved in connection with altering his estimates of the probabilities associated with the set of alternative outcomes.

Often when reviewing the past, whether with pleasure, relief, regret, or deliberate objectivity, we do not consider only the unique trajectory known to occur that carried us through a particular arc of time. We conceive of alternatives and go on to conjure what might have been. We can therefore daydream of either what happened or what is to come. Much of an individual's daydreaming centers upon amending the imagined defects in the sequence of events and rehearsing the brilliant course of events that could ensue. The rehearsal of such sequences in fantasy may even inflate one's estimate of the probability of certain events occurring. Fantasy is a comfortable mood because the experienced frequencies of occurrence can be ignored in arranging the sequences of events. There will result some courses of action that are logically possible although they never occur. This is a common pastime pertaining to realms of publicly dangerous but personally attractive events, such as adventures in sexuality or brutalizing a bully.

Grammatical Competence for Acting and Understanding

I now return to the question asked at the beginning of this chapter—how are people in everyday life able to communicate and understand one another? Since meaning is lodged in the structure of act-wholes, they do so to the extent that they have the same knowledge about behavior. People think about and interpret acts as outlined here, applying the procedures to knowledge of social conduct acquired in the manner described in Chapter 4.

If we wish to know what an individual understands, we must familiarize ourselves with the sets he keeps in mind. We must have available the content of his experience and the likelihoods of events combined in whole acts. Without personal exploration this analysis is difficult to do for individuals. But it can be done for a group or a culture. Through a survey we may establish the frequencies at which combinations of reactions occur in whole acts and calculate an average for the group while appreciating that individual variation is part of the circumstance. In Chapter 9 I will present such an array of conduct for the social relationship I use as a case study.

Incomplete understanding is common. People do not always have knowledge of all alternatives. Nor do they have the same knowledge. Inasmuch as they have diverse interpersonal experiences and assemble different alternatives in the act-structures they conceive, they infer different connotations for given acts. Within repeatedly shared settings, comprehension is easier. In other parts of society or in other cultures, individuals are more vulnerable to misunderstanding because of the different sets of alternatives and probabilities. However, difficulty in fathoming an act (in contrast to incomplete understanding) cannot occur until one has accumulated ample

behavioral data. Therefore, a child in a strange land will not be as surprised and baffled as his parents even though all are equally and simultaneously exposed to the same exotic event.

Such discrepancies in experience make understanding of the same
message less congruent than people imagine it to be. However, in other
ways processes are at work to enhance mutual comprehension. For one,
since behavior perceived from others is unavoidably perceived along with
information about one's own activity, it is often hard to sort out who
contributes what to an event. One may believe he apprehends another
person whereas it is his own contribution that makes the event intelligible.
This is not self-deceit. The nature of interpersonal mind forces perceiving
the combined conduct of self and other. Another help to mutual understanding comes from the way each individual remembers the data of
behavior. I described an interpretive process in which a person considers
his experienced alternatives and their dispersion across all situations and
assesses the act by its relative probability as well. But the whole act, as
mentioned earlier, is in some ways less than the sum of its parts. According
to Bartlett, remembering involves substantial condensation and reorganiza-
tion of subject matter into more familiar form. It is likely that frequencies
are also adjusted, especially by adults, to fit some generalized experience
rather than to preserve exact tallies of reactions to situations. Even an
unusual reaction, unless it was dramatic, may be replaced in memory by
a more plausible and probable alternative. This replacement strengthens the
basis of shared meanings for the consolidations of data converge. One
person's more generalized knowledge comes closer to another's when its
simplified and condensed form has eliminated the sharpest differences.
Conversely, this same process may increase the polarity between the minds
of men from different groups, since the repetition of little discrepancies
may mount to a more obvious contrast.

Having acquired the ability to understand experience and perform these
acts again, the individual develops further. He generalizes to new possibilities. This enlargement is manifest in his comprehension of acts that he
never encountered before and in his performance of acts that he never did
before.

It is possible for an individual to comprehend or perform a novel act by
the achievement of creative combinations. He can imagine a logically
possible reaction, insert it into a format of conduct with known alternatives, and thereby give it significance. In this way new meanings can be
conceived in daydreams, in imagination, and are not necessarily empirical.

So although meaning is behavioral in origin, it extends beyond experience in the same way that matter is tangible in its initial conception but now extends beyond substance. Suppose the individual meets another person who reacts to a situation in a novel way. The novelty is usually a reaction used for the first time instead of more commonly employed alternatives in that situation. Our man is acquainted with the structure of the event and can import relevant material from his knowledge to the situation of the moment. He knows of his own reactions to those reactions of others in that situation. That is, he has following clues as well as preceding clues and alternative clues. The novel reaction acquires intelligibility when fitted into this structure.

There are several classes of events that do not conform to this condition. Those uncommon and sometimes bizarre reactions are taken as manifestations of madness. I will identify some of them in Chapter 7.

By the procedure of creatively combining known elements of conduct, the individual can perform a novel act. This experienced ability to generalize has led man to govern himself according to the grammar of behavior. Noting a set of alternative reactions to a situation, he says there is a choice and imputes responsibility to the actor for his conduct. The notion of free will is based on the premise of sets of alternatives in situations. If every situation were followed solely by one reaction, the postulate of free will would be absent from his social institutions because there would be no empirical ground for dealing with the prospect. Moral and legal systems make man accountable for the consequences of his actions on the assumption that he is not instinctive, that he selects from a set of alternatives available to him in the situation to which he reacts.

PART TWO

Methods

6

Sampling a Repertoire

It is time to look at impartial information that could shed light on some of the issues presented in Part One. Hence I turn to the matter of measuring behavior. What good can be gotten from examining actions depends in turn on how well they are described. We cannot avoid affecting our methods as we try to improve our knowledge, and as we better the way in which we study acts, our understandings sharpen.

I undertook to collect a body of behavioral evidence and to arrange it to fit the contours of whole acts. These four chapters of Part Two are devoted to an outline of the procedures I followed. My discussion here represents a radical shift in subject matter. I will not return to the issues of Part One until Part Three, where the case study described here becomes the data for analysis. In this part I will give an account of my method in substantial detail, because I have been unable to find in social science literature explicit discussions of how several measurement techniques would apply to interpersonal acts. This step-by-step narration will be useful to those who plan to carry out similar research.

Readers not intending to perform behavioral research will find the details less engrossing. The procedures should at least be skimmed. Understanding the type of information collected and the way it is prepared for use (especially in Chapters 6 and 9) is needed to appreciate the material of Part Three.

A study of behavior could be accomplished by focusing on one or a few particular individuals or on a relationship between categories of people. I chose the latter. There is an advantage to using a social relationship for this type of inquiry. People are interacting everywhere all the time. More data is available than one needs in order to learn about social conduct, and we commonly pay attention to only a portion of what is happening. If one chooses to study interpersonal behavior from the standpoint of an individual, the subject matter is all his conduct when he is within sensory access of others. However, each person has special qualities in his behavior. Though these qualities enable us to appreciate him as an individual, they do not permit ready generalizations. It is easier to develop laws from behavior in a social relationship that endures while individuals in it come and go. Accordingly, I used a social relationship as my case study.

A Repertoire and Its Populations of Acts

The example to be described has some unique aspects, yet it fits within a larger array of conduct in society. I will briefly define the elements of this system to provide a common ground for discussion. A *social relationship* is a link between persons in two positions. A *position* is a unit of a social structure. Many positions can be easily identified for they are named explicitly, such as a job in an organization or a party to a contract. These positions include teacher, mayor, salesclerk, wife, lessee. A position need not be formally designated. The category of outsider summarizes a person's identity in relation to others and is therefore a social position. So is shopper, boyfriend, tourist, passerby, onlooker, and inhabitant.

Most positions imply the existence of at least one other; for example, friend and friend, enemy and enemy, husband and wife, reporter and respondent, parent and child, employee and coworkers, supervisor and subordinates, teacher and students. But few positions are linked to only one other. The *social structure* is a network of social positions. For example, in the home a man has one relation to his wife and another to his children. If the dwelling houses an extended family, the man may also have active relationships with grandparents, in-laws, and siblings. The partners in these various relationships are themselves directly involved with one another. Thus while the man has one relationship with his wife and another with his child, wife and child are also linked by their direct relationship. When individuals interact their conduct may be described according to their positions.

The acts observed in a given social relationship comprise its *repertoire*. It is the pattern of all interpersonal behavior performed by persons in one social position with those in another position. The factory foreman uses one repertoire when interacting with subordinates, a different repertoire when in contact with his peers, and still another when dealing with his plant's top management. Together these articulating patterns are the set of repertoires for the position of foreman. Since social positions are cross-linked, there are more repertoires than there are social positions. Simultaneous contact among people in several relationships breeds a scene of complex interaction. For example, the courtroom judge acts under conditions of simultaneous access to his bailiff, clerks, the plaintiff, the defendant, their lawyers, and onlookers in the room. Each of these people also confronts the same interpersonal situation from his own position, calling an ensemble of repertoires into play.

The character of human social life given to us by a repertoire conceals in its averaging process the details of personal and environmental differences. It does not refer to particular individuals who happen to occupy the social positions at any given time. Yet one must begin by studying specific relationships to arrive at an empirical description of a repertoire.

The idea of a population is useful here. A population is an aggregate of things or events that can be identified and enumerated. Applied to interpersonal conduct, the behavior associated with a given social relationship is a *population of acts*. It is the local crowd, a portion of the repertoire for a given position in a given relationship in a given time and place. For example, the general conduct of husband with wife is a repertoire. The conduct of a particular husband with his wife is a population of acts. Variations among populations of acts reveal how different people and surroundings affect a repertoire that exists in the abstract throughout society. A repertoire may therefore be defined as the set of act-populations accompanying a certain social relationship wherever it is found, whereas a population of acts is the behavior of specific individuals in that relation in specific places and times.

Of course, there are crucial differences between a population of acts dwelling in an environment and a biological population. A repertoire is not a species. It is not composed of independent living creatures who can reproduce themselves. Acts are behavioral events, not organic entities. They do not die but vanish. The utility of the concept is the method of study it implies rather than the similarity in subject matter. The idea of population suggests the technique of a census to draw a sample of interpersonal acts. Several surveys would pave the way to portraying a repertoire from the evidence gathered and would deliver the material for analysis.

The social relationship I use as a case study is that of psychiatric aides with patients in mental hospitals. The aide position is sometimes called attendant, or orderly, or nursing assistant in some institutions. It is not a well-publicized hospital job, although about 100,000 people in the United States are so employed. Aides are important in psychiatric care because they are the most numerous category of personnel. There are more of them than all the other types of workers in the mental health professions combined. Also, since there is a shortage of trained professionals, the aides—who are not extensively trained for their job—are the institutional staff members who have the most contact with patients.

The relationship between aide and patient is especially appropriate for the study of interpersonal behavior, since interpersonal contacts are a primary concern in psychiatric treatment. Even the handful of patients in individual psychotherapy or in group psychotherapy find themselves in the company of aides during most of the day. Aides are therefore strategically placed and may help or undermine a patient's treatment experience. This quantitative advantage is not merely relevant to psychiatric matters. The hospital is a home for the people in it. Yet the privacy of home life is curtailed. Because of the open and transient nature of institutional life, access to the hospital is easier for researchers than is access to private homes. To be sure, this access impinges upon the kind of behavior that goes on, but the hospital is still a site of a wider range of behavior, including more intimate forms, than can be found in many places except in the home.

This privileged accessibility is enhanced by the aides' modest position in the hospital hierarchy. I say this in appreciation of aides' willingness to cooperate with social scientists. A researcher has to earn the trust of his subjects in a field setting. At higher echelons in the organization, status concerns and rivalries pile onto the task of establishing sound research relationships, and a group—like the aides—that does not generate these extra problems makes it easier to carry out an impartial survey.

This relationship is also interesting because mental hospitals have much dramatic folklore associated with them. Citizens having no direct exposure to life in these institutions think of them along with prisons as behavioral cesspools for society, with madmen stalking and raging in their confines. Some writings of former mental patients portray insane asylums as places of brutality. Along with acknowledging some kindness and humanity, their accounts are replete with instances of callous treatment and beatings by ward attendants. (Beers, Maine) Even hospital employees returning to their homes after work are likely to narrate unusual events of the day. All this adds up to a popularized sketch of the mental hospital as a turbulent and pitiable scene.

My aim was to study a population of acts between aides and patients impartially and to avoid deciding what is important, proper, or expected. This openness would enable me to learn the content of the social relationship, the stuff of everyday life as well as dramatic incidents. I also sought to know how many acts occurred in the population for a given time period. Something of the quality of social life is implied by the relative numbers of acts in relationships.

Because I will allude to the program piecemeal in several chapters, here is a timetable of the phases of my research: I became aware of the difficulties in describing and interpreting interpersonal behavior in 1958 and spent most of the next two years trying to clarify the issues. The period September 1959 to July 1961 saw three research assistants and me carrying out an observational field survey to assemble information about conduct in the aide-patient relationship. From 1962 to 1965 I worked on a part-time basis on the problem of classifying the data. At the end of that span I had achieved the first taxonomy of actions. After a lapse of three years I returned to this task with another research assistant and produced a revised classification in 1968. That year I began to analyze the information, and I completed the inquiry in 1969.

The Sample Survey

Populations of acts contain multitudes of episodes that vary in type, duration, and frequency. They are amenable to study by a survey based on a sampling design. No difficulty is raised by the fact that acts are brief events that spring into existence and end as fast. On a different time scale the same can be said for human lives. Life is short, the poets say, a fleeting vapor, but a day. Individuals or events are parts of their respective populations for a while; then they are gone and are replaced by others. This transience does not interfere with the taking of a census of either persons or acts.

The census design was based on assumptions about the times and places that acts occur in the population, but difficulties arose in defining some of the features of behavior on which the sample could be based. Acts were the units to be noted, measured, and analyzed. Yet the survey would be carried out first, and events would be classified after the field records were made.

So I did not know what the units would be. Hence I could not say what the probability of act-selection in a population would be. Accordingly, I had to establish a sampling design that focused on whom to observe when and where rather than on acts themselves.

The survey stages are related to one another. Whatever is not accomplished during one stage, or whatever bias is introduced at one stage, can often be accomplished or corrected at another stage provided the researcher comprehends what he has done and what adjustment has to be made. Such adjustments, perhaps resulting in information that is not quite so precise as the product of a more straightforward sample, are far more common than the latter circumstance. Superb sampling designs well fitted to populations are realized, if at all, only at a stage of a science when its subject matter is well known. This is not so for interpersonal behavior. One is in the position of needing information at the beginning of the census that is available only after the work is complete. So judgment, informal knowledge based on experience, and reading have to guide the initial decisions. If one keeps track of early decisions and is aware of their implied assumptions about behavior, some adjustments can be made later to improve the precision and accuracy of the information assembled.

1. *Sites*

Almost all contacts in the relationship between aides and patients take place within the confines of mental hospitals. Since the behavior might vary from one setting to another, I arranged to carry out the behavior census in two institutions. They are located in the same metropolitan area. Both house male and female patients with a wide range of ages and with a wide variety of diagnosed illnesses.

One hospital is a small, private psychiatric institution of 200 beds. As a treatment center it emphasizes a psychoanalytically oriented program of one-to-one relationships between staff members and patients. Most of the patients in this hospital have high-status socioeconomic backgrounds. They live on wards housing from fifteen to forty persons, in separate bedrooms, with shared multiunit toilets, nicely furnished living rooms, and dining rooms located on each ward. As a teaching unit for a nearby medical school, this hospital conducts several training programs for different professions simultaneously, including a full psychiatric residency program. Each year between fifteen and twenty physicians become apprentices at the hospital. There are also a number of graduate students present who receive field work experience and clinical training supervised by members of the departments of Psychology and Social Work. There are also several fourth-year students from the affiliated medical school and a score of budding psychiatric nurses from the hospital's own school of nursing. All these students, along with the hospital's ample staff of psychiatrists, social workers, psychologists, and nurses, are well in evidence and have much contact with patients. The psychiatric aides comprise 30 percent of the hospital's staff, and about 25 percent of the aides are college students or college graduates.

The other hospital is a large state institution of 3,000 beds. Its professional treatment personnel are few in number, and much of their contact with patients is centered on diagnostic efforts at the time of admission. The hospital is generally understaffed. It emphasizes recreational activities as forms of treatment—ball games, basket weaving, table games, and movies —and the director once observed ruefully that with the staff available it could be no different. The therapy program was typically talked of in deficit terms: this is all we are able to do so we make the best of it. Most of the patients in this hospital have lower-status socioeconomic backgrounds than their counterparts at the private institution. The patients here live on wards housing over one hundred patients each, sleep in large dormitories, share multiunit toilets and daytime living areas furnished mainly with chairs and tables. Several large central eating halls, some in separate buildings, provide cafeteria-style meal services to the patients of most wards. The state hospital also has a psychiatric residency program, a more modest one, and it has few trainees in the psychology and social work professions at any time. Aides make up 70 percent of this institution's staff, and few of them have any formal education beyond secondary school.

How generalizable will the findings of this survey be to the repertoire at large? My experience in research and as consultant during the past decade makes me think these two settings are nicely chosen for comparative purposes. They span a range of the types of institutions and patients, and the findings may be applicable to other hospitals. Of course, each institution is different in some ways from all others.

Knowledge of mental hospital settings told me that differences in conduct would be found in various places and times within them. Psychiatric aides located on different wards may confront different types of situations with patients. There is a progression of wards from those that have patients who are calm and able to take care of themselves, to those housing patients who are more agitated and in poorer communicative contact with their environment, to those whose patients are extremely withdrawn and unable to accomplish the elementary activities of daily life—such as eating, going to the toilet, and dressing—by themselves. I estimated that an aide spends about one-quarter of his work time at an off-the-ward site, such as playing fields, gymnasium, coffee shop, and auditorium. Consequently, I broke down the environment into sites reflecting these differences. I made up lists, in consultation with psychiatrists and other professionals, for the different areas of each hospital and the types of patients housed there or the types of activities that could occur there. I then grouped these sites into what seemed to be homogeneous clusters according to the possible situations that aides could confront. I matched the groupings of sites in both hospitals in order to establish comparability of the data to be collected. I could not have known ahead of time how many acts would be in the populations, so I assumed a rough correspondence between numbers of acts and numbers of aides. These partitionings yielded strata that were approximately equal for the numbers of aides involved, except for one larger stratum in the private hospital and two larger strata in the state hospital. These larger groupings were established because the sites that were grouped together were so similar.

This procedure yielded ten site groupings that reflected the variety of milieux found in each mental hospital. A list of the sites is given in Table 6-1, page 101. Later I sampled from each of the groupings proportionate to their number in the total population. Since the sampling fraction was the same for each group of sites, no adjustment would be required later for combining the data of several sites into a single estimate of the population.

2. Durations and Times

Next I made decisions based on the time-bound character of the aide-patient relationship. There are more aides on duty at certain times of the day and week than at other times. This implies different frequencies of acts at different times.

Aide-patient contacts during nighttime hours are meager. The wards are quiet. Few patients are awake. A patient returning from the toilet may ask for a cigarette, and the two may stand in the dim corridor chatting for a while. If a patient cannot sleep, the aide may prepare a glass of warm milk for him. If sleeping is more difficult, the aide will let the patient sit up for a while and may call the night nurse to provide a sedative. The pace is slow, and interactions fall largely in these categories. Few other situations are the offspring of those hours. To be sure, this means that the night shift is a time for a certain kind of interaction. As such it deserves to be included in the fullest description of the repertoire. On the other hand, it comprises a small amount of acts in any population, and the cost of adding this knowledge systematically to the whole is high because visits by observers would net little information compared to the time and effort invested. I therefore excluded the period from 11 P.M. to 7 A.M. from the boundaries of my survey population and sought information about behavior during the waking hours of the day.

My next decision concerned the length of each unit of observation. A subtle danger in sampled observations is that the time spans may be too short, so that fragments of acts are noted and too much is missed. If the sample is made up of brief observation periods and several events are occurring at once, the observer may be prone to record the briefer events that he is able to perceive entirely and to omit the longer ones whose beginnings or ends do not fall within his observation period. Complex actions may be unrecognizable at a glance. The research team directed by Barker and Wright observed and recorded the behavior of children in a midwestern town for eight full days. The episodes so recorded ranged in duration from a few seconds to 121 minutes. The age of the child involved was directly related to the length of his behavior episodes. More than 70 percent of the recorded events were shorter than two minutes. Even for the oldest child observed, an eleven-year-old, less than 2 percent of her behavior episodes lasted longer than fifteen minutes. Considering these time ranges, and also that the aides and patients in my study were adults, I established a two-hour unit of observation and parceled the waking hours of the day into adjacent two-hour periods. I also established a rule that if an episode lasted longer than the scheduled end of the observation unit, the researcher was to remain beyond that time in order to record the event in its entirety.

My final decision dealt with the days of the week. Just as there is a cycle of activity during the day, there is a longer one that occurs over the length of the week. Aides coming into contact with patients find that week after week the evenings at the movies repeat themselves, as do the mornings to shave or to give haircuts, as do the patients' weekend visits home. Because the different days may be linked to different activities, I cited them as seven separate possibilities.

I then created a roster of sampling units consisting of given days of the week for given two-hour periods from 7 A.M. to 11 P.M. Using a table of random numbers, I selected occasions for visiting each of the ten sites. To ensure the dispersion of the observation units per site, once the day and time of observation had been selected for a given site, neither that day nor that time were drawn again for that site. The same day/time observation unit could, however, be selected for another site. I sampled the site-groupings proportionately and drew correspondingly more observation units for the larger groups referred to above. Save for these exceptions, I selected two units of observation for each stratum. The two hospital samples were independent of each other; that is, the selection of combinations of times and days and sites for one hospital did not depend on the selections for the other.

This stage of sampling produced a total of 54 observation units (representing 108 hours) to be carried out in both hospitals, with at least a pair of units allocated to each site in each hospital.

3. *Persons*

I have already noted that since classification would follow the field observations, acts themselves could not be the basis of the sample design. So the third stage of the sample concerned which aides to observe.

It is sometimes difficult to distinguish a social position from others around it. Distinctions can be coarse or fine. The finer they are, the more effort is required to ascertain whether an individual is or is not a genuine incumbent of the position, for his attributes will overlap with those of other persons in other positions. For example, if one studies the so-called top management of an industry, it is a challenge to know where the top ends and middle management begins. The decision might vary according to the size of the corporations involved. In the same way it can be difficult to locate the boundary between an urban and a suburban area. The city limit may run between two rows of houses whose density on both sides is the same. If a community—rather than the formal city lines—is to be demarcated for study, it is necessary to make an arbitrary cut somewhere along gently graded changes in neighborhood character. Similarly, the lines between aide and other staff positions are often indistinct. In spite of the plan to watch only psychiatric aides, practical problems arose in identifying those persons. There are other staff members who—while technically not aides—resemble aides in time and place and content of interaction with patients. Affiliating student nurses and practical nurses begin on the wards as untutored in psychiatry as are most aides. Medical tasks are a small part of their daily concerns. They deal with patients in an almost identical range of life events as do aides and are often relied on by the administration to cover wards as aides. There is some overlap of activities in the other direction as well. In spite of regulations to the contrary, aides sometimes distribute medicines and make entries in the patients' records. The dress or uniform of the affiliating student nurse, the practical nurse, and the aide are alike. It would not have been appropriate to our observations to call attention to the interest of researchers by asking personnel to identify themselves, but an observer arriving at a site often could not be confident whether a particular individual was an aide without making inquiries. There were, however, relatively few people in these other positions. Accordingly, I chose to err on the side of inclusiveness and grouped the above-mentioned students along with aides, except when they were accompanied by registered nurses or were handing out medicines. From now on I will speak of these three types of positions as aides.

The observer would select an aide to watch by going to the site and finding one. If there was no aide to be found, he wandered about the site until one appeared. If two or more aides were located in the same place, he noted whether both were involved with the same patients. If they were, he made records of all together. If they were not, he used a random procedure for selecting one of the aides to begin the observations. (I used my watch, glancing at it and invariably finding that its second hand pointed more in the direction of one aide than the other.)

Observing individuals to gain information about acts may result in some types of behavior being overlooked and the variation in the population being underestimated. The acts of each individual are not independent of one another, and only collections of acts performed by each person could be selected. This clustered sample in the third stage of selection, though it enlarges the sampling error, cannot be avoided if act categories are unknown and people rather than acts are to be selected. However, since individual aides differ in their conduct with patients, both in quality and in rate of interaction, some of the clustering effect can be mitigated by sampling many persons. This tactic would enhance exposure to the entire range of conduct in the population. This adjustment is not as satisfactory as giving all combinations of acts equal probability in selection. But it is a strategy suited to the circumstances.

We therefore investigated how many different aides had been observed. We analyzed the field records for each hospital and judged that a minimum of 90 and a maximum of 189 different aides were observed in the private hospital; in the state hospital a minimum of 96 and a maximum of 160 different aides were observed. The observations were made at a dozen or more different sites in each hospital. The field visits to both hospitals were spread over a period of two years, and the second visit to the same site occurred on another day at another hour. Given these circumstances and the fact that job turnover among aides at both hospitals was fairly high, the chance is small that the same aide turned up several times on more than one ward during our field visits. However, aides from various wards may have also been observed at recreation sites. Yet the minimum number of 90 different persons seems numerous enough to represent the range of behavioral styles to be found in a setting.

Another aspect of cluster sampling in this study deserves mention. Different sites at different times and days of the week had different numbers of aides present. In about half of our observation visits, we found only one aide on duty at the site. He provided all the behavior information available. The record was therefore continuous for him in all his interaction for the two-hour period. Since his cluster of acts comprised the entire set of actions that could be observed, his conduct was equal to the conduct of aides at that site at that time. There was no selection bias or error. That cluster sample was identical to a nonclustered sample for that observation unit. On other occasions there were two or more aides present. At those times selection of one aide meant ignoring all the others' acts. More rarely, mostly at parties and at recreation and in the dining halls, several aides could be observed at one time because they were involved in the same activity with patients, and we made records of all their conduct.

Field Observations

Over a period of two years, four trained observers, including me, took turns visiting designated sites in both hospitals and tried to make a full record of events that occurred when aides and patients had sensory access to one another. (I will describe in Chapter 7 some of the criteria for sensory access and use.) We recorded only the conduct of aides with patients, even when there were other staff members and visitors present. If aides were not on the scene, we did not record patients' actions. Table 6-1 lists the sites tapped for observations at the hospitals, briefly describing them according to the ten strata into which they were grouped and the number of hours of recording that took place at each site.

Table 6-1. Sites within each hospital and hours of recording

Sites Within Hospitals [a]	PRIVATE HOSPITAL Hours of Recording	STATE HOSPITAL Hours of Recording
1. Admissions ward—Male (M)	4	4
2. Admissions ward—Female (F)	4	6
3. Maximum security ward—M	3.5	—
4. Maximum security ward—F	4	4
5. Geriatric ward—M	—	4
Geriatric ward—F	—	2
Geriatric ward—M & F	4	—
6. Other locked ward—M	—	4
Other locked ward—F	4.5	—
Other locked ward—M & F	9[b]	—
7. Open ward—M	—	10.5[c]
Open ward—F	—	12.0[c]
Open ward—M & F	3	—
8. Canteen or Coffee Shop	3.5	3
9. Gym, Outdoor Field	5	2
10. Party, Dance, Picnic	3.5	3.5
Totals	48.0	55.0

[a]There was no separate maximum security ward for acutely disturbed male patients at the state hospital; a wing of the admissions ward housed this group. Only the private hospital had wards housing both male and female patients, and they were matched by pairs of wards at the state hospital. The private hospital had few open wards; the state hospital had few locked wards.

[b]Two wards.

[c]Three wards.

This table first appeared on page 654 in *American Journal of Sociology* (published by The University of Chicago at The University of Chicago Press), vol. 74, No. 6, May 1969, as part of my article, "Behavior Rhythms in Mental Hospitals," pp. 650–665.

In the state hospital some of the observation units drawn in our sample, when visited, turned out to have no aides on duty. On one ward, for example, the patients were calm and collected and were behaving in a responsible manner without supervision, and no aides appeared during the entire two-hour unit of observation. The observer was ushered in and shown around the ward on this occasion by a patient trusty who carried the keys. That visit therefore netted no record of events. Out of the scheduled thirty observation units of two hours each, observers spent a total of five hours at sites in the state hospital when aides were not present. As a result the observations in that setting totaled fifty-five hours. Failing to observe aides on those sites means that, if the population is to be described correctly, those sites *should* be given less representation. They do not represent a loss of information, and no new observation units need be added to replace the five hours. The size of the sample is merely reduced by that number of hours without distorting the definition of the relevant population.

The fact that aides were not present at those sites at those times tells something about the customary locales within the hospital environment for the aide-patient relationship. In the state hospital aides are assigned mainly to sites where overt signs of illness abound, and acts belonging to that population are sparse where patients are composed and able to take care of themselves. In the private hospital aides are assigned pervasively. There were always one or more present during our designated observation times. Thus in the private hospital a larger portion of the population of acts involves patients who behave more normally. Our twenty-four visits of approximately two hours each yielded records for forty-eight hours in the private hospital.

There were some discrepancies between the allocated hours and the actual length of observation. Although the units were scheduled to be two hours each, occasionally our observation time did not coincide perfectly with an activity. For example, an observer arrived at an auditorium in one of the buildings to observe aides and patients in recreation together from 9 P.M. to 11 P.M., but the party ended at 10 P.M. After an additional half hour of cleaning up by aides and patients, the activity terminated, everyone left, and the hall was darkened. In Table 6-1, the instances of observation hours not divisible by two reflect actual recording times resulting from one or more of these circumstances.

We visited the sites ahead of time so that we would be more familiar to staff and patients when we reappeared. Staff members and patients knew that we were coming and that our interest was in everyday life at the hospital. While not concealing ourselves when we came to observe, we tried to avoid interaction with them and to restrict our activities to recording. In making the records, the observer noted the conduct of aides in the presence of patients and also recorded what patients were doing at the time. The aide chosen was observed as long as possible. Occasionally the pace of recording made it necessary to stop observing in order to complete a lengthy record. On these occasions, after completing the record, the observer would begin his aide selection procedure again. Thus if only one aide was on duty at the site, his course of interaction was followed throughout. If more than one were present, the observer sometimes lost track of a given aide when he stopped to complete a written record and then took up observing another aide when he was finished.

Each observer made on-the-spot records and wrote openly except at parties and picnics. At times brief events drew his attention, at times more extended ones. He noted episodes ranging from the momentary "Have you got a light?" to transactions lasting more than an hour. He tried to record one episode completely before turning to another, even if the later one was more dramatic. When faced with a decision of how inclusive to be, he chose to err on the side of providing fuller pictures rather than sketchy pieces. He described the surroundings, the circumstances leading up to the event, the sexes and approximate ages of the participants, the physical objects employed, and what was said and done.

Before and during the span of field visits, we repeatedly discussed and agreed that we did not presume to know what is good or bad, important or unimportant, or relevant or irrelevant in the aides' relations to patients. We knew neither which actions were critical in the social relationship nor what effects were wrought by different interpersonal styles. Our emphasis on impartiality did not seem difficult to sustain because we conducted practice sessions before visiting the sites and reviewed the purposes of the survey several times during its course. It helped us in this effort to imagine that we were working for a scientist who wanted a record of interpersonal behavior but had not informed us of his main interests. Accordingly, we did not establish specific behavior categories in advance for these field observations. We made exhaustive records of events in everyday English. Some indirect evidence that we were impartial came from several of my outside colleagues who, upon learning of the nature of our records, criticized me for carrying out what they labeled purposeless observations.

Here is an example of a field record:

#170/Hospital:Private/Site:f/Date:4–12–60/Time:9–11 AM/*Observer:JJ*
Setting: Living room of ward. Female aide sitting on couch with two female patients. Aide is smoking and listening to the two patients talk.
P-A: "Who wants to go for a walk? Short walk? Long walk?"
A-P: "I'd love to go for a walk, but we have clinic."
P: "Short walk _____ "
A: "Good."
Aide and patient get up to go for a walk.
(This patient had been moaning how tired she was to other patients, and had been stretched out on couch. The female aide's voice seemed pleased at the idea for a walk. The two got up looking pleased with selves for idea of walk.)

There is a fourth stage in sampling, determined by the observer's capacities and dispositions. Examining the records after the field survey, I learned that the aims for thoroughness were not always achieved. Some of the records were incomplete or ambiguous. It is easy to understand why this should happen. Contacts between aides and patients sometimes came thick and fast. Each episode contained myriad aspects, and it was a practical impossibility for an observer to note and enumerate all of them. For him to try writing faster in order to miss nothing was as futile as trying to count raindrops. It was not raindropping, it was raining.

7

Classification

In the early stages of a science, specimens are usually gathered before classification begins. But a specimen collected by a photographic plate, a fossil indentation, or a written record does not yield utterly unclassified information. The researcher has registered what his instrument is able to record. Certain properties of the subject matter have been noted; others have been disregarded. If the English language is used to make records of interpersonal behavior, an enormous amount of organization is thereby imposed. It leads to a corollary of Protagoras' ancient claim: man makes the measure of all things.

Although interpersonal behavior has been observed and recorded, this process does not imply that acts have been captured and may then be exhibited. The events must be transformed into categories. This categorization is not fully achieved by field records. The taxonomic task is to systematize the information gathered, following conventions to decide when an event is a repetition of another and when it is different and assembling the data in the structural form of unit acts.

The task is rugged and critical. Barker, who undertook the quest for a human behavior taxonomy, remarked on how little guidance was available and concluded that "investigation must follow the canons of discovery rather than those of scientific verification." It is indeed more of a groping venture than a well-established procedure. There is no taxonomic scheme independent of its aims. Its purpose influences the definition of what characteristics of the subject matter will be considered essential. In the beginnings of studying behavior, a prime goal should be a classification that is impartial to known theories.

How much classification should be sought? A student, appreciating the subtleties of interpersonal exchanges, may want to preserve the entire record even if it is unwieldy. But dealing with behavior so kaleidoscopic makes generalizations hard to phrase. To gain more useful facts, we must discard some information. The classification must achieve some reduction of data and yet stop short of dismissing all distinctions, for that would prevent comparative or quantitative analysis. The taxonomist consigns some nuances to oblivion and aims for a general representation of the entire record. Events that are vaguely bounded, with more similarity than compellingly unrelated features, are placed in the same category delineated by some primary properties. Darwin wrote that "when a young naturalist commences the study of group organisms quite unknown to him, he is at first much perplexed in determining what differences to consider as specific, and what as varietal; . . . His general tendency will be to make many species . . . if his observations be widely extended, he will in the end generally be able to make up his own mind: but he will succeed in this at the expense of admitting much variation,—and the truth of this admission will often be disputed by other naturalists."

A behavior taxonomist should not cherish illusions about perfect instances or ideal types in establishing a classification. Mendeleev's Periodic Table initially presumed to list perfect types of elements in each category. However, some of the original elements, for example, thorium, turned out to be an element-family, a cluster that we now call an isotope. In some cases, by peculiar patterns of radiation, an isotope may emit particles that result in a transformation from the unstable element to another more stable one either higher or lower in the tabled list of elements. Thus the study of isotopes has become a study of variants and transformations, a far cry from the neatly compartmented Periodic Table. The rule for tolerating this state of affairs is that a category's internal diversity should be softer than the differences noted across the junctures of categories. One way of dealing with similarities is to invoke the criterion of confusion, or interchangeability, to decide where to draw boundaries. Events assigned to one class should be easier to confuse with one another than with those assigned to other classes. The category or class will not stand for any actual event in all its detail. It is abstract. By ignoring certain details, you emphasize other features. In this way the properties of the class will be a more stable cluster than will the properties of individual acts. Since the category recurs, one can treat events according to their commonalities and enumerate occasions that repeat themselves.

If, in the course of classifying, scanning new data prompts a realization that events have been misallocated, the entire set of categories may be altered accordingly. This principle of successive approximation is illustrated as follows.

Suppose that you have moved into a new home and are confronted with the problem of storing sheets, pillowcases, blankets, towels, and many related items (as well as some oddities like a hair dryer and light bulbs) in a closet that has adjustable shelves. You review the items to be stored, arrange the shelves, and begin to place the goods upon the shelves. After proceeding for a while, the way the closet begins to fill up tells you that your initial estimate was skewed. It turns out that although you have eight sheets, when you fold them neatly they take up less space than anticipated. Meanwhile, you discover that you have more oddities to store in that closet than you realized, including children's bathtub toys, a folding rack for drying clothes, a bathroom scale, and some extra toiletries. You remove some of the goods, rearrange the shelves, and then complete the storage task. Two months later you realize that the matter of fit pertains not only to the size of objects but to their frequency of use as well. If you are thorough, you may remove the goods, rearrange the height of a shelf or two, and re-store all the goods in an order that not only uses space well but also leaves the items used most often readily accessible. Reviewing your effort, you see that the initial try at storage was absolutely valid for the *specific items* inserted in suitable places. The reason for the first rearrangement was that *the entire set* of objects to be stored was then taken in consideration. The reason for the second rearrangement was that the *quantitative aspect* of use of all objects in the set was further taken into consideration. The final arrangement will have its deficiencies. For example, the bathroom scale turns out to sit shallowly on its shelf and leaves an unfilled area between it and the shelf above it. In another place, the purchase of some extra sheets requires careful storage just short of cramming. Yet considering the entire set of objects for which storage was required and the different frequencies of their use, you have arrived at an overall arrangement that is nearly optimal.

This procedure confers a different pattern and significance upon categories than if one develops them in advance and applies them repeatedly. This classification depends on the set being treated. A category will be recognized according to its membership in the set. It may be recognized differently in another set. Does this principle of relativity imply an abandonment of universals? We give up the standard yardstick, but the procedures and principles of categorization remain universal methods to be applied to all sets.

Conventions for Classifying Field Records

The results of the classification described in this section, the final set of categories of situations and reactions, are presented in Figures 7–1 and 7–3. The reader may be helped by studying those categories before reviewing the method outlined here. I will present the steps of my classification procedure as conventions flowing through several stages of decisions about similarities and differences among events. I established these rules in a diary that I kept during that experience. As can be imagined, the canons of exposition make this outline more coherent and logical than the course of my own taxonomic efforts.

The four stages (A, B, C, and D) described below should be repeated for successive samples of the written records, randomly selected. Dealing with this portion of the whole limits and spaces the initial labor—which is most difficult. The amount of records in the sample is more manageable. This procedure avoids fatigue and leaves one responsive to the records longer. It is therefore easier to consider all the events simultaneously. It also reduces the chances of being influenced by frequencies in establishing categories, so fewer infrequent acts will be overlooked.

Each sample should be used to establish a set of categories that fits its portion of the evidence. Upon classifying that portion, assemble all the categories into a single distribution with the number of events represented by them noted as well. Some distinctions made in the classification of the first sample may be contradicted by the second one. This may highlight the unevenness of applying a distinction and prompt a more explicit resolution of the issue. Each new systematization will result in a more orderly body of categories.

A. *Identify Situations*

Situations are classified first because they contain the contact opportunities and are the beginnings of acts. The classification begins by a review of the records to become acquainted with what was noted. This should establish a universe of information to take precedence over informal knowledge and expectations. The records are the data. Leave them intact. It is not an occasion to add memories or to clarify awkward phrasings.

Define and compile a list of situations based on a careful scanning of the records.

1. Every situation must be included in this first listing. Because of the detail confronted and the thoroughness required, one begins by looking at the records through a newborn's eyes. The beginning is the most difficult. Adults forget the long effort they took to synthesize sensations into the first few things they perceived in infancy. The classification has something of the character of an infant's experience in confronting his environment, for the cues are legion, their enumeration is a chore, and conquest over the haphazard array is snail-like and taxing.

2. Every situation (or contact opportunity) requires sensory access between aides and patients. Each record should be coded for the number of aides present. If the record lists the same situation for two or more aides simultaneously, credit it for each of them. In this way the frequencies of events will be correlated with the number of aides involved. If n number of aides are present in a situation, there are n acts to be classified, for each of them is assumed to react—whether they react similarly or differently. Thus if three aides walking together pass a lone patient, three acts occur although there is only one patient. If the record lists two different situations for the same aide (or for each of two or more aides), list each situation for each aide accordingly.

Sometimes contact opportunities occur in an overarching situation involving many people and enduring for a substantial period of time. A party, for example, or mealtime in the dining room, is a large event in which people are concentrated in an area and given many opportunities for interaction. In such cases, assume that if two people are overtly interacting, others do not have access to them and there are no contact opportunities pertaining to them. Intrusions are exceptions to this rule. If while one person is chatting with another, a third walks over and asks for a cigarette, the start of a new situation takes place. It occurs in the midst of another event, and both events must be categorized and counted.

Do not be selective. Do not presume to know in advance what is important and what is not. List every discernible situation.

3. The action part of the situation is what the individual says and does. Pay attention first to the sequence of his motions, verbal and otherwise, and then to the objects involved in the action—such as a cup of coffee, a hypodermic syringe, an automobile. Additional features of the situation may be described as fully as given in the records. The sex and costume of

participating individuals, the geographic location and particular site, the weather conditions and day of the week may be cited. Since some of these factors exert influence upon conduct, their consideration in classification is a prelude to the study of determinants of acts as well as an aid to grouping events into appropriate categories.

4. Because the classification of acts uses written records, the procedure rests ultimately on understandings of words by the classifier. Beyond this unavoidable circumstance, I recommend minimal reliance on implicit and covert understandings to identify situations. However, there are two cases in which the onset of a new situation may occur without any change in sensory access. One concerns a change in the salient time of interaction and the other a change in the salient topic.

Overt interaction may be triggered by time schedules. For example, men may be sitting in a dormitory when suddenly one calls out to the other, "It's time to eat." He did not react only to the behavior of others within sensory access but also to some knowledge about a schedule and the time of day as given by a clock. Clock time is an objective cue for the situation. But distinguishing 7:30 A.M., 12 noon, and 5:30 P.M. as the starts of scheduled dining periods depends upon covert understandings. Such understandings cannot be altogether avoided by the classifier. Some identification of situations will presuppose knowledge of such things as time schedules.

Sometimes a new situation commences through actions of the interacting individuals themselves. For example, some persons are working together and then break for relaxation together. How does one decide whether this shift in topic is a situational change or a continuation of the same event? This can be rephrased as an issue of how long in duration and how internally complex can behavior be and still be called a single act? My solution is to rely on criteria for deciding the *ends* of acts. Once the end of one act is identified, a new situation begins even if the participants are still behaving in each other's company. The method for establishing ends of acts is given in section D.

According to some students of behavior, the most exhaustive catalog of observable conditions will still be too rawboned for describing the relevant aspects of an interpersonal context. Emphasizing the import of contexts in interaction, Goffman writes that any encounter can be understood initially in terms of the membrane of common social understandings in which it is enclosed, which are created as much by "rules of irrelevance" that exclude consideration of certain conditions as by other rules that indicate what properties of the situation should receive attention. He concludes that "it is to these flimsy rules, and not to the unshaking character of the external world, that we owe our unshaking sense of realities."

For several reasons I suggest limiting the citation of background understandings. The classifier will not know all the covert rules and all the contextual features of the situation. Without inordinate time and effort a full list cannot be made. One must therefore limit oneself to some subset. Which features shall they be? The important conditions, of course, the ones that make a difference. The trouble comes in trying to include all of these and to exclude more trivial ones on the basis of preliminary knowledge and assumptions. It would be helpful to know in advance what criteria to use in classification, but this is exactly what is unclear. Even well-known beliefs can be treacherous, for behavior often violates some covert agreements. Given an initial commitment to impartiality and to avoidance of presuming causes and consequences of actions, at this stage it is wise to limit the account to observables. They at least lend themselves to similar measurement and analysis. I concede that background expectations play a part in interaction. One of the things people do when they meet is try to learn about one another's covert social attributes, such as occupation or political outlook. On the other hand, the subtleties of social existence are often correlated with its more obvious features. There is some relation between occupational status and the uniform one wears, the manner of dress and grooming, and the objects used in activities—such as apron, cash register, or mop. The initial portrayal of situations can be both objective and indicative if it notes the onset of access, some observable features of the context, and the actions of participants.

Do not move on to further steps until this step is completed. The procedure will go faster once the identification of situations is complete. The records will be more familiar, and the list of situations will become guides to locating reactions.

B. *Group the Situations*

After completing the initial list of all contact opportunities in the sampled records, assemble the situations into groups having the same features.

1. There is no definitive guide to whether a contact opportunity is a different type of situation or is a repetition of another type. Some decisions will be easy because the similarities are obvious, as when two or more

different occasions involve the same behavior and the same objects. For example, in a family one will note repeated occasions of persons sitting and watching television together, of people eating a meal, of one person cleaning a part of the house in the presence of others, and of a mother putting her child into bed and trying to lull him to sleep. Where situations embody distinctive features as well as similar ones, the classifier must decide whether these are minor gradations of a single theme or noteworthy divergences. I have found several techniques helpful:

a. If a difference is to be ignored in order to accept a similarity, let the similarity be in behavior and the difference in some condition—such as the objects involved or the location of the event. Suppose a camper wanders a short distance away from his group while on a hike, and another camper starts off in the wrong direction upon leaving the camp dining hall, and a third camper walks into the wrong bunkhouse in the campsite area. The sites of these events might be ignored and a grouping established on the basis of the behavior.

b. When a judgment of similarity or difference appears difficult, try phrasing each situation a little more abstractly in order to get an inkling of what features may be identified as dominant.

c. The classification procedure will later include a review of the complete set of situational groupings. If in doubt on this first attempt at grouping, preserve the distinction. If in doubt on the second try, make the consolidation.

2. Often the mood to consolidate is roused by implicit aspects of situations, for the classifier will know things that are not obvious. If he utilizes all his information, his grouping will be erratic because he is aware of more facts concerning some interpersonal spheres than others. If he ignores his knowledge, some of his groupings may seem unnecessarily obtuse, for his additional knowledge when applied might result in different clusters. In this stage be cautious about asserting a personal understanding. Turn to this source of assistance later in order to resolve difficult cases.

The following decision highlights this problem and indicates its significance. In the state hospital, large numbers of patients were sometimes observed being marshalled for an activity. The beginnings of hours recorded and words spoken by aides made it easy for me to conclude that these were scheduled activities. In the private hospital, there may have been just as many scheduled activities, but they often happened for individuals rather than for groups of patients. These were harder to discern. For example, the scheduled appointment of a single patient with his private psychotherapist could be at an untypical time—say ten minutes after the hour or ten minutes before. The absence of clock clues and of group movement could have led me to underestimate the amount of scheduled activity in the private hospital. This may have led to a finding I report in Chapter 9, that scheduled activities for patients were more numerous in the state hospital. So the allocation of data to a qualitative category (i.e., "It is time for a scheduled activity") will affect quantitative findings. To introduce additional assumptions or complicated techniques of inference in order to compensate for this possible sampling error may be harder to defend and perhaps more distorting. It is an unresolved and challenging problem in the systematic classification of behavior.

Another difficult decision concerned individuals who refused to engage in optional activities or individuals who refused or delayed performance of obligatory acts in the institution. I knew which acts were required and which were optional. The distinction is common to many spheres of life and involves background understandings. Legislators, for example, have the option to participate in testimonial dinners but are obligated to attend working sessions of their legislative body. Some take all their options and skip many of their obligations in an election year. Should the distinction be preserved? I decided to preserve it in sorting the situations in my first attempt at grouping. It happened that the application of another criterion in a later phase (section F below) confirmed the distinction.

3. The situational groupings need not be equal in complexity, in numbers, or in apparent significance. This step is an establishment of types. It may well result in variations among groups that reflect natural differences in behavior. One must allow the chance that a category will contain a singular situation and not be a cluster at all. Every event must be given its place. Categories that occur only once during a prolonged series of observations represent rare situations. They too are valid aspects of interpersonal life.

C. Identify Reactions to Situations

Every situation is followed by a reaction. For each situation on the list, cite the behavior of every individual within sensory access who is an incumbent of the position being studied. His actions should be described in the same way used to portray the conduct of persons that were identified in the situation (see A–3). Included here could be the report that no overt change in behavior took place.

1. If a group of two or more patients pass one aide who is alone and he delivers a generalized greeting, only one reaction has occurred. Conversely, it is possible for an aide to combine two reactions in responding to a situation.

2. Situation and reaction often overlap. In making the classification explicit, replace this blend in time by a distinct order of situation followed by reaction. However, several acts may overlap in time. If, in reacting to the situation cited in A–2 above, an individual gives the solicitor a cigarette while continuing to converse with another person, he is interweaving his reactions to the two situations.

3. Several events were grouped together to establish some situational categories (see B). It is possible that reactions to each of those events in the set were different, and all should be duly noted. Furthermore, a reaction to one situational category is not necessarily unique to that cluster. It may appear in several different groupings.

The structure of the whole act will be noticeable at the completion of this step. Each act will be composed of two elements, a situation and a reaction, each involving the behavior of one or more persons. A group of similar situations will be associated with a set of alternative reactions, and the number of persons observed to perform each reaction will tell how frequently each reaction took place.

D. *How to Identify the End of an Act*

Interpersonal behavior is a flowing array, each phase overlapping with and conditioned by the preceding phases. It is also a series of discrete units, the arrangements of behavioral events into categorical chunks that we isolate, name, and count. These two forms are equivalent to the conversion of speech into grammatical sentences. Written language is not, as Sapir claimed, "a point-to-point equivalence . . . to its spoken counterpart." Careful attention to speech reveals that talkers often run on without producing simple declarative sentences. Yet they are readily understood, and in the act of transcribing some endings may be arbitrarily assigned.

Acts also appear to be both sequential and discrete. This is a problem for classification. Records of behavior show continuity and relatedness. Every reaction becomes part of a new situation as an encounter unfolds. Adding the reaction may alter former circumstances, and a long transaction whose contents change abruptly may be recorded. Situations are often nested inside each other, the dominant contextual features persisting through many acts. For example, steel workers high atop a construction job will take time out for lunch and relaxation. They can eat and drink, chat with one another, and even play checkers. But perched as they are on the girders of an unfinished building, they are constrained from engaging in some activities that would be feasible on the ground and with which their nether companions occupy themselves during the same breaks. Therefore, some forceful conditions remain during the course of the day. Within that period we customarily judge that numerous interpersonal acts have occurred.

Given these connections in behavior, the classifier needs a way of identifying acts that are in some respects joined. Scan for conditions that are altered in the course of interaction to identify changes in situations. A change in salient topic could be a new situation (see A–4). For example, the shift in the use of objects in interaction from buckets, rivets, and hammers to lunch boxes and magnetic checkerboards may be objective indicators of a change in topic for a high-steel crew.

The differences between an episode continuing on the same topic and the onset of a sufficiently different topic are not always so clear as those in the example of the construction workers. Often the junctures in interlocking sequences will elude the classifier if he is not familiar with the situations. He cannot always tell when one act ends and another begins. It may appear that cessation of sensory contact following a reaction is an objective criterion of the termination of an act. But what if people give up sensory access and then reunite within seconds or minutes? What if the earlier topic or focus of interpersonal activity is continued in the reunion?

This criterion might be acceptable if other aspects make it manifest that a change in situational topic has occurred. But often there is no such change. A mother may be giving her children lunch, leaving them repeatedly to fetch things and do things in other parts of the house. The intermittent contacts do not appear to be separate whole acts but rather suspensions of topical continuity because of trips out of the kitchen. For the children at lunch, as for individuals in other situations, their orientation to the future spanning the intermittent periods of contact with their mother provides hidden continuity to that interaction. A secretary may answer the telephone in the midst of a conversation with someone else and then go back to that conversation and its subject matter when the brief duty engendered by the phone call is consummated. Shall the reunion be tagged the beginning of a new act? This is the reverse of the question stated above. In the construction worker case apparent continuity could perplex the classifier because *topical* changes suggest disjunctions. In the latter instances *sensory contact* is obviously broken and then reestablished, yet the classifier holds on to what happened before and joins it to events that follow to impose continuity. Because participants do the same, relying on their memories to link parts of an event, we cannot use cessation and onset of sensory access to tell when an act begins and when it ends. A behavior sequence may have gaps between its segments and still be a unit act. The classification problem is how to determine the end of an act so that it is not confused with the delay or the prolongation of a reaction over intermittent sensory contacts.

If I assume that individuals adjust perceptions of act units to include breaks in contact, I must also assume that the participants establish the units to which they respond. This brings the measurement of behavior to the edge of a morass of covert processes and subjectivity. But one can skirt the morass. There is a solution based on understanding the nature of the field records. The task of behavior systematics is not begun purely and without some prior categorization. Classification takes place through field workers' use of language in recording observations. Language is a codifier. It accomplishes differentiation, exclusion, and establishment of behavior categories for those who use it. After all, it is possible to describe much of what one person does with another by referring to muscle contractions and motion through space and thereby avoid the use of interaction-relevant words. In everyday descriptions, English-speaking people rarely say, "She raised her fist and conveyed it forcibly to his nose." Most people say "She hit him" or some equivalent unit phrase. Each phrase is a *linguistic gestalt,* encompassing events as they are registered in human experience in a certain milieu. Describing events becomes so conventional that people do not exalt their linguistic portrayals with the name of systematic classification, but they perform the same process. When people describe acts, they establish configurations that they recognize in a way comparable to other classes of events they have categorized. Their descriptions overlook short breaks in sensory access if they conclude that the behavior unit spans the breaks. Field records, then, are repositories of categories of action.

There is a hitch to using field records to locate boundaries of acts. Descriptions enmesh behavior in a linguistic format peculiar to the users. The categories are not the same for all who speak the same root language. People in certain social statuses own vernaculars that differ from those used by others. We acknowledge this by referring to the language of business, the language of love, the language of the underworld, and so on.

Maurer has shown that every part of the interaction among a pickpocket and his assistants and their intended victim has a category in the argot of pocket-picking. Each label refers to a complex of body movements that are grouped as a significant act in the sequence. Briefly, the mark (intended victim) is fanned (contacted to locate the loot) by the claw (pickpocket) and then pratted (maneuvered into position) by a stall (assistant) who shades (covers or detracts from) the claw as he scores (removes the loot). The men who accomplish this series of body signals summarize the stages of the entire operation according to a division of labor significant to themselves. They encode behavior according to categories shared by their group and not necessarily known to outsiders.

So the behavior taxonomist confronts the problem of linguistic relativity. Since the categories used by participating actors embody units of experience significant to them, the classifier can *rely on descriptions used by persons in the social position being studied* to identify the ends of acts. The closer his units fit the descriptions of actors, the more likely he is to achieve a culturally valid partitioning of the material gathered through observation.

To accomplish this requires a separate stage of research. It should take place after completing the first classification of situations (A and B) and will entail interviewing people who were observed earlier or interviewing others in the same social positions.

After the field survey was completed and the first identification of situations was made, three researchers (including me) interviewed forty to fifty aides—not necessarily the ones we had observed. We employed a technique that I and others (e.g., Collier) had used before in which records or diagrams or photographs of the informants' own behavior are presented to them for comment. We used small cards, and typed on each card one of the situations identified in step B of the classification procedure. Keeping the records anonymous, we queried the aides at one hospital about what we had observed in another setting. We interviewed on sites similar to those at which the records had been made and explained this cross-hospital feature to the aides.

The interviewer shuffled the deck of situation cards and showed about twenty-five of them, one at a time, to each informant. The interviewer asked whether the informant had seen the event in his hospital and, if so, what had taken place. We sought reports of events rather than policies. Policies were usually broached as "In that case I would . . ." and we countered this by interjecting "Tell me about the last time you saw this happen" or "What did the aide do?"

Using the cards created an easier atmosphere than the direct confrontation of an interviewer leveling questions, and we gathered abundant testimony and detailed anecdotes from our respondents. We tape-recorded these interviews and later transcribed them. The aides' remarks could then be treated as objective data, not to be used as information about the occurrence of acts but as delineators of act-boundaries.

To identify the ends of acts, scan the two sets of descriptions, the observers' field records, and the transcriptions of informants' testimony in the interviews. Where the participants' descriptions fit well with a segment or several segments of a reaction depicted in the field records, substitute their phrasing for that depiction and the end-boundary of the reaction thus will be established.

Testimony being what it is, an interview in which an informant is asked to describe behavior with which he is familiar taps a combination of past perceptions and anticipations. He relies, as does everyone, on a frame of thought in which memory and orientation to the future pertain to the same set of acts. In Chapter 4 I described the individual's idea of an act as that of an ensemble and noted that when he thinks of a situation, he is prompted to think of the set of alternative reactions to it. His memory differs from his anticipations only in the probability values he assigns to alternatives. He may discard a reaction he observed for a substitute that he conceives to be highly probable. Therefore, the classifier should use the participant's description only if it parallels an event reported in the observational records. Verbal testimony is not enough. It must be correlated with observation. Informants' phrases are not to be brought into the classification if the behavior described has not been noted by observers.

It became easier to establish the end of an act by matching aides' descriptions of their reactions to the events logged in the field records, especially if four or five aides reported the same reaction to a situation.

E. *Code All the Observational Records*

After the guides for situations and reaction categories have been established from the several samplings, replace all the records used and classify the events in the entire set of records. It is necessary to repeat the classification because many revisions have occurred since the initial designations were made. Further adjustments may be prompted by new materials, that is, while reading records not sampled for categorizing. Some informants' descriptions that were not used earlier may now match some of these newly discovered reactions.

I proposed that the classifier should hold on to his doubts about similarity between situations and preserve distinctions in his first grouping (see B–1–c). Observable characteristics, such as words spoken, gestures made, objects involved, and aspects of context, were to be the bases for grouping situations in that step. In this reclassification, be more severe about the tendency to preserve distinctions. If judgment cannot give explicit guidance and there are only vague feelings that a situation is different from the cluster in which it might be placed, quell the feelings and consummate the merger.

One event should be coded for every actor (being studied) observed in every situation. If an aide behaved toward a group of patients as a group, I coded his conduct as one reaction. If he dealt differently with individual patients within the same situation, I coded each reaction as a separate event. If an aide dealt similarly but pluralistically with patients who were part of a group, that is, if he treated patients as individuals within the broader context of a situation, I coded each instance as a separate reaction. For this the record sometimes contained a guide to the number of events, and I coded one event for each variant explicitly mentioned. For example, the record noted that one aide wandered about the cafeteria while patients were eating, saying, "Are you getting enough to eat?" "Don't eat food dropped on the floor." "How are you today?" "Hello, Joe." I coded four events for this entry, though not all in the same category.

F. *Consolidate the Situational Categories*

The field records have by this time been codified in a way that affords information not available initially. The taxonomic procedure can now reach beyond surface properties of events. No two situational groupings at this stage will be altogether similar, yet some will appear alike, and matters of similarity or difference can now be resolved.

1. In its extreme, this is a question of the universal and the unique. In its graded form it is the matter of sameness and difference. How can one decide that two things are or are not alike?

Given any two or more groupings of situations whose overt properties leave the matter in doubt, a rule enunciated by Peirce can be applied: If two classes of situations have no differences in reactions to them, then there are no significant differences between the two classes of situations. This pragmatic principle is used in many spheres. For example, we test a solution for acidity or alkalinity by applying some of it to paper treated with litmus dye. If the paper turns red, the solution is acid; if the paper turns blue, the solution is alkaline. The chemist notes the reaction of the paper in order to discriminate among the liquids. This technique of classification is like perceiving. Perception is categorizing a sensory array partly according to knowledge about one's reaction accompanying that array. Similarly, classify interpersonal situations by how people react to them.

2. For such a complex phenomenon as an interpersonal event, the first statement of this technique is incomplete. Litmus dye may be adequate for discriminating an acid from a base because a single dimension—the degree to which hydrogen ions are present in excessive concentration—has been isolated as the key property. No such thematic isolation is yet available in the study of interpersonal behavior. A situation will not always be followed by the same reaction on the part of different individuals that confront it. Several alternative reactions may occur (see C–3). The pragmatic principle must therefore be extended to compare the *sets of reactions* associated with two or more situations being considered for consolidation.

In the classification round completed (step E), the data were left amenable to consideration of sets of alternative reactions as a basis for further clustering or for preserving distinctions.

3. Along with referring to sets of reactions comes the need for a quantitative evaluation of supposedly equivalent sets. Different reactions that occur in a situation occur with assorted frequencies. Just as it is rare that the probability for one alternative will be 1.000 (that is, that there will be only one reaction to a frequent situation), it will be rare to find equal probabilities for several alternatives.

"How shall we decide whether two collections are to belong to the same bundle?" asked Russell. "Find out how many members each has, and put them in the same bundle if they have the same number of members."

4. First note the qualitative similarity of reactions. Then check the similarity in *proportional frequencies of occurrence*. I refer to proportional frequency because one may find a group of situations that was observed thirty times apparently similar to a group that happened ten times. If reactions A, B, and C took place 3, 15, and 12 times respectively for the first group, and reactions A', B', and C' happened 1, 5, and 4 times respectively

for the second group, the merger is justifiable on the basis of qualitative and quantitative similarity between the sets of reactions.

Some categories kept separate because of doubt in the first two rounds of clustering (B and E) will now appear alike because their sets of reactions are similar. Other tentative dissimilarities will be confirmed by the lack of equivalence in their sets of reactions or by unequal relative frequencies between similar reactions. Examples of both outcomes appear on page 124.

5. This technique for consolidating categories does not change the pattern of reaction alternatives or their frequencies. The act is made more general but is not otherwise altered. One may wonder about the implication that a possible later comparison between the two or more types of events has been barred by the merger. Comparison would have shown that the same set of reactions occurs in the same proportion in both types of situations.

We will not find that all interpersonal acts have the same amount of complexity or duration or frequency. Do not insist upon questionable unions just to achieve a more condensed set of categories. The systematization is supposed to be exhaustive and representative. If an uncommon situation or reaction is noted, one that cannot readily be placed with others, leave it alone. Neither force group membership on it nor expel it from consideration.

G. *Merge the Reaction Categories*

Follow the procedure outlined for situations in step B to group reaction categories by their overt similarities. Reactions are alike if the descriptive phrases of participants refer to the same action or if they are similar to descriptions in the written records.

While situations were consolidated on the basis of similar reaction sets (step F), at this stage reactions—the key elements of behavior to be studied and compared later—are never to be grouped according to their appearance in similar situations. After all, if a group of situations with similar sets of reactions were consolidated into a single class, their reactions still persist as separate categories (see F–5).

Like the initial establishment of situational clusters, the classifier may confront doubtful cases here too. Earlier groupings or discriminations among reactions may be adjusted at this time. If a revision is introduced, the consolidations made in step F (in which sets of reactions were compared) must be reviewed, recalculated, and reclassified accordingly.

Apply simple generic descriptive labels to the reaction categories (as is shown in Table 7-3).

One may come across records that are ambiguous or too meager to identify a reaction conclusively. It is the price paid for moments of fatigue when recording observations. These too are data. If the fragments of information are sufficient to indicate that something did happen even though the record is not complete or clear enough to tell what happened, the instance is to be listed as Not Ascertained and will appear in the description of the population of acts.

The Situations

Reviewing all classified groups, I phrased each situational category to reflect qualities common to the events it subsumed and omitted features not shared by all in the cluster. To simplify the description, I gave main play to verbs and nouns and used few qualifying adjectives. The resulting list of situations is given in Figure 7-1.

A repertoire encompasses a set of situations grouped together by the social relationship in the same way that a situation groups together a set of reactions. Just as a given reaction can occur in different situations, a given situation can occur in different repertoires. If the social relationship studied is one involving a position whose incumbents (like patients) live almost their entire lives in the presence of those in the other position (like aides), it is plausible that situations of daily existence will find their way into the repertoire. The list shows a broad range of contact opportunities for aides with patients. Some are familiar circumstances everywhere in society, such as passing or meeting someone (2 in Figure 7-1), having a conversation (4), being engaged in recreation (6), attending a party (7), and noting a newcomer in the neighborhood (25). Other situations are familiar in institutions or in the home, such as the arrival of time for a scheduled activity (3), playing pranks (13), or dining (14). Some of the situations appear in work repertoires. For example, situation 12 could be rephrased as follows: "An employee complains or denounces the company (or insults a foreman)." Situation 15 occurs in schools and in army camps during cleanup periods: "A student (or soldier) is not where he is supposed to be (or wanders away from his group)."

Each category has a unitary form. For example, patients at recreation

Figure 7-1. Situations for psychiatric aides with mental patients

1. A patient requests an item (e.g., socks, cigarette) or service (open the window) or information (what's for dinner).
2. An aide and a patient pass each other or meet.
3. It is time for a scheduled activity (e.g., to wake up, eat, sleep, dress, or receive medicine) for patients.
4. A patient makes a remark or is having a conversation with an aide (about his own interests, family, illness).
5. A patient performs an unusual verbal act (rants, mumbles, or yells incoherently).
6. Patients and aides are at recreation together (playing a game, exercising).
7. Patients and staff members are at a party (or picnic or carnival).
8. An aide is working on the ward, and some patients are nearby.
9. Patients are in the day room, and the aide is not engaged in ward work.
10. A patient asks to be let off (or onto) the ward (or to make a phone call).
11. A patient is in distress (crying, afraid, or berating himself).
12. A patient complains or denounces the hospital (or insults an aide).
13. A patient is making mischief for someone (teasing, tickling, hiding shoes).
14. Patients are eating in the dining room.
15. A patient is not where he is supposed to be (or wanders away from his group).
16. Some patients are on their way from one place to another.
17. A patient delays or resists doing a required activity.
18. A patient performs an unusual physical act (gyrates, lies stiffly on the floor, or eats food spilled on the floor).
19. A patient refuses an invitation to join in an optional activity (go for a walk, play a game).
20. A patient is negligent or destructive toward objects.
21. A patient performs a usually private gesture in public (walks about undressed, masturbates, or makes a sexual advance).
22. A patient attacks someone (by hitting or throwing something or by threatening).
23. Patients invite an aide who is not busy to join them in recreation (or for coffee).
24. Someone (a visitor, taxi driver) comes to the ward (or there is a phone call) for a patient.
25. A new patient is on the ward.
26. A patient smiles and his false tooth drops out.

NA Situation not ascertained: records incomplete, ambiguous, or lost.

(6) and patients inviting an aide to join them in recreation (23) are listed separately. The reason is that either circumstance was observed alone. It was often possible to note an aide's reaction to patients at recreation before the patients invited him to join in. The two are therefore classified separately.

Situation 1 (A patient requests . . .) is of taxonomic interest. It is an outcome of the procedure for consolidating categories according to similar frequencies for similar reactions. In step B of my classification I listed three distinct categories of asking for a service, requesting an article, and asking for information and kept them separate in the early classification rounds. Then in step F I sought candidates for mergers. The aides' reactions were the same in content and in proportional frequency for all three types of requests, and I brought them together in a single category.

In contrast, situations 17 (A patient delays or resists doing a required activity) and 19 (A patient refuses an invitation to join in an optional activity) reflect a distinction that survived my attempt at consolidation. As noted in step B–2, I made a distinction at first. Then in step F I found that the sets of reactions to these two situations differed. Aides sometimes compelled patients to perform obligatory activities, but they never used coercion in situation 19. So I preserved the separation.

Classification posed challenges for some cases in which patients seemed upset or disorganized. The variety of disturbances manifested by patients was large. Sorting common forms was easy. For example, if a patient cried about being locked up, I coded it 11 (A patient is in distress); if he expressed anger about being locked up, I coded it 12 (A patient complains . . .). But other forms of disturbance were uncommon. It was perplexing to sort these disparate and unusual forms. Descriptions deal aptly with events that are familiar to us. Uncommon events elude familiar words. Though I felt less secure in moving from specific events to a general class, I finally grouped unusual events according to the primacy of three themes: uncommon verbal behavior (5), uncommon physical gestures (18), and performing an ordinarily private act in public (21). Figure 7-2 contains the categories of both common and uncommon forms of upset. It illumines that twilight zone where personal judgment guides decisions about the frequencies of situations. In saying that certain verbal and physical gestures are uncommon, I draw upon my own experience rather than upon some comprehensive survey reporting statistical distributions of events.

My judgment also led me to conclude that forms of upset such as being

Figure 7-2. Events subsumed by categories of upset or disturbance

Uncommon	*Common*

Uncommon

5. A patient performs an unusual verbal act:
   - Rants, mumbles, or yells incoherently
   - Asks a nonsensical question repeatedly
   - Makes an irrelevant request repeatedly (e.g., asks for permission to put on socks although already wearing a pair)
   - Makes animal-like noises (e.g., in response to questions)

18. A patient performs an unusual physical act:
   - Gyrates and whirls
   - Lies stiffly on the floor in front of a doorway
   - Eats food spilled on the floor
   - Performs motion rituals (e.g., twists neck and shuffles rapidly in place while holding arms stiffly angled out from body)
   - Manifests tics

21. A patient performs a usually private gesture in public:
   - Walks along corridors or into living room dressed only in underwear, or naked
   - Performs a physically affectionate gesture toward person of same sex (e.g., lays head in lap)
   - Makes a heterosexual advance (e.g., attempts to embrace other)
   - Masturbates

Common

11. A patient is in distress:
   - Cries, sobs
   - Is afraid and ready to flee
   - Berates himself
   - Expresses worry about own illness or fate of own family

12. A patient complains or denounces the hospital:
   - Curses
   - Insults a staff member
   - Criticizes a hospital arrangement (e.g., loudly declares impatience with "the way everything is locked up around here")

20. A patient is negligent or destructive toward objects:
   - Sits on ping-pong table
   - Teeters on chair so that only one or two chair legs touch floor
   - Kicks furniture
   - Slams door furiously (i.e., enough to crack pane of glass in door)
   - Shreds napkins

22. A patient attacks someone by hitting or throwing something (or by threatening):
   - Slaps face
   - Raises fist and threatens (or wields object and threatens)
   - Hurls object at someone

in distress (11), complaining or denouncing an organization (12), being negligent or destructive toward objects (20), or attacking people (22) happen everywhere in our society. We have all acted these ways at times in our lives. Note that I placed in category 20 (A patient is negligent or destructive toward objects) an instance of a patient's shredding napkins. Some readers will look askance at such a classification and believe it to be strained. The act seems of insufficient magnitude to fit their meaning of negligence or destructiveness. Striving to classify according to objective properties rather than exclusively social interpretations and being governed by the principle that each event has to fit somewhere in the set, I found situation 20 the most acceptable category. It was acceptable enough to make unnecessary the creation of a separate category for shredding napkins.

Add these to the other familiar situations mentioned above, and it appears that the conduct of patients in mental hospitals is mostly like that of people everywhere. Only the unusual verbalisms (5), unusual physical gestures (18), and ordinarily private actions done in public (21) are rare outside the institutions. We have all done some of these things at one time or another. It is the frequency, the repetition, or the severity of such performances that leads to branding individuals as crazy and to consigning them to mental hospitals. Mental illness, however, refers to more behavioral forms than those of situations 5, 18, and 21. Schizophrenics characteristically show little interest in their environment and are prone to sit quietly and be withdrawn. By the classification method used, such conduct on the part of patients would not have been distinguished from that of patients who were not withdrawn but who were sitting quietly watching television (e.g., 9).

For other than uncommon upsets I did not persist in trying for groupings. Nor was I selective in the classification. I assigned every recorded event to a category and permitted an event to remain distinct even if it resulted in a lone entry. That is how the situation of a patient's tooth popping out when he smiled, which was observed only once, remained a separate category (26). I considered classifying it as a patient in distress (11), but it was different from the other events grouped there and required an additional inference about how the patient felt, so I left it alone.

Finally, the list of situations in Figure 7-1 contains the important residual category of Not Ascertained. Occasionally a field record noted that a contact opportunity between aides and patients occurred but that its nature could not be discerned. Records were inadvertently left incomplete in the midst of observing. Or a record was lost after being numbered and partly classified. These things should not happen ideally. Yet they do occur in behavioral research, just as faulty or erratic measurements creep into laboratory or into field procedures of other disciplines. Though the event cannot be fully reported, the record contains some information, and this circumstance can be acknowledged in a standard way. It is preferable to list the event as Not Ascertained rather than to risk distortion either by placing it in a specific category through guesswork or by discarding the remnant of data.

The Reactions

Figure 7-3 is a roster of the reaction categories. There are twenty-four reactions plus the residual category of NOT ASCERTAINED. Each entry is tagged by a brief phrase such as FULFILLS REQUEST (a) or CONVERSES (b). This generic label subsumes a set of specific reactions that constitutes the behavior grouping. So, for example, one form of conversing (b) is to stop to talk to another and to ask how he is getting along.

If a description in the language of aides was utilized in the classification, it is cited here in quotation marks. The quotations for a category thus indicate something about the content, scope, and duration of the reaction as the participants classify it. Some expressions are distinctive to the subculture of these informants, almost idiomatic. Consider ". . . did not know what was going off at the time" (q) and ". . . lets it go at that" (l and x). Aides use these descriptions to portray aides' behavior. Not all reactions were mentioned in the interviews, and I could not achieve the full calibration of act units to informants' phrases. In these instances I used the observers' notes and tried to follow the aides' leads from their other remarks to locate the ends of acts. For one category, BRIEFLY AGREES OR DISAGREES (m), there was no informants' testimony available at all.

The twenty-four reactions comprise a set. While some categories may seem unsatisfactory, it will not be easy to change them without considering the gaps and overlaps that might be created in connection with other categories in the set. Exceptions to this are CARES FOR OR SERVES (n), TEACHES OR CORRECTS (p), and REASSURES AND TRIES TO REMEDY (q). Each of these may be broken down into two parts; for example, CARES FOR, and SERVES. With all classifications there is the problem of deciding where to draw the lines between categories. These three reactions were left as composites because—considering the aides' own descriptions—the separations appeared less apt for the behavior observed. With more information at hand perhaps separations would appear justified.

Some academics do not like the category TEACHES OR CORRECTS (p). It seems too catchall for them. They claim that not all the actions subsumed by it are instructive or corrective. However, it is a label referring to a gesture to instruct or correct. The label does not guarantee the effects of the move, for that would be defining interpersonal acts according to their presumed consequences. Many thoughtful persons in teaching positions are hard put to know just how their overt efforts affect the students exposed to them. For the same reason these categories cite action rather than consequences. The aide may tell a patient to do something (c), but we cannot assume that the patient then does it. The aide may entreat a patient not to worry or to "get hold of yourself" (q), but it does not follow that the patient is thereby reassured. Nor can a category itself be interpreted as neutral or joyful or sinister. In Chapter 5 I showed how the meaning of an act comes from a comparison with its alternatives.

The main difference between TELLS OR REMINDS TO DO SOMETHING (c) and SUPERVISES ACTIVITY (h) is that in the latter reaction the aide remains in sensory contact with the patient whereas in the former he may not. Sometimes both reactions seemed applicable, and my choice was dictated by cues supplied by descriptions from aides' interviews. Otherwise, which of the two categories was used depended on what the record of the event revealed about the duration of contact. If contact was prolonged, I assigned the reaction to h.

While reaction c has the flavor of a command and is at least a direct request, reaction j (SUGGESTS ENTERING ACTIVITY) applies when the patient is offered the option for the activity.

Comparing FULFILLS REQUEST (a) and PARTICIPATES FULLY (i), a is a specific response to a patient's immediate request. Reaction i is a broader response of the aide to patients in more diffuse interaction. Generally, a was used when the reaction was sufficient to the situation and did not lead to or entail further interaction with patients, whereas i was used if the patient's request was an invitation leading to further interaction. Moreover, whereas reaction a seems to result from a patient's imposing his will upon the aide, in i there is an implication of equality or exchange, with patient and aide influencing one another. In situations where an aide's reaction is specific and does not lead further, if an aide fulfills a request and also imposes his will, this event can be designated by combining reaction a with

Figure 7-3. List of reactions

a) FULFILLS REQUEST
—"Goes and gets it for him."
—"Does it for him."
—"Answers him."
—"Gets up and lets him out."

b) CONVERSES
—"Stops to talk and asks how he's getting along. . ."
—"Talks with him."
—Asks questions, gives advice and opinions, tells jokes.
—"Comments on the situation."
—"Sits down and talks with them."
—"Welcomes him to the ward and takes a little while to get acquainted."
—"Keeps up a conversation."

c) TELLS OR REMINDS TO DO SOMETHING
—Tells him to make his bed, keep a doctor's appointment, get a haircut, etc.
—"Goes through the ward saying that it's time [to wake up, go to activity, etc.]."
—Calls patients and hands out medicines.
—"Reminds him to be sure to sign out [or to put on socks] before he leaves."
—"Goes and tells the patient."
—"Tells them we are ready to close up so hurry and finish eating."

d) SHOWS NO OVERT CHANGE IN BEHAVIOR
—"Keeps right on walking."
—"Doesn't stop to make conversation and keeps on with his picking up."
—"Gives no recognition and doesn't say anything to them."

—"Walks by without any sign of attention."

e) LEAVES THEM TO THEMSELVES
—"Looks on and lets the party run its course."
—Plays a separate game with an aide.
—Sits and reads.
—"Stands in back of the room and watches them."
—"Talks with other aides."

f) GREETS
—"Says 'Good morning' and continues on."
—Hands him a partly smoked cigarette without speaking.
—Stays in one place and jokes with patients who pass by.
—"Moves among the tables making small talk like 'How are you today?'"

g) TELLS TO STOP
—"Tells him to put some clothes on."
—"Tells him he is supposed to stay with his group."
—"Tells him this is not the time or place to act this way."
—"Calls to him that he shouldn't do this and to sit down."
—"Tells him to stop."

h) SUPERVISES ACTIVITY
—Clears the doorways and directs traffic.
—Changes the television program from news report to fictional drama.
—"Asks the patients if they mind moving while he is cleaning out there."
—Directs traffic, keeps them in line.
—Escorts them.
—"Goes off together with them."

Figure 7-3. (continued)

i) PARTICIPATES FULLY
—"Stays right in with the group, walks around, talks, sings, and dances with the patients."
—Works with the patients and follows their suggestions on what to do.
—"Goes along with them."

j) SUGGESTS ENTERING ACTIVITY
—"Encourages the patients to mingle and to be out there dancing."
—"Asks a patient who is standing nearby to sit in at the game."
—"Tries to get something for them to do [as watch television, knitting, play baseball, play game]."
—"Invites him again and tries to convince him that this is part of the treatment program."

k) COMPELS (TO STOP OR TO DO IT)
—"Eases him out of the day room and brings him back to his bedroom."
—"Catches him and brings him back."
—"Insists that he do it, and guides him out of bed with his arm around him."
—Tries to force-feed him.
—"Walks him over to a chair and gets him to sit there."
—"Gets the patients separated."
—Holds the attacker.
—"Stops him from going further."
—"Walks him out of the office and back to the day room."
—Pulls him off the table.
—"Insists that he do it [that drunk patient stay awake to avoid risk of coma; that agitated patient sit

down] and guides him . . . with his arm around him."

l) PERMITS
—"Lets him act on his own."
—"Doesn't try to force him."
—"Permits him to do this."
—"Lets it go at that."
—"Smiles at it and permits him to do this."

m) BRIEFLY AGREES OR DISAGREES
—Says uh-hmm and nods his head.
—Shakes his head.
—Acts as if he understands, agrees or shakes his head.

n) CARES FOR OR SERVES
—"Goes ahead and washes, dresses, or feeds them."
—Helps them to bed.
—"Fixes up a tray and brings it to the table."

o) ASKS ASSISTANCE
—Asks him where another patient is.
—Tells of own troubles.
—Asks patients to tell the others.
—"Asks them to get up and help him clean up."

p) TEACHES OR CORRECTS
—"Sits there and makes him ask nicely before he does it."
—"Instructs them as to how to play and tells them when they make mistakes or good moves."
—"Asks him what he is talking about and to speak clearly."
—Says loudly that he wishes people would stop putting their cigarette butts in the flower pots.
—Tells him to sit straight on the chair.

Figure 7–3. (continued)

q) REASSURES AND TRIES TO REMEDY
  —"Asks the patient what was
    bothering him and reports it to
    the nurse."
  —Suggests what might be done.
  —"Explains to the other patient that
    the one who hit him is sick and
    did not know what was going off
    at the time."
  —Says "That must be an uncom-
    fortable feeling."
  —Says "Get hold of yourself" and
    massages his back.

r) WITHDRAWS
  —Becomes quiet and leaves.
  —Leaves game after a while.
  —"Informs them that some other
    time he would go but at present
    he was busy."

s) STIPULATES A CONDITION
  —"Tells him to wait a minute until
    he finishes what he is doing."
  —"Checks in the nurses' station to
    see whether or not he is allowed."
  —Agrees for a short, rather than
    long, walk.

t) REFUSES
  —"Tells the patient he is able to
    get it himself or do it himself."
  —"Says he doesn't know."

u) BANTERS
  —When asked for bacon, brings a
    piece two inches long.
  —Asks patient who is in pajamas at
    midday why he can't sleep.
  —"Laughs and imitates him."
  —Tries to pinch and wrestle with
    him.
  —Says "Boo!" as he passes.

v) PARTICIPATES PARTLY
  —"Lets the patient do the talking."
  —"Listens to him."
  —Plays the game and does not make
    extra comments.

w) ASKS WHAT IS THE MATTER
  —"Asks him what was the matter
    and why he did not join in."
  —"Asks him why he is acting that
    way and what the trouble was."
  —"Asks him what was wrong, and
    did he want to talk about any-
    thing."

x) PERMITS UNDER A CONDITION
  —"Lets him go but does not let him
    out of sight."
  —"Looks out of the nurses' station
    to see if it will go on, and when
    it doesn't he lets it go at that."

NA) REACTION NOT ASCERTAINED

TELLS OR REMINDS TO DO SOMETHING (c) or with STIPULATES A CONDITION (s).

Unless otherwise stated, STIPULATES A CONDITION (s) is a form of fulfilling a request or accepting an invitation along with some qualification or additional gesture to imply strongly that the action would not be performed if this were not also done. The difference between s and PERMITS UNDER A CONDITION (x) is that s is used if the aide's accommodation to the patient is explicitly subject to a condition, whereas x refers to a patient's behavior being allowed to continue under a condition. Reaction x is usually a matter of avoiding active interference. Others observing the aide will note that he pays attention to what is going on but that he does not move to affect the situation as long as it remains below a certain threshold—of intensity, volume, or duration. Reaction s is a matter of the aide's attempting to alter the circumstances under which he himself will perform some action. It usually involves bargaining with a patient who makes a request or gives an invitation.

Like studies of sound that are validated by a baseline category of silence, this roster of reactions includes the important one of SHOWS NO OVERT CHANGE IN BEHAVIOR (d).

Three reactions, SHOWS NO OVERT CHANGE IN BEHAVIOR (d), LEAVES THEM TO THEMSELVES (e), and WITHDRAWS (r) seem members of the same family. One distinction between d and the other two should be implied by my discussion of this reaction in Chapter 5. If there is no noticeable difference in the aide's conduct, it is classified d, whereas for e or r the aide commits a new action. Sometimes aides were observed near patients, available but not interacting with them. For example, an aide may be found sitting reading a newspaper in the nurse's office while patients are watching television in the day room. Such instances are usually classed as reaction e. Reaction e does not have the looked-right-past-him character that is possible for d, nor does it convey the erstwhile interaction denoted by r. Where e denotes interacting with persons other than those in the relationship being studied (for example, talking with other aides rather than with patients), interaction with patients is positively excluded unless patients intrude into the ongoing interaction. Thus e takes the aide out of contact opportunities with patients by virtue of the reaction itself. Reactions d or r—since they do not refer to direct engagements in interaction with others—do not eliminate new contact opportunities with patients immediately, according to the criterion of sensory access.

One difference between TELLS TO STOP (g) and COMPELS TO STOP OR TO DO IT (k) is that the latter invariably includes at least touch contact, usually pressure, perhaps to the point of grasping, grappling, or pulling. Direct physical force in k can be used to make the patient cease an action, make the patient perform an action (like getting out of bed or eating), or cause the patient to move from one location to another. In this last form the patient may continue the behavior that was part of the situation to which the aide reacted by compelling the patient to move. For example, if a patient is leaning against a door and is crying to get out, an aide may lead the patient away while the latter continues to sob. Reaction k may therefore remove the patient from one place and confine him to another without directly suppressing the patient's behavior that was part of the original situation.

I classified as a greeting an instance of an aide's handing a partly smoked cigarette to a patient (f in Figure 7-3). It is a gesture of inclusion where scarcity of smoking materials makes the conservation of cigarettes pertinent. Workmen share them at work breaks. Soldiers do on the battlefield. At some parties it is a form of greeting to offer the newcomer a "joint" of marijuana that is being passed around, instead of an alcoholic drink. GREETS (f) is related to CONVERSES (b) in the same way that PARTICIPATES PARTLY (v) is related to PARTICIPATES FULLY (i). Reaction f is a salutation but not a joining; v entails performing an activity but not contributing further to its interpersonal aspect. For example, an aide may be engrossed in a game of checkers or cards or ping-pong and yet show little personal communication with others in the game. Reaction v would apply because this category, like the others, refers to the behavior of one person toward other persons; it does not refer to the overt conduct of a person toward nonhuman aspects of the activity. Classifying a reaction as v implies that other reactions in that set designate fuller participation.

Some reaction categories seem more complicated than others. For example, TELLS TO STOP (g) has one central message while REASSURES AND TRIES TO REMEDY (q) has a double theme. Such disparities among the categories held my attention during classification. At first I had an urge to simplify, to create units that seemed equal in scope and complexity. But the descriptions in the field notes and in the informants' testimony consistently reflected such differences. Some reactions were more elaborate than others, took longer, had identifiable elements that occurred together almost all of the time. I chose to be faithful to the record and to establish categories that reflected the events as they occurred. Taking each reaction category as one of the total set should not be assumed to imply an equality among their messages. Some reactions communicate more than others.

Sense Modes Stimulated

Spoken language is the most important form of social interaction. Its possibilities have been exploited remarkably by humans. But interpersonal action begins with and is based on all forms of sensory communication, not only on what reaches the ears. Yet there is no tried and true notational system for nonverbal gestures. In this section I describe conventions I followed to decide which receptors were stimulated in a given act.

This coding of the field records augments the sorting of behavior into the reactions that are listed in Figure 7-3. There are many nonverbal gestures alluded to in those reactions. This addition does not fill gaps in an incomplete roster of conduct but is a source of further information. It will be used to test the idea about sensations of social intimacy that I offered in Chapter 2. This sense mode classification may be useful in other ways as well. For example, in the preceding section, to clarify reaction v (PARTICI-PATES PARTLY) I pointed out that it refers to interpersonal behavior and not to playing a game itself. Some readers may have been skeptical, thinking of how much can be communicated by competitors even though they do not speak directly to one another. The lobbing of tennis balls during courtship is decidedly different from the play between husband and wife. My remarks about reaction v should not be interpreted as referring only to audible messages. The supplementary coding described in this section deals with sensory data in general and should help define v and other reactions.

The field records were not always explicit about which receptors were involved in acts. I therefore did more research during the months I classified the records of sensory stimulation. I watched other persons interacting to learn the aggregates of receptors commonly affected in the specific reactions that I was trying to code. Figure 7-4 contains the decisions I made about sensory stimulation in social conduct. Note that it is the stimulation of other persons, not of the individual performing the reaction, to whom these decisions apply. Also, the matter of intentional or accidental use of a sensory channel was not an issue. I coded observable evidence.

The decisions in Figure 7-4 refer to the reactions of aides with patients according to survey records. Those decisions were sometimes conditioned by my later observations of people in interaction. For example, if an aide

Figure 7–4. Coding decisions for sensory stimulation of reactions

Sight
—Gestures
—Signals with hands or body
—Shrugs shoulders
—Listens to the other

Hearing
—Calls
—Laughs
—Speaks
—Whistles or hums

Smell
—Is close to the other's nose

Touch
—Taps on the arm
—Brushes by the other

Pressure
—Grabs the other's shirttail and pulls him
—Pulls
—Grabs
—Shoves

Sight and Hearing
—Converses, chats

Sight and Smell
—Gestures very close

Sight and Touch
—Shakes hands

Sight and Temperature
—Stands very close, almost touching

Sight and Taste
—Passes cigarette for puff

Sight, Hearing, Touch, and Temperature
—Has arm around other's shoulder while chatting

Sight, Hearing, Smell, Pressure, and Temperature
—Utters soothing noises while maneuvering other into a comfortable position

Sight, Smell, Touch, and Pressure
—Dresses the other and handles him while doing so

Sight, Touch, Pressure, and Temperature
—Dances with the other (dance forms in which people hold one another, rather than the noncontact forms)

Touch and Temperature
—Puts arm around shoulder or waist

Touch and Pressure
—Guides
—Tickles
—Massages

Pressure and Temperature
—Embraces
—Grips and holds

Not Ascertained:
Information incomplete

spoke to a patient, unless the record noted that the aide "called to the patient" I assumed that visual as well as auditory stimulation took place. When in doubt, however, I refrained from crediting the stimulation of a given receptor. So I assumed that the loud declaration about cigarette butts cited under reaction *p* (TEACHES OR CORRECTS) in Figure 7-3 was directed toward anyone within earshot and that no particular visual stimulation accompanied it.

Of course, other instances of the reactions might show different combinations of receptor stimulation. Reactions display varied sensory stimulation in their delivery, and we know almost nothing about this stimulation by types of behavior. Some of these variations may well be the countenances people allude to as "It was the *way* he did it" or "It was *how* he said it" to declare that ostensibly the same behavior carries different messages.

The criterion for smell stimulation is that the other person's face be very close to the actor. It is a debatable criterion. Man is believed to have sensitive olfactory organs but ones that adapt to given levels and types of odors. Therefore, such proximity is probably not required for smell to be stimulated during a reaction. Yet sensation involves a change in the level of stimulation. On this count human olfactory stimulation is probably negligible until another comes very close to one's nose. The liberal use of perfumes and colognes in certain situations enlarges the range at which a change in sensed odor can occur. But this rarely happens in the hospital, and I credited smell only when the patient's nose was very close to the aide.

A person's skin is a source of considerable radiant heat, and temperature can be sensed by any part of the body, but I required that two people had to be in body contact (or very close) rather than only in limb contact. The criterion is that the feel or closeness had to last more than a moment so that heat's slow transmission could have occurred. Thus temperature can be sensed when two people are dancing together or when they are wrestling but not when one has merely gripped the other by the shoulder.

In one instance an aide who was smoking a cigarette passed a patient and handed the butt to him (reaction *f* in Figure 7-3), and the patient began smoking it. It is debatable whether this should be scored as stimulating taste. I did so because I assumed that a wet mouthpiece was sensed by the patient.

Reaction *d* (SHOWS NO OVERT CHANGE IN BEHAVIOR) does not necessarily lack sensory impact. The aide may continue an action he performed before a situation arose. If he whistled while he worked, classing his reaction to a new situation as SHOWS NO OVERT CHANGE IN BEHAVIOR (d) signifies that he did not alter his conduct. Therefore, patients' hearing was stimulated by the whistling in reaction d. In another instance an aide walking along a corridor brushed by a patient who started to speak to him. I coded this reaction d and credited it with sight and touch stimulation.

I also followed a convention to avoid double counting when one reaction was used in combination with another. For example, in one case an aide reacted to a patient who was in distress by trying to comfort him (see q in Figure 7-3). The aide leaned close to the patient, massaged his back, and uttered soothing tones. I coded this remedial effort as stimulating sight, hearing, smell, pressure, and temperature. Intermittently, during moments of calm for the patient, the two had a conversation. The aide related an ancedote about an occasion when he was drunk in the Navy. The function of this anecdote was perhaps to distract and thereby ease the patient's tension, but I classified it according to its overt properties as conversation—not reassurance—because it occurred while the patient was calm and because I would not presume its effect on the patient. At the same time, I avoided double scoring of sensory modes. So for this second reaction (b in Figure 7-3) in the situation, I credited only sight and hearing stimulation even though sometimes the aide continued to clasp the patient as the conversation took place.

Strategy, Labor, and Controversy

Classification is a task so central to a discipline that there is nothing more fundamental to appeal to as a criterion for the adequacy of its accomplishment. Tiryakian noted its commanding place in a science, saying that the explanation of reasons for a classification is equal to "the codification of the existing state of knowledge in a discipline." The findings of all empirical research, the data of all human discourse, rest upon the set of categories used to refer to events.

To fit act units to their everyday experience, I relied on the testimony of participants in interaction. I expect that an improved systematics will move away from, as I tried to do, the popular ·technique referred to by the German word *Verstehen*. Roughly translated as understanding-through-empathy, it calls for putting oneself imaginatively in the place of persons acting and thereby experiencing social life as participants do. Weber favored the procedure, expressing interest in a sociology whose categories of events would be based on the subjective viewpoints of the individuals whose behavior was being studied. (He also recognized that an empirical anchor was needed to ensure the validity of such understandings.) Understanding-through-empathy depends too critically upon gifts not shared by all researchers. Some men accomplish it at times, but a social science cannot be based on the technique. We must develop conventional ways of describing and interpreting, methods that men can be trained to use even if they are not well endowed with rapport. This challenge, developing conventional procedures for ordinary men to use in dealing with an extraordinary topic, has imposed hardships on the classification of interpersonal acts.

Disagreements wait for any try at systematizing behavior. Reviewing the collection of events grouped together as categories in Figures 7-1 and 7-3 will set one wondering about alternative groupings. Classification invites debate. Some will clamor for distinctions that were not made. Addressing himself to the same field records, a different classifier may feel that my categories are bare and omit data that makes a difference in understanding. Someone else's try, if he used the same field records and similar principles, could yield a related but different set of categories for several reasons. One might make different cuts, preserving distinctions that were obliterated here and not acknowledging discriminations that were noted there. Perceptions and descriptions can be scaled differently to yield acts of other sizes, complexities, and durations. Finer situational groupings would result in more uniformity of reaction within each cluster. Numerical comparisons other than proportional frequency would yield different clustering decisions. Hence different outcomes could emerge in the stage of consolidation, according to similarities in the set of reactions. It would not be surprising to find someone else's categories intermediate with mine. Like the classification of situations and reactions, the decisions for sensory stimulation are also open to challenge. The conventions I used represent a try at measurement in an area where tradition provides little guidance.

The findings about behavior that I will report in Part Three rest on the outcomes of the procedure that I used and outlined here. I could dwell again and again during my presentation on the problem of behavior systematics. How adequate are the categories? Are they most natural? Are they too ungainly? Uneven? There will be a long search for an effective way of sorting out and summarizing the properties of acts, and the search will be accompanied by dogged controversy. Act-boundaries will prove to be as difficult to establish as was the taxonomy of pigeons or the ordering of subatomic particles. The issue is a persisting one but not a paralyzing one. Approximations are useful. We can explore in the meantime without waiting for an unchallengeable classification of the evidence.

Visions of an exhausting procedure will be aroused by this description of classification. In naturalistic observation, achieving a taxonomy is an arduous, painstaking task needing both bulldog tenacity and the ability to pace oneself in the work. Those who have done it know this. They know in addition that the effort fosters a ruthless attitude toward gratuitous assumptions about the nature of one's subject matter. Classifying is a teacher and a disillusioner. If the former is more powerful, one will emerge better equipped for further research and discovery. If the latter impact is greater, it often marks the point at which one abandons research in the discipline.

8

Estimating the Population of Acts

We are less interested in the particular sample of events classified than in the population from which it is drawn. Once the data are classified, the dispersion of acts in the population can be estimated. Estimation depends on the relation between the units of the population and the basis of the sample. In its simplest form, if the sample were designed according to acts, one could count the number of events assigned to each reaction category and multiply them by the ratio of population size to sample size in order to arrive at the estimate. In this case, however, acts were not elements in the sample design. Sites in the hospital, days and times, and aides were the elements. Some expected omissions and biases have therefore appeared. For example, on some occasions during observation periods, there were more aides present than the researcher could effectively observe. He chose among them and did not record what the others did. In the estimation stage I had to compensate for those who were neglected. I made several adjustments to rescale the sample information.

In this chapter I will first describe adjustments made for the survey data to compensate for such inequalities so that the estimation properly describes the population of acts. I will then treat a number of related methodological issues and how they might be resolved.

From Sampled Observations to a Probability Statement of the Population

To estimate how many acts were in the populations, I reviewed each assumption and decision that was incorporated into the actual sample or deliberately left out of it in order to gauge its effect upon the information at hand. I found three features of the sample to guide me in adjusting its tallies to improve the estimate:

1. *From the number of hours of observation in the sample to the number of hours defined as the time-size of the population*

Human existence, including its social relationships, has a daily and weekly activity cycle of work, play, and rest. Should one want to compare several relationships, such as aide with patient, teacher with student, parent with child, or counselor with camper, a similar amount of time would be needed for a baseline. The span of a week would confer a vantage for comparison.

While the entire weekly period covers what all persons in one social position may do with those in another, what each individual does can only happen during the time he is present and in contact. Where formal participation through work in an organization is involved, this is usually a forty-hour period per person. I therefore fixed a forty-hour period per week as the time-size of the population of acts. Forty hours also represents an aide's work week. This repeating span of time is accompanied by a repetition of opportunities for contacts between aides and patients in characteristic situations. The population of acts could therefore be described as if it were performed by a typical aide. One could multiply it by the number of individuals in that social setting to arrive at values for the aggregate. In this way one can speak interchangeably of aides and of a single aide while referring to the same behavioral description. Suppose there were a difference between the conduct of a particular aide and the conduct of the aggregate. The most straightforward comparison to make would be between the person's conduct during a forty-hour weekly period and the generalized description of the act-population calibrated to the same number of hours per week.

Aides were observed forty-eight hours in one hospital and fifty-five in the other. Since the temporal boundary of the population is a forty-hour period, the tallies for all events in the sample had to be reduced proportionately. This procedure requires multiplying every frequency of the classified acts by its appropriate condensing fraction. In the private hospital this fraction is 40/48. For example, if an event in a given category was noted to occur eighteen times during the forty-eight hours of observation in the private hospital—and if this were the only correction to be made—that event would be estimated to occur only fifteen times (five-sixths of eighteen) in a forty-hour period in that hospital. In the state hospital the correction factor was 40/55.

This adjustment often resulted in fractions for a forty-hour period. But these are easy to interpret. For example, if an act is listed to occur .75 times per week, this means that it occurs approximately three times in four weeks.

2. *From each observed situation to the number of aides present during that period of time*

On pages 96 and 99 I called attention to a moot assumption, that each individual would contribute about the same number of acts to the population. Not knowing in advance how to design a sample that would tap behavioral events directly, I fitted the selection procedure to people. An aide reacts to every situation he confronts and can only confront situations that take place when he is on duty. The more aides on duty, the more likely a situation occurring at that time will take place in the presence of an aide. At both hospitals, more aides were on duty during the day shift (7 A.M. to 3 P.M.) than during the evening shift (3 P.M. to 11 P.M.). Hence what patients did in the daytime was more likely to confront aides. The daytime situations comprised a larger part of the population of acts than did situations which happened in the evenings when fewer aides were present.

The selection of observation times in the sample was random and not proportional to the number of aides present, while opportunities for aides to confront and react to situations were guided by the work schedules reported in the preceding paragraph. As a result, there was a relative oversampling of times containing fewer aides and undersampling of times containing more aides. This called for an adjustment in estimating the population values, a compensation that would restore the appropriate relative frequencies to events whose likelihoods of selection had been made unequal.

Using information about the numbers of aides present at the time, I gave each situational frequency *a weighting according to the relative number of aides present*. In this way an event recorded during an observation unit that undersampled the number of aides was multiplied by a factor that increased its frequency enough to offset the undersampling. Another event recorded during oversampling was multiplied by a factor that decreased its frequency proportionately. The resulting frequencies then reflected the number of aides on duty at the different sites and times.

After the field survey was completed, I secured information about the number of aides on duty by checking the supervisors' lists of aides scheduled for duty and the hospital attendance records. At the state hospital a consistent pattern of three aides present during the day shift (7 A.M. to 3 P.M.) for every two aides on duty during the evening shift (3 P.M. to 11 P.M.) was manifest for each day of the week during the entire field survey. Schedules at the private hospital were more uneven. Overlapping shifts were common there, and Saturdays and Sundays were given as days off somewhat more often than were other days of the week. I will describe the correction for the data of the state hospital. Because its aide schedules varied more, more arithmetic calculations and a greater variety of weightings were applied to the private hospital data, but the corrections were similar in principle to the adjustments made for the state hospital.

Let the number of events noted in the state hospital equal 100 percent. Our observations were scattered almost evenly throughout the day, so that day shift and evening shift observations each contributed about 50 percent of the recorded events. But at this hospital the staffing ratio was almost exactly three aides present on the day shift for every two aides present on the evening shift. On the assumption that the relative number of aides present is equivalent to the relative number of situations confronted, situations occurring during the day shift should reflect about 60 percent of the aides' population of acts whereas evening shift situations should represent about 40 percent.

To weight the number of events by the number of aides present, the frequencies for morning visits were multiplied by a factor of 1.2 (i.e., 60/50), and the frequencies for evening observations were multiplied by a factor of .8 (i.e., 40/50). Thus the events recorded for the day shift aides came to represent 60 percent of the entire population; the events contributed by the evening aides, 40 percent. For example, if one type of situation noted in the classified records was tallied ten times during the day shift and another type of situation was tallied ten times during the evening shift (a total of twenty situations), this corrective weighting alone would yield an estimate of twelve of the first type and eight of the second type (for a total of twenty situations). No harm is done by this correction if the *same* event was observed equally during each period, for multiplying each portion of a homogeneous aggregate to reach a certain figure is equivalent to multiplying the entire aggregate by a single factor that yields the same figure. The frequencies estimated for those situations evenly distributed over all times of the day and week will not be affected, since the increased frequencies for one time will be offset by the reduced frequencies for another time. This also reveals that the procedure does not change the overall number of acts. All frequencies are weighted relative to all others by adjusting each event in inverse proportion to the probability of its having been observed.

3. *From assumed equality between day and evening shifts in observation hours to actual sampling fractions*

In establishing the weightings described in step two, I assumed that hours of observation were equal at various times of the day. In fact, the actual distribution of recording observations was as follows: at the private hospital, twenty-five hours during the day shift and twenty-three hours during the evening shift; at the state hospital, twenty-eight hours during the day shift and twenty-seven hours during the evening shift. It is not tenable to assume that behavior observed at one time of day is representative of behavior at another time of day. Aides differ in their conduct toward patients at different times, synchronized with the daily cycle of living. For example, in the mornings aides waken patients and help them get dressed. If a large part of the observations of aides' behavior had been made between 7 A.M. and 9 A.M., one would portray aides as being disproportionately engaged in such activity. Therefore, it is appropriate to adjust for the times of observation during the day. Accordingly, I introduced a slight correction to compensate for the relative difference between hours of observation and shift hours. I will illustrate its computation with the case of the state hospital. (Again, although the principles and methods were the same, there were more computations for the private hospital data. Six correction factors were established, based on discrepancies between the proportions of time in the six periods during the week when different numbers of aides were on duty and the proportions of actual hours of recording in each of those six periods.)

At the state hospital two time periods were identified for different numbers of aides on duty during the week—the day shift and the evening shift. These are of equal length, fifty-six hours each. The hours of recording should have been equal too, but 51 percent of the observation hours occurred during the day shift period and 49 percent during the evening period. To correct for this, I multiplied day shift frequencies by .98 and evening shift frequencies by 1.02.

In the actual calculations the three adjustments were multiplied together to result in a composite weighting that was used to convert observed sample frequencies to estimates of population frequencies. For example, each event noted at the state hospital during the *daytime* was estimated by the three corrections .727 [40/55] × 1.20 [60/50] × .98 [49/50] to represent .86 of an act in that population. Because of the particular corrections made, several factors partly canceled each other out.

These corrections refer to aspects of sampling bias that are amenable to quantitative adjustment. The outcome of estimation was affected by procedures in earlier stages. The adequacy of observer records bore upon knowledge of events. The categories established in classification, and decisions about similarity or difference that resulted in some situations and reactions being grouped together and others being kept distinct, influenced frequencies of types of events. Other sampling designs could have introduced other distortions while perhaps avoiding some of those mentioned here.

In all, 678 events were classified from the field records at both hospitals. After the corrective weightings were applied, the total number of acts was estimated at 537 for the two populations.

Reliability and Validity

In this section I treat some standard concerns about measurement as they apply to interpersonal behavior. It is customary to ask to what extent the same findings would be gotten if the research were repeated (reliability) and to what extent those results reflect the subject matter as it is theoretically defined (validity). I will describe several checks on the possible extent to which errors and bias may have crept into this survey, point to assumptions whose effects on this measurement of social conduct were left uncontrolled, and suggest some classes of inquiries that can be carried out to assess such a research program.

1. *In the Field Survey*

A challenge is commonly raised about the pitfall of directly observing behavior. The observer will affect the conduct of others who are aware of his presence and interest in them. People who know they are being watched respond to such knowledge. As a result, an observer may see events that do not usually happen and may fail to see other acts because his presence has inhibited their occurrence. Another type of influence of researchers upon the subjects they study has been reported by Rosenthal. He demonstrated through several experiments that humans, and even rats and worms, behave selectively or are recorded as behaving selectively according to some expectancy or bias on the part of the observer. So participation of a human observer is said to have an impact on the information assembled.

The problem of observer-effect is cast into perspective by realizing that it intrudes in other disciplines too. In quantum mechanics, Heisenberg identified the effect of the measuring instrument upon the measurement of the velocity and position of subatomic particles and showed that every observation of position would alter the velocity by an unknown and unknowable amount. Heisenberg's arguments about the imperfectibility of measurement applied to very small particles and were pivotal in changing that discipline from a deterministic to a statistical mechanics. Some writers claim that Heisenberg's insight cannot be applied to macroscopic spheres of study. I think it can. It is a tenet of the theoretical limits to precision in any science. The reason is, as stated in Chapter 3, that along with any perception of objects in one's environment there is a portion of input that is perception of oneself as part of that environment. Through this perceptual blending, every researcher is intimately coupled with the events he is observing. Because of this blending the researcher must assume that his information does not necessarily represent events that occur when his measurement is not taking place. Therefore, all scientists interfere with what they study. The matter of observer-effect is two-staged. Even if the scientist does not directly affect the behavior of what he studies, he will affect his own perception of those events.

There is further resemblance between the methods of quantum mechanics and social science. In physical research, measurements of wee particles are achieved by bombarding them with electrons in a particle accelerator and by watching the results of the collisions. A measurement uncertainty emerges from an interference with the phenomenon by objects of the same order of magnitude and complexity as the phenomenon itself. In studies of interpersonal behavior, the researcher whose presence can directly affect the behavior of people he observes is also of the same order of magnitude and complexity as those whom he watches.

One can argue that the particle-missile used in an accelerator is merely an agent of the scientist and not the ultimate interpreter of findings. This is another issue, not one of observer-effect. Wiener wrote pessimistically of this problem for social science, insisting that the coupling between researcher and people studied was more problematic because "we are too much in tune with the subject matter of our investigation." He believed that we could only cope with this difficulty if we could accomplish large numbers of observations and thereafter treat our data statistically in terms of population averages. Massive statistical evidence may lend confidence to findings. One may also check for evidence of unwanted involvement, as I did.

a. During the field work we tried to record evidence which suggested that aides and patients were responding to our presence. We wondered whether we could do better than the report of Barker and Wright on the behavior of children in a midwestern town. According to their research team's records, out of 5,975 observed episodes, 1,887 of them (or 32 percent) involved an interaction between a child and an observer. The authors give a plausible reason for this large percentage. Many of the children were charming and irresistible. An observer found it hard to maintain his aloofness if approached by them.

In our work we strove to be unobtrusive and to minimize overt interactions. Yet some patients did try to interact with us, and some staff members were obviously sensitive to our presence. While our records may not reflect all the influence that was transmitted, out of the 678 events classified there were twenty instances, or 2.9 percent, in which the observer knew or suspected that he was involved.

b. There was no prior basis for assessing reliability of the observers' records because I established the categories of behavior in classification after the field survey. The observers also rotated in assignments to various sites in the two hospitals. Inasmuch as behavior of patients differed among the sites, some diversity among observer records is to be expected. Is there any evidence of bias in the observers' perceptions of conduct?

One type of information pertinent to the conduct of mental patients is the record of their upsets or disturbances (see Figure 7-2). These instances are usually dramatic. They are also relevant to mental illness itself. If observers were biased in their recording, this bias could well show itself in reports of these events. Investigating this possibility, I found that differences among observers' reports were strongly related both to their different amounts of observation and to the different sites of their observations. Where the frequencies in reporting such situations did not parallel the amount of observation time, the difference was clearly related to the places visited. Observers on the admissions ward and on the maximum security ward reported more instances of all these types of upset. The two observers who worked in both hospital settings showed this pattern. Relative to their hours of observation in the private hospital, observer number two contributed disproportionately fewer citations of disturbance, and observer number three contributed disproportionately more of such citations. Observer number three had visited the male maximum security ward both times. But in the state hospital, where observer number two visited the ward housing the acutely ill male patients, the disproportionate citations of tumult by observers numbers two and three were reversed.

c. I made a parallel investigation into how much each observer contributed to the report of each type of reaction of aides. Again, the findings suggested that differences among observers' records leading to differences in classification can be attributed mainly to differences in their field assignments. While observers numbers two and three worked in both hospitals, observer number one worked only in the private hospital and observer number four only in the state hospital. Observer number four's notes contained fewer instances of reaction a (FULFILLS REQUEST) and more of reaction b (CONVERSES) than did the records of the others. To anticipate a finding I will report in Chapter 11, I suggest here that these records reflect a difference between the two populations. Of course, observer number four's field records contributed to establishing that difference. But several kinds of evidence will confirm the institutional difference rather than reflect the recording unreliability of observer number four. Another disparity that seems to stem from a difference in field assignments is the disproportionate contribution to reaction h (SUPERVISES ACTIVITY) by the records of observer number two. He happened to be present at more parties and picnics than the others, and on these occasions aides commonly superintended the goings-on.

Reasons can be put forth for expecting the observers' records to be different. It is hard to know how much to attribute to observations made exclusively in one hospital that we know is unlike the other, to observations made at sites and times that we know are unlike other occasions, and to personal differences among observers in recording styles. Since observers numbers two and three visited both hospitals, similarities and differences between them should bear upon the matter of observer reliability more critically. It turns out that their field notes make disproportionate contributions in the classification of only two reactions. Significantly more instances of *e* (LEAVES THEM TO THEMSELVES) and somewhat fewer of *d* (SHOWS NO OVERT CHANGE IN BEHAVIOR) were classified in the records of observer number three than in any of the others. This pattern does seem to express a difference in reliability among the observers. In classification, if there is no noticeable difference in the aide's conduct the reaction should be categorized *d* (SHOWS NO OVERT CHANGE IN BEHAVIOR), whereas if the aide commits a new action or gesture while remaining apart from patients the event should be coded *e* (LEAVES THEM TO THEMSELVES). This distinction suggests that the amount of information in an observer's record could be critical. An observer who recorded more information might have included more evidence for changes in aides' gestures. This could account for the fact that observer number three's records yielded more instances of reaction *e* and fewer instances of reaction *d* than did those of the others. My research assistants were competent and committed, but apparently their competence and commitment did not fully match the zeal of the director of this study. I am observer number three.

d. Did the sample survey yield a representative picture of the population? The greater number of observation hours than the amount in the population time period may have helped here. Every social relationship has a repertoire that includes types of events which occur infrequently. In some relationships the rare events are crucial. The people of many cultures have maxims vouching for the decisive place of the rare situation in friendship. They take the form "You only know who your true friends are when you are in trouble or in need." But rare events are more likely to slip through an observational sampling net. Yet a category for an event can only be established through classification if the event is noted at least once. Had our observations been forty hours per hospital rather than forty-eight or fifty-five, fewer kinds of situations would probably have been noted. The larger time sample probably ensures a better representation of the various types of acts in a repertoire.

2. *In the Classification*

a. The behavior descriptions to be presented are from a single prolonged taxonomic effort, with much revision. I first classified the field records in 1962 to 1965. I did not know during the task which records referred to which hospital because I and a research assistant transcribed the identities to an anonymous code and worked from this reference file. If I found two events that seemed similar according to the classification procedure, I had no direct way of knowing whether I was establishing a category based on two events from two different hospitals or two from one of the institutions. After a lapse of three years I again classified the records with the help of another research assistant. This effort netted new understandings of the task, and I altered some earlier decisions accordingly. Because of this I was prevented from checking the reliability of the *classification* by a statistical comparison of the two tries.

b. A strain lurks between the ideal of objective measurement and the insight that people's perceptions of behavior differ according to differences in their backgrounds and makeup. The insight seems to challenge the adequacy of behavioral research, for objectivity is adherence to conventions that can be shared by all. It implies that the measurements should be free from the bias of a particular culture or of a particular individual. Yet the wedge between objectivity and subjectivity has never been the validity of one kind of data over another. It has been the methodological problem of dealing with subjective material. As I reported in Chapter 7, I tried to dissolve the wedge by using a more objective and a more subjective classification in tandem. I relied first on observer records and then on the actors' own descriptive vocabulary as two sources of the same information in order to identify the boundaries of acts and to consolidate the reaction categories.

In the interviews, when we presented little cards bearing descriptions of anonymous patients in situations that were based on the field records, there was no indication of how many times those situations occurred or of the reactions observed. We did not ask aides about the frequencies of events. Nor did I take into consideration, while establishing reaction categories, the number of times that aides mentioned various actions. The aides' descriptions were thus independent of quantitative conclusions and estimates made on the basis of the sample survey. (There is a lack of independence, however, that I cannot fully assess. In this study I am a ubiquitous agent— the phraser of situations, the editor of aides' testimony, the matcher of their comments to the categories, the classifier of field records into categories of acts.)

If the aides responded openly, their testimony should be based on experience. If the descriptive phrases they had ready for denoting acts were related to their experience, these should refer to the most frequently observed events. Claparède, studying the behavior of witnesses, concluded long ago that with lapse of time there was a tendency to testify in the direction of the probable. Infrequent reactions, not being seen as often, should be mentioned less often. Therefore, if the reaction categories described in aides' vernacular were equal to or subsumed a larger proportion of all the behavior in the population, it would signify that their testimony and the results of the sample survey were in accord about the relative frequencies of events.

I made an audit and found that the testimony was used to establish 81.6 percent of all categories describing aides in the private hospitals and 81.9 percent in the state hospital. These categories turned out to hold 84 percent of the acts in the private hospital population and 83.5 percent of the state hospital act-population as estimated from the field survey. If aides in recounting behavior tend to report the most familiar and probable acts, this match confers an aura of reliability upon the *estimate* of frequencies in the populations.

Maybe a double bias operated. Perhaps aides were on their good behavior in the presence of observers, and when interviewed the aides also reported good behavior. From events seen and described, it does not seem that aides tried to slant their reporting or conduct favorably. Aides often neglected to mention what might be considered approved conduct on their part. At the same time, several aides reported instances of forcing patients to do things (see *k,* COMPELS TO STOP OR TO DO IT, Figure 7-3) and of admonishing patients (see *g,* TELLS TO STOP, Figure 7-3) under circumstances that their supervisors would not approve. One aide reported that he overturned beds to get patients up in the morning. (We did not observe this in our field survey, so it was not included in the population of acts.)

c. Once acts were classified using aides' own testimony as boundary-givers, it was clear that some acts took longer to consummate than others. Although acts differed in the time taken for consummation, I counted each classified event as a unit act. With this in mind I can imagine what must have happened in the course of a field observation. The observer would begin with a randomly selected aide and stay with him as long as possible, recording his conduct within access of patients. The researcher would break off observing the aide if he needed extra time to complete his written record. Acts of longer duration, because they take more time to consummate and are thus under way more of the time, are more likely to be occurring either at the start of the observation unit or at the return to observation after completing a written record and are more likely to be sampled. It follows that events of short duration would be undersampled. They would also be undersampled if an observer stopped to complete a record before continuing his observation, for more short-duration events than long-duration events could occur in that interval. Then, if all were treated as units in the tallies of classified acts, the relative number of long-duration events would be overestimated.

I cannot resolve this problem here, but I will offer some considerations. Most of the time the observer could and did record everything an aide did in the presence of patients. There were not many breaks during which recording went on without observing. There were therefore few *onsets* of observation during each visit. Second, if an onset of observation began with a long-duration event, it often began in the midst of it rather than at its exact beginning. The first portion of that event may have taken place while the observer was recording another act. In such instances there may still have been enough information to discern the nature of the event. In these cases the observer took relatively less time to record long-duration events and proceeded to the next event sooner. Perhaps this compensated for oversampling prolonged actions.

Third, a certain act may be more available by being in existence longer, but if the observer begins noting it when too much of the act has been completed, the entire event may remain incognito because the record would be inadequate. Its mention in the record would be relegated to the category of NOT ASCERTAINED, acknowledging the margin of error without implying that the record was associated with a longer- or shorter-duration event. It is less likely that briefer events are noted in fragments. The briefer event is likely to be observed long enough for adequate identification if it is noted at all. The result of this difference may be that more portions of prolonged acts are cited as NOT ASCERTAINED. That is, shorter-duration acts would be undersampled, whereas longer-duration acts would contribute disproportionately to the residual category of NOT ASCERTAINED.

An alternate sampling method that avoids this particular distortion would be to select individuals and follow them continuously for long periods. Even if the observer were able to keep pace in his recording, this strategy is inferior to taking spaced samples unless the total amount of observation in the survey is enlarged considerably. Spaced observations favor the recognition of long-term patterns of conduct and are less subject to overrepresentation or underrepresentation of actions that occur in cycles, as might happen when the individual being observed is in an extreme temper. Also, there may be seasonal variations that would be missed if all observations were made, say, during the summer months alone. Thus the spaced sample may be more representative than continuous observations of a few persons, even if the continuous hours of observation total more than in the intermittent samples. Our survey, stretching as it did over two years, with ample intervals between visits, allowed time for the appearance and disappearance of temporary moods in the settings. Natural fluctuations in conduct had a chance to average out.

9

Behavior Tables

In the preceding chapters I described a method of collecting and organizing information about interpersonal behavior. The task is like making a census of animals on an island. To conduct the survey, one must define several boundaries that bear upon which animals will be found. Some of these are whether to set the island's limits at high tide or at low tide and whether nocturnal creatures will be included along with those abroad during the day. Procedures have to be devised for classifying the fauna and for deciding whether look-alikes are alike or not. Where systematization is the prime job, inferences about the importance of types should be minimized. Then, compensating the tallies according to the times of day and tide levels when observations were made, one will transform the count into a guess at the numerical size of the population.

Now that I am about to disclose the findings about aides' behavior, I must encourage you not to become dismayed when, in this chapter, you discover a lengthy table of data and an equally long text defining and discussing it. Like a horse-racing dope sheet or a tabular summary of stock market transactions on a major exchange, the format of information offered here will be strange only at first. When its code is learned, it is easy to read. It can be referred to rapidly, and information can be snatched from it at a glance. It contains far more information than is utilized in the analyses that follow. The table may serve beyond the pages of this volume should you wish to study it for questions I do not deal with here.

The ideas explored and tested and the discoveries reported in Part Three can best be understood if you are aware of the nature of the information I refer to again and again. Otherwise, Part Three will seem abstract. Its gaps will be the gaps of concrete examples. Those examples are included, but the examples are predominantly the systematic knowledge contained in the tables of this chapter rather than the anecdotes and impressions that served in Part One.

The behavior table, 9-1, is a summary whose format fits the definition of the whole act: a situation followed by a set of alternative reactions, each having its own probability. As I show with Matrices 9-3 and 9-4, Table 9-1 can be condensed further by a procedure that makes access to the information even quicker and easier. I will identify the main entries and briefly define their properties.

The Situation (S)

The upper left-hand corner of every numbered section in the behavior table describes the beginning of an act, the immediate observable circumstances to which an aide responds. Entry 1 in Table 9-1, for example, discloses a situation in which a patient requests an article or information or a service.

Twenty-six situations are identified in the two hospitals. Most of them are familiar and reflect routine aspects of daily life as well as the particulars of hospitalization. In Chapter 7 I remarked on parallels between these situations and those in other locales. Perhaps no relationship in society is exempt from some of the situations.

Descriptions of behavior are phrased in the singular but also refer to patients and aides acting in concert. Masculine gender is used throughout, but the events were observed for female patients and female aides as well.

The Reaction (R)

The table first cites a situation and then lists the set of reactions that were observed to follow it. Each reaction is the core and completion of an act. For example, as shown in situation 1, one reaction of the aide is to fulfill the patient's request (*a*). Another is to refuse it (*t*).

The reaction category is set in small capitals. Then examples of specific conduct covered by it in that situation are given in parentheses. If the phrase is a quotation, that phrase was heard in the interviews that followed the field observations.

The aide's behavior can be simple (a single category) or compound (a combination of categories). For example, in situation 1 some aides tried to

Table 9–1. Aides' probable reactions to situations with patients in two mental hospitals (based on a forty-hour week).

Situations and Reactions	Private Hosp: 200 beds			State Hosp: 3000 beds		
	Frequencies	p(R)	p(S)/p(S)p(R)	Frequencies	p(R)	p(S)/p(S)p(R)
1. A patient requests an item (e.g., socks, cigarette) or service (open the window) or information (what's for dinner). The aide	30.15	1.000	.118	28.00	1.000	.100
a) FULFILLS REQUEST (E.g., "Goes and gets it for him." "Does it for him." "Answers him.")	24.42	.810	.096	20.70	.739	.074
t) REFUSES (E.g., "Tells the patient he is able to get it himself or do it himself." "Says he doesn't know.")	4.12	.136	.016	3.52	.126	.013
p-a) TEACHES OR CORRECTS (E.g., "Sits there and makes him ask nicely before he does it.") and FULFILLS REQUEST	.50	.017	.002	2.92	.104	.010
t-p) REFUSES and TEACHES OR CORRECTS	.61	.020	.002	.86	.031	.003
u) BANTERS (E.g., When asked for more bacon, brings a piece two inches long.)	.50	.017	.002	—	—	—
2. An aide and a patient pass each other or meet. The aide	16.04	1.000	.063	38.58	1.000	.138
f) GREETS (E.g., "Says 'Good morning' and continues on." Hands him a partly-smoked cigarette without speaking.)	7.49	.467	.030	11.94	.310	.043
b) CONVERSES (E.g., "Stops to talk and asks how he's getting along.")	1.86	.116	.007	12.46	.323	.045
d) SHOWS NO OVERT CHANGE IN BEHAVIOR (E.g., "Keeps right on walking.")	3.07	.191	.012	4.12	.107	.015

c) TELLS OR REMINDS TO DO SOMETHING (E.g., Tells him to make his bed, keep a doctor's appointment, get haircut, etc.)	1.54	.096	.006	5.76	.149	.020
o) ASKS ASSISTANCE (E.g., Inquires where another patient is.)	—	—	—	2.58	.067	.009
c-b) TELLS OR REMINDS TO DO SOMETHING AND CONVERSES	—	—	—	.86	.022	.003
NA) REACTION NOT ASCERTAINED.	2.08	.130	.008	.86	.022	.003
3. It is time for a scheduled activity (e.g., to wake up, eat, sleep, dress, or receive medicine) for patients. The aide	**12.42**	**1.000**	**.048**	**30.40**	**1.000**	**.109**
c) TELLS OR REMINDS TO DO SOMETHING (E.g., "Goes through the ward saying that it's time." Calls patients and hands out medicines.)	7.56	.609	.029	22.24	.732	.080
n) CARES FOR OR SERVES (E.g., "Goes ahead and washes, dresses . . . them." Helps them to bed.)	4.04	.325	.016	5.24	.172	.019
o) ASKS ASSISTANCE (I.e., Asks patients to tell the others.)	—	—	—	1.20	.040	.004
c-n) TELLS OR REMINDS TO DO SOMETHING AND CARES FOR OR SERVES	—	—	—	.86	.028	.003
n-b) CARES FOR OR SERVES AND CONVERSES (E.g., "Sits down and talks with them.")	—	—	—	.86	.028	.003
d) SHOWS NO OVERT CHANGE IN BEHAVIOR (E.g., "Gives no recognition and doesn't say anything to them.")	.82	.066	.003	—	—	—

Table 9-1. (continued)

Situations and Reactions	Private Hosp: 200 beds			State Hosp: 3000 beds		
	Frequencies	p(R)	p(S)p(R)	Frequencies	p(R)	p(S)p(R)
4. A patient makes a remark or is having a conversation with an aide (about his own interests, family, illness). The aide	28.08	1.000	.109	11.94	1.000	.043
b) CONVERSES (E.g., "Talks with him." Asks questions, tells jokes, gives advice and opinions. "Comments on the situation.")	13.92	.496	.054	6.96	.583	.025
r) WITHDRAWS (E.g., Becomes quiet and leaves.)	4.82	.172	.019	2.06	.173	.008
m) BRIEFLY AGREES OR DISAGREES (E.g., Says uh-hmm and nods his head; shakes his head.)	4.30	.153	.017	2.32	.194	.008
d) SHOWS NO OVERT CHANGE IN BEHAVIOR (E.g., "Doesn't stop to make conversation and keeps on with his picking up.")	2.14	.076	.008	–	–	–
v) PARTICIPATES PARTLY (E.g., "Lets the patient do the talking." "Listens to him.")	1.04	.037	.004	.60	.050	.002
b-o) CONVERSES and ASKS ASSISTANCE (I.e., Tells of own troubles.)	1.04	.037	.004	–	–	–
b-r) CONVERSES then WITHDRAWS	.82	.029	.003	–	–	–

5. A patient performs an unusual verbal act (rants, mumbles, or yells incoherently). The aide

	16.60	1.000	.065	16.66	1.000	.059
d) SHOWS NO OVERT CHANGE IN BEHAVIOR (E.g., "Gives no recognition and doesn't say anything to him.")	7.28	.438	.029	5.84	.350	.021
g) TELLS TO STOP (E.g., "Tells him this is not the time or the place to act this way.")	6.24	.376	.024	.60	.036	.002
m) BRIEFLY AGREES OR DISAGREES (E.g., Acts as if he understands; agrees or shakes his head.)	2.04	.123	.008	3.18	.191	.012
b) CONVERSES (E.g., "Comments on the situation." Asks questions, gives advice and opinions,)	—	—	—	2.92	.175	.010
p) TEACHES OR CORRECTS (E.g., "Asks him what he is talking about and to speak clearly.")	—	—	—	.86	.052	.003
b-q) CONVERSES and REASSURES AND TRIES TO REMEDY (E.g., "Asks the patient what was bothering him and reports it to the nurse.")	—	—	—	.86	.052	.003
p-d) TEACHES OR CORRECTS then SHOWS NO OVERT CHANGE IN BEHAVIOR	—	—	—	.60	.036	.002
d-g) SHOWS NO OVERT CHANGE IN BEHAVIOR then TELLS TO STOP	—	—	—	.60	.036	.002
d-m) SHOWS NO OVERT CHANGE IN BEHAVIOR then BRIEFLY AGREES OR DISAGREES	—	—	—	.60	.036	.002
m-g) BRIEFLY AGREES OR DISAGREES then TELLS TO STOP	—	—	—	.60	.036	.002
NA) REACTION NOT ASCERTAINED.	1.04	.063	.004	—	—	—

Table 9-1. (continued)

Situations and Reactions	Private Hosp: 200 beds			State Hosp: 3000 beds		
	Frequencies	p(R)	p(S) p(S)p(R)	Frequencies	p(R)	p(S) p(S)p(R)
6. Patients and aides are at recreation together (playing a game, exercising). The aide	17.71	1.000	.069	14.00	1.000	.050
i) PARTICIPATES FULLY (E.g., "Stays right in with the group, walks around, talks, sings, and dances with the patients.")	8.25	.466	.032	5.24	.374	.019
p) TEACHES OR CORRECTS (E.g., "Instructs them as to how to play and tells them when they make mistakes or good moves.")	1.43	.081	.006	3.78	.270	.013
v) PARTICIPATES PARTLY (E.g., Plays the game and does not make extra comments.)	1.86	.105	.007	1.46	.104	.005
j) SUGGESTS ENTERING ACTIVITY (E.g., "Asks a patient who is standing nearby to sit in at the game.")	1.04	.059	.004	2.06	.147	.008
i-r) PARTICIPATES FULLY then WITHDRAWS (I.e., Leaves game after a while.)	2.06	.116	.008	.60	.043	.002
e) LEAVES THEM TO THEMSELVES (E.g., Plays a separate game with an aide. "Talks with other aides.")	2.46	.139	.010	–	–	–
v-p) PARTICIPATES PARTLY then TEACHES OR CORRECTS	–	–	–	.86	.062	.003
NA) REACTION NOT ASCERTAINED.	.61	.034	.002	–	–	–
7. Patients and staff members are at a party (or picnic or carnival). The aide	10.06	1.000	.039	21.62	1.000	.077
e) LEAVES THEM TO THEMSELVES (E.g., "Looks on and lets the party run its course.")	3.28	.326	.012	5.66	.262	.020

f) GREETS (E.g., Stays in one place and jokes with patients who pass by.)	2.46	.245	.010	4.46	.206	.016
h) SUPERVISES ACTIVITY (E.g., Clears the doorway and directs traffic.)	2.46	.245	.010	4.46	.206	.016
i) PARTICIPATES FULLY (E.g., "Stays right in with the group, walks around, talks, sings, and dances with the patients.")	.82	.081	.003	4.12	.191	.015
j) SUGGESTS ENTERING ACTIVITY (E.g., "Encourages the patients to mingle and to be out there dancing.")	1.04	.103	.004	2.92	.135	.010
8. An aide is working on the ward and some patients are nearby. The aide	**6.16**	**1.000**	**.024**	**21.06**	**1.000**	**.075**
o) ASKS ASSISTANCE (E.g., "Asks them to get up and help him clean up.")	1.74	.283	.007	8.42	.400	.030
h) SUPERVISES ACTIVITY (E.g., "Asks the patients if they mind moving while he is cleaning out there.")	.50	.081	.002	6.02	.286	.022
i) PARTICIPATES FULLY (E.g., Works with them and follows their suggestions on what to do.)	1.04	.169	.004	2.58	.122	.009
j) SUGGESTS ENTERING ACTIVITY (E.g., "Tries to get something for them to do [like play baseball].")	1.24	.201	.005	1.46	.069	.005
d) SHOWS NO OVERT CHANGE IN BEHAVIOR (E.g., "Doesn't stop to make conversation and keeps on with his picking up.")	1.64	.266	.006	.86	.041	.003
p) TEACHES OR CORRECTS (E.g., Says loudly that he wishes people would stop putting their cigarette butts in the flower pots.)	—	—	—	.86	.041	.003
o-h) ASKS ASSISTANCE and SUPERVISES ACTIVITY	—	—	—	.86	.041	.003

Table 9-1. (continued)

Situations and Reactions	Private Hosp: 200 beds			State Hosp: 3000 beds		
	Frequencies	p(R)	p(S)/p(R)	Frequencies	p(R)	p(S)/p(R)
9. Patients are in the day room and the aide is not engaged in ward work. The aide	**8.62**	**1.000**	**.034**	**16.40**	**1.000**	**.059**
e) LEAVES THEM TO THEMSELVES (E.g., Sits and reads. "Talks with other aides.")	7.51	.871	.030	7.98	.487	.029
j) SUGGESTS ENTERING ACTIVITY (E.g., "Tries to get something for them to do [like watch television, play a game, knitting].")	—	—	—	4.90	.299	.018
b) CONVERSES (E.g., "Sits down and talks with them.")	1.11	.129	.004	2.06	.126	.007
e-j) LEAVES THEM TO THEMSELVES then SUGGESTS ENTERING ACTIVITY	—	—	—	.86	.052	.003
h-e) SUPERVISES ACTIVITY (I.e., Changes the TV program from news to fictional drama) then LEAVES THEM TO THEMSELVES	—	—	—	.60	.036	.002
10. A patient asks to be let off (or onto) the ward (or to make a phone call). The aide	**17.62**	**1.000**	**.069**	**4.38**	**1.000**	**.016**
a) FULFILLS REQUEST (E.g., "Gets up and lets him out.")	9.98	.566	.039	2.06	.470	.008
s) STIPULATES A CONDITION (E.g., "Tells him to wait a minute till he finishes what he is doing." "Checks in the nurses' station to see whether or not he is allowed.")	5.58	.317	.022	1.46	.334	.005

d) SHOWS NO OVERT CHANGE IN BEHAVIOR (E.g., "Gives no recognition and doesn't say anything to him.")	1.24	.070	.005	—	—	—
e) TELLS OR REMINDS TO DO SOMETHING (E.g., "Reminds him to be sure to sign out [or to put on socks] before he leaves.")	—	—	—	.86	.196	.003
c-a) TELLS OR REMINDS TO DO SOMETHING and FULFILLS REQUEST.	.82	.047	.003	—	—	—
11. A patient is in distress (crying, afraid, or berating himself). The aide	7.60	1.000	.030	9.62	1.000	.034
q) REASSURES AND TRIES TO REMEDY (E.g., Says "Get hold of yourself" and massages his back. Suggests what might be done.)	4.92	.647	.020	5.32	.553	.019
k) COMPELS [TO DO IT] (E.g., "Insists that he do it [that agitated patient sit down] and guides him . . . with his arm around him.")	—	—	—	2.58	.269	.009
b) CONVERSES (E.g., "Keeps up a conversation.")	1.04	.137	.004	—	—	—
u) BANTERS (E.g., Says "Boo!" as he passes.)	—	—	—	.86	.089	.003
q-g) REASSURES AND TRIES TO REMEDY and TELLS TO STOP (E.g., "Tells him this is not the time or the place to act this way.")	—	—	—	.86	.089	.003
b-q) CONVERSES and REASSURES AND TRIES TO REMEDY.	.82	.108	.003	—	—	—
q-k-b) REASSURES AND TRIES TO REMEDY and COMPELS [TO DO IT] (E.g., "Insists that he do it [that drunk patient stay awake to avoid risk of coma] . . . with his arm around him.") and CONVERSES	.82	.108	.003	—	—	—

Table 9–1. (continued)

Situations and Reactions	Private Hosp: 200 beds			State Hosp: 3000 beds		
	Frequencies	p(R)	p(S)/p(R)	Frequencies	p(R)	p(S)/p(R)
12. A patient complains or denounces the hospital (or insults an aide). The aide	12.82	1.000	.050	4.04	1.000	.014
d) SHOWS NO OVERT CHANGE IN BEHAVIOR (E.g., "Walks by without any sign of attention.")	3.90	.304	.015	2.32	.574	.008
m) BRIEFLY AGREES OR DISAGREES (E.g., Says uh-hmm and nods his head; shakes his head.)	4.35	.339	.017	.86	.213	.003
q) REASSURES AND TRIES TO REMEDY (E.g., "Asks the patient what was bothering him and reports it to the nurse." Suggests what might be done.)	–	–	–	.86	.213	.003
NA) REACTION NOT ASCERTAINED.	4.57	.357	.018	–	–	–
13. A patient is making mischief for someone (teasing, tickling, hiding shoes). The aide	3.94	1.000	.015	12.80	1.000	.046
l) PERMITS (E.g., "Smiles at it and permits him to do this.")	3.94	1.000	.015	3.78	.295	.014
g) TELLS TO STOP (E.g., "Tells him this is not the time or the place to act this way.")	–	–	–	2.92	.229	.010
u) BANTERS (E.g., Tries to pinch and wrestle with him.)	–	–	–	3.78	.295	.014
d) SHOWS NO OVERT CHANGE IN BEHAVIOR (E.g., "Walks by without any sign of attention.")	–	–	–	.86	.067	.003
d-g) SHOWS NO OVERT CHANGE IN BEHAVIOR then TELLS TO STOP	–	–	–	.86	.067	.003
k) COMPELS [TO STOP] (E.g., "Stops him from going further.")	–	–	–	.60	.047	.002

	5.51	1.000	.021	9.20	1.000	.033
14. Patients are eating in the dining room. The aide						
n) CARES FOR OR SERVES (E.g., "Fixes up a tray and brings it to the table." "Goes ahead and . . . feeds them.")	3.69	.669	.014	1.72	.187	.006
h) SUPERVISES ACTIVITY (E.g., Directs traffic, keeps them in line.)	—	—	—	2.58	.280	.010
e) LEAVES THEM TO THEMSELVES (E.g., "Stands in back of the room and watches them." "Talks with other aides.")	.82	.149	.003	1.72	.187	.006
f) GREETS (E.g., "Moves among the tables making small talk like 'How are you today?'")	.50	.091	.002	1.72	.187	.006
f-e) GREETS then LEAVES THEM TO THEMSELVES	—	—	—	1.46	.159	.005
n-f) CARES FOR OR SERVES and GREETS	.50	.091	.002	—	—	—
15. A patient is not where he is supposed to be (or wanders away from his group). The aide	6.08	1.000	.024	6.70	1.000	.024
k) COMPELS [TO STOP] (E.g., "Catches him and brings him back.")	1.86	.306	.007	3.18	.475	.012
g) TELLS TO STOP (E.g., "Tells him he is supposed to stay with his group.")	2.14	.352	.009	2.06	.307	.007
l) PERMITS (E.g., "Lets him act on his own.")	—	—	—	1.46	.218	.005
x) PERMITS UNDER A CONDITION (E.g., "Lets him go but does not let him get out of sight.")	1.04	.171	.004	—	—	—
g-x) TELLS TO STOP then PERMITS UNDER A CONDITION	1.04	.171	.004	—	—	—

Table 9-1. (continued)

Situations and Reactions	Private Hosp: 200 beds			State Hosp: 3000 beds		
	Frequencies	p(R)	p(S)/p(S)p(R)	Frequencies	p(R)	p(S)/p(S)p(R)
16. Some patients are on their way from one place to another. The aide	6.82	1.000	.028	5.24	1.000	.019
h) SUPERVISES ACTIVITY (E.g., Escorts them. "Goes off together with them.")	6.82	1.000	.028	5.24	1.000	.019
17. A patient delays or resists doing a required activity. The aide	4.73	1.000	.018	7.30	1.000	.026
κ) COMPELS [TO DO IT] (E.g., "Insists that he do it, and guides him out of bed with his arm around him.")	2.08	.440	.008	3.52	.482	.013
i) SUGGESTS ENTERING ACTIVITY (E.g., "Invites him again and tries to convince him that this is part of the treatment program.")	2.04	.431	.008	.86	.118	.003
l) PERMITS (E.g., "Doesn't try to force him.")	—	—	—	2.06	.282	.007
k-l) COMPELS [TO DO IT] (E.g., Tries to force-feed him.) then PERMITS	—	—	—	.86	.118	.003
j-l) SUGGESTS ENTERING ACTIVITY then PERMITS	.61	.129	.002	—	—	—
18. A patient performs an unusual physical act (gyrates, lies stiffly on the floor, or eats food spilled on the floor). The aide	8.47	1.000	.033	3.44	1.000	.012
u) BANTERS (E.g., "Laughs and imitates him.")	3.52	.415	.014	—	—	—
g) TELLS TO STOP (E.g., "Calls to him that he shouldn't do this and to sit down.")	2.48	.293	.010	.86	.250	.003

i) SUGGESTS ENTERING ACTIVITY (E.g., "Tries to get something for him to do [play game].")	.61	.072	.002	.86	.250	.003
f) GREETS (E.g., "Says 'Good morning' and continues on.")	1.04	.123	.004	—	.250	.003
k) COMPELS [TO STOP] (E.g., "Walks him over to a chair and gets him to sit there.")	—	—	—	.86	.250	.003
g-l) TELLS TO STOP then PERMITS	—	—	—	—	—	—
l) PERMITS (E.g., "Permits him to do this.")	.82	.097	.003	—	.250	.003
19. A patient refuses an invitation to join in an optional activity (go for a walk, play a game). The aide	**7.05**	**1.000**	**.027**	**4.30**	**1.000**	**.015**
j) SUGGESTS ENTERING ACTIVITY (E.g., "Invites him again and tries to convince him that this is part of the treatment program.")	3.73	.529	.014	1.72	.400	.006
l) PERMITS (E.g., "Lets it go at that.")	1.04	.148	.004	2.58	.600	.009
w) ASKS WHAT IS THE MATTER (E.g., "Asks him what was the matter and why he did not join in.")	1.24	.175	.005	—	—	—
NA) REACTION NOT ASCERTAINED.	1.04	.148	.004	—	—	—
20. A patient is negligent or destructive toward objects. The aide	**7.37**	**1.000**	**.029**	**.86**	**1.000**	**.003**
k) COMPELS [TO STOP] (E.g., "Walks him out of the office and back to the day room." Pulls him off the Ping-Pong table.)	2.06	.280	.008	.86	1.000	.003
p) TEACHES OR CORRECTS (E.g., Tells him to sit straight on the chair.)	2.85	.387	.012	—	—	—
b) CONVERSES (E.g., "Comments on the situation.")	.82	.111	.003	—	—	—
l) PERMITS (E.g., "Lets it go at that.")	.82	.111	.003	—	—	—
w) ASKS WHAT IS THE MATTER (E.g., "Asks him what was wrong, and did he want to talk about anything.")	.82	.111	.003	—	—	—

Table 9-1. (continued)

Situations and Reactions	Private Hosp: 200 beds			State Hosp: 3000 beds		
	Frequencies	p(R)	p(S)/p(S|p(R)	Frequencies	p(R)	p(S)/p(S|p(R)
21. A patient performs a usually private gesture in public (walks about undressed, masturbates, or makes a sexual advance). The aide	5.29	1.000	.021	2.92	1.000	.010
g) TELLS TO STOP (E.g., "Calls to him that he shouldn't do this..." "Tells him to put some clothes on.")	3.68	.696	.015	2.06	.705	.007
k) COMPELS [TO STOP] (E.g., "Eases him out of the day room and brings him back to his bedroom.")	1.00	.189	.004	—	—	—
n-k) CARES FOR OR SERVES (E.g., "Goes ahead and ... dresses him.") and COMPELS [TO STOP]	—	—	—	.86	.295	.003
u) BANTERS (E.g., Asks patient who is in pajamas at midday why he can't sleep.)	.61	.115	.002	—	—	—
22. A patient attacks someone (by hitting or throwing something or by threatening). The aide	1.22	1.000	.004	6.70	1.000	.024
g) TELLS TO STOP (E.g., "Tells him to stop.")	—	—	—	2.32	.346	.009
k) COMPELS [TO STOP] (E.g., "Gets the patients separated." Holds the attacker.)	.61	.500	.002	1.46	.218	.005
q-w) REASSURES AND TRIES TO REMEDY (E.g., "Explains to the other patient that the one who hit him is sick and did not know what was going off at the time.") and ASKS WHAT IS THE MATTER (E.g., "Asks him why he is acting that way and what the trouble was.")	—	—	—	.86	.128	.003
x) PERMITS UNDER A CONDITION (E.g., "Looks out of the						

nurses' station to see if it will go on, and when it doesn't he lets it go at that.")	—	—	—	.86	.128	.003
g-k) TELLS TO STOP then COMPELS [TO STOP]	.61	.500	.002	—	—	—
q) REASSURES AND TRIES TO REMEDY	—	—	—	.60	.090	.002
w) ASKS WHAT IS THE MATTER	—	—	—	.60	.090	.002
23. Patients invite an aide who is not busy to join them in recreation (or for coffee). The aide	4.75	1.000	.018	1.20	1.000	.004
i) PARTICIPATES FULLY (E.g., "Goes along with them.")	2.28	.480	.009	1.20	1.000	.004
s) STIPULATES A CONDITION (E.g., Agrees for short, rather than long, walk.)	1.65	.347	.006	—	—	—
r) WITHDRAWS (E.g., "Informs them that some other time he would go but at present he was busy.")	.82	.173	.003	—	—	—
24. Someone (a visitor, taxi driver) comes to the ward (or there is a phone call) for a patient. The aide	2.75	1.000	.011	.86	1.000	.003
c) TELLS OR REMINDS TO DO SOMETHING (E.g., "Goes and tells the patient.")	2.75	1.000	.011	.86	1.000	.003
25. A new patient is on the ward. The aide	.61	1.000	.002	.60	1.000	.002
b) CONVERSES (E.g., "Welcomes him to the ward and takes a little while to get acquainted.")	.61	1.000	.002	.60	1.000	.002
26. A patient smiles and his false tooth drops out. The aide	1.04	1.000	.004	—	—	—
q) REASSURES AND TRIES TO REMEDY (E.g., says "That must be an uncomfortable feeling.")	1.04	1.000	.004	—	—	—
NA Situation not ascertained: records incomplete, ambiguous, or lost.	7.06		.028	1.46		.005
TOTALS	256.57		1.000	280.28		1.000

instruct patients to ask nicely in addition to either fulfilling or refusing their requests (acts 1-*p-a* and 1-*t-p*). In situation 15 (a patient wanders away from his group) the aide first asked the patient where he was going and told him to remain with the group; when the patient did not do so, the aide allowed him to go but kept him in sight (act 15-*g-x*). Different aides may utilize different sequences in performing compound reactions. The table cites the most common sequence.

If the reaction could not be clearly identified from the field records, it is entered in a residual category, REACTION NOT ASCERTAINED. It appears as the final entry for an act-whole (see situation 2).

It happens that 128 different simple and compound acts are listed in the table. That many situation-reaction combinations subsume the 678 events recorded in the field (see page 145). So the classification introduced a 5.3:1 summarizing ratio (of events to categories) while preserving much of the diversity in the relationship.

Table 9-1 is only an inventory of contacts between aides and patients and only portrays aides' behavior in the presence of patients. It is therefore an incomplete picture of the conduct of aides and of patients. It does not tell how they act when they are not in each other's presence. As for other staff members, although they were sometimes present in the scenes outlined here, the behavior table does not describe the reactions of nurses, doctors, other patients, other staff members, or visitors to situations with patients.

Frequencies of Situations and of Reactions

For each hospital, the numerical entries in the left-hand column for situations give the estimated number of times the situations occur in a forty-hour period. These are often fractions because the tallies were adjusted in the estimate. But acts only occur as entireties and should be interpreted as such.

This information is given separately for each hospital, and the two can be compared. For example, an aide in the private hospital receives about thirty small requests from patients (situation 1) every forty hours, whereas in the state hospital these are somewhat less frequent (twenty-eight times every forty hours). The situation of an aide's working on the ward in the presence of patients (situation 8) will happen more than three times as often in the state hospital as in the private hospital (twenty-one times vs. six times).

Situations are numbered in the order of their overall frequency in the two act-populations. In a given population, the sum of situational frequencies equals its number of acts. This figure appears at the end of the table. There are about 257 acts in the private hospital and 280 in the state hospital population.

The frequency of a situation is broken down into frequencies for the different reactions that follow it. For example, in the private hospital the aide fulfills the patients' requests (act 1-*a*) more than twenty-four times in a forty-hour period. He refuses those requests (1-*t*) about four times in the same period. The sum of all instances of reactions to a situation equals the situation's frequency.

If the row for a reaction is blank (indicated by a dash), that reaction was not observed in that hospital. See, for example, the empty rows for act 1-*u* in the state hospital and act 2-*o* in the private hospital.

The reactions are lettered in order of their overall frequency in the two populations and are listed in order of frequency within each situation across both settings.

I do not report behavior by sites within the hospitals for a number of reasons. Several milieux are not well matched across the institutions because of differences in housing arrangements for patients (Table 6-1). Therefore, such refined comparisons are not feasible. Also, if the estimates were to be sorted into ten types of sites, there would be too few instances of each act at each site and consequently a large number of blank rows. Site often seemed irrelevant in the classification. I found that I consolidated events from several sites into a category without discerning anything in the record other than the initial site listing to convey a difference in the nature of the event.

The behavior table contains information about patients as part of the situational descriptions. But the table tells how often the situations take place for aides, not the rates at which patients perform those events. For example, patients may also request information or cigarettes (situation 1) from other staff members in the same forty-hour period. Moreover, the table does not fully describe what patients do. The acts of the most normal patients in the state hospital are underrepresented because fewer aides are assigned to wards where patients are calm and composed (see pages 101–102). Sometimes there were no aides present on those wards during our visits, so no records were made of patients' behavior. Still, aides have the most pervasive contacts with patients in mental hospitals, more than any other staff group. What patients do in their presence is roughly indicative of patients' conduct in general.

p(S): Probability of the Situation

The likelihood of any situation relative to all situations in a hospital is calculated by dividing its frequency by the total number of acts. This fraction appears for each situation at the top of the right-hand column of numbers for each hospital. For situation 1 in the private hospital, $30.15 \div 256.57 = .118$, which figure indicates that nearly 12 percent of all contact opportunities are likely to begin with the patient making a request of an aide. The sum of all situational probabilities in a population equals 1.000, as shown by the bottom line of the behavior table.

The situations range widely in likelihood. Most acts in a population are repetitions of common situations. In the private hospital more than half (51.1 percent) of all interaction between aides and patients involves the first seven of the twenty-six situations. In the state hospital the first seven situations provide 57.6 percent of the contact opportunities. The behavior table tells us that aides in the state institution deal with patients on matters of scheduled activities (situation 3) more than twice as often as in the private hospital. Mealtime contacts (14) are also more likely at the state hospital. A plausible reason for this is that patients at the state hospital are served at scheduled sittings in large dining halls, so a multitude of contact opportunities are available to an aide in attendance. In the private hospital, patients are fed in small dining rooms on their own wards. They may enter and seat themselves individually during the serving hours. There an aide may be on the ward yet not in the dining room. Or he may be in the dining room with but a few patients present at the time. A related reason helps explain why situations 2 (An aide and patient pass each other or meet) and 9 (Patients are in the day room and the aide is not engaged in ward work) occur much more often in the state hospital. It is partly due to the sheer number of patients—who are available to be passed or met—on the wards or on the grounds of the state institution. About 3,000 patients live in eighteen buildings there. Contrast that density with the sparse distribution of 200 patients among twelve buildings on equal-size grounds at the private hospital.

How alike are the situations confronting aides in the two hospitals? Since one of the hospitals is a private institution and the other state-supported, and since they house patients from different socioeconomic backgrounds, we would expect some differences. The correlation coefficient for the paired situational probabilities is .66, which is statistically significant but not strong. Some notable disparities in situational probabilities in the two act populations have been mentioned in the paragraphs above (situations 2, 3, 9, and 14), and in the preceding section (situation 8). Situations 4 (A patient makes a remark or is having a conversation with an aide) and 10 (A patient asks to be let off or onto the ward, or to make a phone call) also show sharply different likelihoods in the two populations. In Chapter 13 I will offer an explanation for these differences.

p(R): Probability of the Reaction

The center column of numbers for each population gives the relative likelihood of each reaction in each situation. It is computed by dividing the reaction's frequency in the situation by the situation's frequency in the hospital. For example, in the private hospital if a patient makes a request of an aide (situation 1), there is an 81 percent chance that the aide will simply fulfill the request (a). This statement about reaction a is a conditional probability. It depends upon the occurrence of that situation. In another situation (e.g., situation 10, A patient asks to be let off the ward), reaction a has a different likelihood relative to its alternatives. Compare also the p(R)s for acts 2-d and 4-d in both hospitals.

When summed, the probabilities for reactions in a situation equal 1.000.

p(S)p(R): Probability of the Act Occurring in the Population

For each hospital the number in the right-hand column for each reaction to each situation gives the likelihood of that act relative to the probabilities of all acts. It is computed by multiplying the probability of the reaction to the situation by the situation's probability. For example, it is likely that in the private hospital greeting patients upon passing or meeting (see 2-f) comprises three out of every hundred acts performed by an aide. In the state hospital this same act is likely to occur more than four times in a hundred acts.

The sum of all these fractions is 1.000, the aggregate probability of the entire population in a setting. Since the sum of the probabilities of acts associated with a situation must equal the probability of the situation, that is, $\Sigma\, p(S)p(R) = p(S)$, it is difficult to cite exact relative probabilities across all situations within three decimal places. Small variations may appear for acts of equal frequency (compare 14-*h* and 19-*l* in the state hospital). Except for such rare instances, small numerical differences do reflect differences in likelihood. I calculated the fractions to four decimal places and then rounded them. Usually one does not report data to the second or third decimal place without determining in advance whether the sampling error is small enough to sustain that degree of precision. If the error is, say, 5 percent, then reports of findings that pretend accuracy to one-tenth of a percent are presumptuous. However, though the precision implied by the numerical entries in Table 9-1 may be unwarranted, I will use those values in subsequent analyses for two reasons. Using three decimal places permits me to assign probabilities other than zero to rare acts without inflating their likelihoods so that they become indistinguishable from more common acts. For example, in the state hospital, acts 1-*p-a* and 1-*t-p* would be indistinguishable at two decimal places unless 1-*t-p* were assigned zero likelihood. Also, the calculations to three decimal places will make it easier to demonstrate the potential of this approach to the study of behavior—a prospect that offsets the somewhat overstated precision.

The table is a composite, portraying behavior associated with scores of individuals as they relate to one another through the positions of patient and aide. It tells of particular individuals who happened to occupy the positions at the times and places we conducted our field survey. Their observed conduct was pooled. No individual patient or aide committing a specific act can be predicted. Still the table is a predictor. While it may be hard to forecast what an individual will do, the behavior of an aggregate of unpredictable individuals may be anticipated. The act is given a separate existence from the specific persons who perform it. Incumbents of the social position will change, but this does not mean the population of acts will change. The population dwells in a niche of a social organization. Its biography is longer and larger than sojourns of particular people in the position. Its pattern is not likely to be mirrored in a single individual, nor is it an idealized abstraction. It is a probability distribution of the various acts.

Why, then, did I estimate the population of acts according to a forty-hour period so that it appears to be the repertoire of a single aide? I did so to arrange the opportunity for comparisons between the individual and the group. Although the probability of a reaction refers to a share in a stock of acts contributed by many persons, sometimes it is convenient to talk of an individual when speaking of a single act. However, if I use the phrase "the aide is disposed to . . ." or "the aide prefers . . ." I speak of the probability of a reaction following a situation and not of inner forces influencing an individual to make a choice.

Compound Acts and Their Decomposition

As just described, the probability of each reaction, p(R), is calculated whether the act contains a single reaction element or several in combination. If one reaction is used, the act is *simple*. If two or more reactions follow the situation in a single event, the act is *compound*. See, for example, act 1-*p-a*. The behavior table is therefore a roster of acts that varies in complexity as well as in frequency and in duration. Of the act total of 537 in both populations, thirty involve combined reactions. I have provided an index of compound acts in Table 9-2. They are identified here as in Table 9-1 and may be located directly in the behavior table.

I first wondered whether compound acts were solely artifacts of the classification. A more refined taxonomy would have yielded more of them. A classification aimed at developing integrated categories of reactions for each observed event—whether or not some were more tangly than others—would have eliminated compound acts. But my classification was guided by the descriptive phrases of aides. It was not based solely on conduct observed, and it resulted in this array.

Other evidence also suggests that compound acts are not artificial products. They appear unequally in the two populations, being twice as frequent in the state hospital. Second, the reactions in a compound act may confirm, contradict, or complement one another. See, for example, acts 4-*b-o* and 15-*g-x* in the behavior table. Third, the compound acts reported comprise only a few of the possible combinations of reactions. Except for one act in the private hospital (11-*q-k-b*) that has as many as three reactions in the same situation, all consist of only two reactions. Even if the possible combinations were limited to two reactions each (that is, *a* with *b, a* with *c, b* with *c,* and so on), there are 276 possible pairs. Only twenty-eight of these combinations—one-tenth of the possibilities—actually appear. Since there are 128 different types of acts in the population, one hundred of them are simple acts.

The reactions most often combined with others are CONVERSES (*b*),

Table 9-2. Index of compound reactions

Situations and Reactions		Private Hospital Frequency	p(S)p(R)	State Hospital Frequency	p(S)p(R)
1	p-a	.50	.002	2.92	.010
	p-t	.61	.002	.86	.003
2	c-b			.86	.003
3	c-n			.86	.003
	n-b			.86	.003
4	b-r	.82	.003		
	b-o	1.04	.004		
5	b-q			.86	.003
	p-d			.60	.002
	d-g			.60	.002
	d-m			.60	.002
	m-g			.60	.002
6	i-r	2.06	.008	.60	.002
	v-p			.86	.003
8	o-h			.86	.003
9	e-j			.86	.003
	h-e			.60	.003
10	c-a	.82	.003		
11	b-q	.82	.003		
	q-k-b	.82	.003		
	q-g			.86	.003
13	d-g			.86	.003
14	f-e			1.46	.005
	n-f	.50	.002		
15	g-x	1.04	.004		
17	k-l			.86	.003
	j-l	.61	.002		
18	g-l			.86	.003
21	n-k			.86	.003
22	q-w			.86	.003
	g-k	.61	.002		
	Totals	10.25	.038	20.02	.070

TELLS TO STOP (g), CARES FOR OR SERVES (n), and TEACHES OR CORRECTS (p). Are these types better mixers than other reactions that are rarely or never linked, such as STIPULATES A CONDITION (s) or BANTERS (u)? What is there about the latter that makes them wallflowers? These are pertinent questions in a grammar of behavior, just as combinations of words are of interest in linguistics. Unfortunately, there are too few cases available in these data for an adequate probe of the topic.

The small number of compound acts in these populations also creates problems in summarizing and analyzing behavior. Compound acts make up less than 6 percent of both act-populations ($30.27 \div 536.85 = .056$). It would be unwieldy to refer to them consistently in a special way in giving quantitative information about reactions. For example, what is the relative probability that an aide will fulfill a patient's request? The answer is not easily available in the behavior table. In situation 1 fulfilling a request (a) may occur alone or in combination with teaching or correcting the patient (p). It is difficult to state conclusions that refer selectively to both simple acts and parts of compound acts. We can, however, decompose a compound act and apportion its probability of occurrence to its elementary reaction categories. This procedure permits a gain in descriptive purity. Some information will be disregarded in this simplification, but whenever it is sought one can refer to Table 9-1. This decision to focus on elementary reactions introduces little distortion since the unit events are overwhelmingly instances of reaction categories used singly. The method used to decompose acts will therefore affect only 4 percent of the private hospital population and 7.1 percent of the state hospital population.

Decomposition is the procedure for translating the probabilities of a set that includes compound acts into the probabilities of the separate reactions. I will use situation 1 in the private hospital to exemplify the procedure. List *each elementary reaction* that occurs in the situation. Cite all the frequencies for each in the situation and add them together.

$$
\begin{array}{lrl}
1\text{-}a & 24.42 + .50 = & 24.92 \\
t & 4.12 + .61 = & 4.73 \\
p & .50 + .61 = & 1.11 \\
u & .50 \quad\ \ = & .50 \\
& \Sigma = & \overline{31.26}
\end{array}
$$

The sum will be a little greater than the total frequency estimated for that situation, since some acts are counted more than once because of their compounding. Next, calculate the relative frequencies of each reaction's occurrence in the situation, as described earlier in this chapter for $p(R)$.

$$
\begin{array}{lrl}
 & & p(r) \\
1\text{-}a & 24.92 \div 31.26 = & .797 \\
t & 4.73 \div 31.26 = & .151 \\
p & 1.11 \div 31.26 = & .036 \\
u & .50 \div 31.26 = & .016 \\
\hline
 & \Sigma = & \overline{1.000}
\end{array}
$$

Now use the notation $p(r)$ to designate the probability of an elementary reaction in a situation, thus distinguishing it from $p(R)$, which is the probability of a simple or compound reaction. To align these fractions with the population estimate, multiply each by the probability of the situation (.118 in this instance). The right-hand column in the final calculation is a simpler description than that found in Table 9-1, for there is but one probability value assigned to each elementary reaction in the set for the situation.

$$
\begin{array}{lrl}
 & & p(S)p(r) \\
1\text{-}a & .797 \times .118 = & .094 \\
t & .151 \times .118 = & .018 \\
p & .036 \times .118 = & .004 \\
u & .016 \times .118 = & .002 \\
\hline
 & \Sigma = & \overline{.118}
\end{array}
$$

Its notation is $p(S)p(r)$. This statement does not imply that each reaction necessarily occurs by itself. It does permit a more convenient summary of behavior. Sometimes there will be a rounding error in calculating $p(S)p(r)$. The probability of a reaction should be rounded upward or downward according to arithmetic rules. Since the sum of the resulting fractions must not exceed the total probability of the situation, the fractions must sometimes be rounded in the wrong direction to accommodate this restriction. If a tie occurs between a lone reaction and one that is combined with another, round the lone reaction's probability upward.

The Transition Matrix

Although the two parts of an act overlap in time, the $p(R)$ entry in the behavior table expresses a sequence in the likelihood of transition from each situation to each reaction. I broached this idea of probable sequence in

Chapter 4 by mentioning the Markov process. The idea of transition is also found in Shannon and Weaver's formulation of message-sending that has come to be called information theory. They describe a communication system as containing a large but finite number of messages (or signs or reactions) available for use by a particular source (for example, an individual). The communication that can take place is lodged in the potential for selecting a message. That potential, the probability that a given message will be selected from the set under given conditions, is its *transition probability*. This term can apply to the information in Table 9-1. For example, the social relationship, the hospital setting, and the situation can be cited as initial conditions. Given these conditions, each reaction's potential for occurrence is known.

The transition probabilities for all messages in a set can be summarized in a matrix. A matrix is an array (usually rectangular) of numbers that are values for a composite entity—such as a population of acts consisting of situations and reactions. Such arrays permit the recording and calculation of simultaneous changes in the set of composites. In a population of acts, for example, a change in the value of any probability would require a change in the values of at least one other since the sum of probabilities must equal 1.000. One change may require changes in the values of many probabilities in a set. Table 9-1 contains two matrices of transition probabilities, one for each population of acts. But its matrices have some features that make them inconvenient to use. They are spread over several pages because of the qualitative descriptions in the left-hand column. It is not easy to make rapid comparisons among acts, even in the same population. Also, several handfuls of compound acts are present. Their transition probabilities are admixtures that make comparisons difficult.

By performing the decomposition procedure, I simplified the information about the likelihood of reactions. This permits the use of a more condensed matrix, and I arranged the resulting probabilities in Matrices 9-3 and 9-4. The same number and letter is used for each situation and reaction. However, numerical and alphabetical order were established according to frequency across both institutions. Overall frequency in the repertoire need not imply an identical frequency order within a given population. Because the row and column sums in Matrices 9-3 and 9-4 do not show steadily decreasing frequencies, the numbers and letters within each population become mere names of actions rather than ordinal designations.

The numbers in the second column from the right-hand side of each matrix indicate the probabilities of the situations. Matrix 9-3 shows that

Matrix 9–3. Distribution of reactions among situations—Private Hospital

		R	E	A	C	T	I	O	N	S[a]						
		a	b	c	d	e	f	g	h	i	j	k	l	m	n	o
S	1	94														
I	2		7	6	12		30									
T	3			29	3										16	
U	4		57		8									16		4
A	5				29			24						8		
T	6					9				36	4					
I	7					12	10		10	3	4					
O	8				6				2	4	5					7
N	9		4			30										
S	10	40		3	5											
	11		8									2				
	12				15									17		
	13												15			
	14					3	3								15	
	15							11				6				
	16								27							
	17										9	7	2			
	18						4	10			2		3			
	19										14		4			
	20		3									8	3			
	21							15				4				
	22							1				3				
	23									9						
	24			11												
	25		2													
	26															
NA[b]																
Σp(r)		134	81	49	78	54	47	61	39	52	38	30	27	41	31	11
No. of S's		2	6	4	7	4	4	5	3	4	6	6	5	3	2	2

[a]All fractions to three decimal places; decimal points and left-hand zeroes omitted.
[b]Not Ascertained.

Matrix 9–3. (continued)

		p	q	r	s	t	u	v	w	x	NA[b]	p(S)	No. of r's
S	1	4				18	2					118	4
I	2										8	63	4
T	3											48	3
U	4			20				4				109	6
A	5										4	65	3
T	6	5		7				6			2	69	6
I	7											39	5
O	8											24	5
N	9											34	2
S	10				21							69	4
	11		20									30	3
	12										18	50	2
	13											15	1
	14											21	3
	15									7		24	3
	16											27	1
	17											18	3
	18						14					33	5
	19								5		4	27	3
	20	12							3			29	5
	21					2						21	3
	22											4	2
	23			3	6							18	3
	24											11	1
	25											2	1
	26		4									4	1
	NA[b]										28	28	
Σp(r)		21	24	30	27	18	18	10	8	7	64	1.000	
No. of S's		3	2	3	2	1	3	2	2	1			82

Matrix 9-4. Distribution of reactions among situations—State Hospital

		R a	E b	A c	C d	T e	I f	O g	N h	S[a] i	j	k	l	m	n	o
S	1	74														
I	2		47	23	14		42									9
T	3		3	78											24	4
U	4		25										8			
A	5		11		23			5					13			
T	6								19	7						
I	7					20	16		16	15	10					
O	8				3				23	9	5					32
N	9		7			31			2		19					
S	10	8		3												
	11							3				8				
	12				8									3		
	13				6			15				2	13			
	14					10	10	8							5	
	15							7				12	5			
	16								19							
	17										3	14	9			
	18							4			3	3	2			
	19										6		9			
	20											3				
	21							6				2			2	
	22							7				5				
	23									4						
	24			3												
	25		2													
	26															
NA[b]																
Σp(r)		82	95	107	54	61	68	47	68	47	53	49	38	24	31	45
No. of S's		2	6	4	5	3	3	7	5	4	7	8	5	3	3	3

[a]All fractions to three decimal places; decimal points and left-hand zeroes omitted.
[b]Not Ascertained.

Matrix 9–4. (continued)

		p	q	r	s	t	u	v	w	x	NA[b]	p(S)	No. of r's
S	1	12				14						100	3
I	2										3	138	5
T	3											109	4
U	4			8			2					43	4
A	5	4	3									59	6
T	6	15		2				7				50	5
I	7											77	5
O	8	3										75	6
N	9											59	4
S	10				5							16	3
	11		20			3						34	4
	12		3									14	3
	13						10					46	5
	14											33	4
	15											24	3
	16											19	1
	17											26	3
	18											12	4
	19											15	2
	20											3	1
	21											10	3
	22		5						5	2		24	5
	23											4	1
	24											3	1
	25											2	1
	26											0	
NA[b]											5	5	
Σp(r)		34	31	10	5	14	13	9	5	2	8	1.000	
No. of S's		4	4	2	1	1	2	2	1	1			86

situation 1 (A patient makes a request) is the most likely one in the private hospital. It would occur 11.8 percent of the time that aides and patients are within sensory reach. At the state hospital, as shown in Matrix 9-4, the most likely situation is number 2 (An aide and a patient pass each other or meet). Its probability is 13.8 percent of all contacts between patients and aides. At the bottom of the matrix, the row of numbers designated Σ p(r) tells the probability of each elementary reaction for the entire population.

By reading across a row in the matrix, one can learn the likelihoods of different reactions for a given situation. By reading down a column, one may learn the probability of a given reaction in different situations.

Because of the decomposition, aides' conduct with patients is depicted as an exhaustive set of mutually exclusive events in the transition matrices. Where this is unacceptable for certain purposes, the behavior table gives a more accurate picture. For other purposes it will be convenient to use the matrix in which each cell gives the likelihood of any elementary reaction for any situation. In Matrix 9-3 we can see that, of all his conduct with patients, the probability of a private hospital aide's fulfilling their requests ($1-a$) is 9.4 percent. In Matrix 9-4 we can see that of all the state hospital aides' actions with patients, the probability of telling a patient to do something upon meeting him ($2-c$) is 2.3 percent. All the probabilities in the cells of a matrix will sum to 1.000 and will represent the entire population of acts.

The transition matrices show that each situation is followed by one or more reactions and that the reactions are themselves distributed over one or more situations. This twofold mingling is the grain of interpersonal behavior. Each situation is not followed by a single type of conduct, nor are its types exclusive to it.

The information in Matrices 9-3 and 9-4 is partly implicit. Since each cell in a matrix represents a reaction to a situation, one could write .000 for transition probabilities in all the blank cells to express those facts. Each empty cell contains an invisible zero. It is important to interpret an unobserved act as having a zero probability. It connects acts to one another on a continuum of likelihoods rather than making a flat distinction between those that have and those that have not been seen to happen.

As soon as the empty cells in a transition matrix are identified as having zero probabilities, the matrix contains more than merely available facts. It refers to the logically possible and thereby enlarges the significance of what is observed. Perhaps aides in the past did use that reaction in that situation, although it is not employed at this moment in the population. Perhaps aides will perform that reaction in that situation in the future.

Review

To a large extent the behavior table and transition matrices are sources of the same information. The data of each are computed differently for convenience of particular analyses or for securing answers to certain questions. The behavior table is the source of qualitative knowledge. If simpler quantitative information is required, the transition matrices furnish data more quickly. The transition matrix also gives logical alternatives to all specific reactions to a situation and cites the alternative—Not Ascertained—to being unable to categorize an event. Such tables represent a different orientation to the study of interpersonal behavior than the concern with what ought to be. This approach sets up connections between what is happening, what may have happened in the past, and what is possible in the future.

Aspects of this format have already been recommended by social scientists. Cottrell wrote, "Predictions of behavior must be made in terms of probable behavior in a specified situational context as perceived by the actor. This of course requires a vocabulary adapted to situational description. It also requires an enormous amount of research to establish major types of social situational patterns in which the persons must function." Coutu added, "When we say a person . . . [will probably behave a certain way] we mean that it is probable in some context. The process could not possibly occur except in some situation, and probable behavior is herein always treated as a function of the situation, meaning that the tendency varies with the situation."

In addition to meeting the suggestions of Cottrell and Coutu, the behavior table's sampling basis makes it an improved account of life in the two mental hospitals. The account is not different from culture-based categories used by members of a group to discriminate among actions, for it incorporates their codes systematically in step D of the classification. But it balances that information with data gathered according to a probability sample. As such it is superior to ethnographies that list only events recurrent enough to be informally recognized as patterns. This table cites all observed events. One can easily learn about the most regular, frequent, and obvious patterns of conduct. It is understandable that the earliest behavioral summaries would refer to those patterns. However, a full portrayal of interpersonal life gives a wider and deeper perspective. Simmel offered an apt explanation of why the comprehensive view is so important and why the extent of behavioral heterogeneity found in society at any time should receive systematic treatment. He said "there exists an immeasurable number of less conspicuous forms of relationship and kinds of interaction. Taken singly, they may appear negligible. But . . . they alone produce society as we know it. To confine ourselves to the large social formations resembles the older science of anatomy with its limitations to the major, definitely circumscribed organs such as heart, liver, lungs, and stomach, and with its neglect of the innumerable, popularly unnamed or unknown tissues. Yet without these, the more obvious organs could never constitute a living organism. On the basis of the major social formations—the traditional subject matter of social science—it would be similarly impossible to piece together the real life of society as we encounter it in our experience."

Because the survey is impartial, the findings are both a less dramatic and a more accurate portrait of a social relationship. Not every action in it is interesting or exciting. Yet for any given act of interest, one can tell just what proportion of the whole it represents. Probability sampling and estimation permit such quantitative comparisons. The behavior table tells how many acts are to be found in the relationship. In addition, each act's sheer rate of happening is translated into a relative probability by setting the population of acts equal to 100 percent. An event is no longer described alone but according to its membership in the set.

PART THREE

Analysis of Findings

10

Behavior Semantics

❧

The pictures that emerge from the behavior table may appear incomplete. Its situational descriptions are crude. Some information could be refined, and other facts might be added. Nowhere is the sex or age of persons mentioned. Nor does the table cite the types of illness from which the patients suffer. On the other hand, by omitting such information the table focuses more on behavior itself. Free of some particulars, acts may be put alongside one another more readily for comparisons. I will demonstrate what can be accomplished with the data by returning to issues set forth in Part One, testing some of the ideas and showing ways in which they can be developed further.

In Chapter 11 I will compare the actions of aides with patients in the two hospitals. In Chapter 12, by reviewing the nonverbal communication found in the two act-populations, I will hark back to the proposition that sensory distance and social distance are connected. In Chapter 13 I will consider the way sensations and other conditions determine behavior. For all these inquiries I wish to deal with conduct meaningfully. In this chapter, therefore, I will give several examples of how the connotations of acts may be established by using the principles announced in Chapter 5. There I suggested that people find six kinds of meaning in behavior. One of these, connotation, is embodied in conduct itself. It is lodged in action's format just as implications of words are given in the arrangement of a sentence. Structure and meaning are entwined.

The act-whole is a creation, constructed from memories of experiences with others. It is an assembly of a number of mental compartments into which are sorted situations and reactions, along with estimates of how many are stored in each niche. Accordingly, one of the first things to do in order to interpret an act is to round up all instances of the reaction and the alternatives implicated with it wherever it appears. In the case of the aides' repertoire, this is easy to do by inspecting Matrices 9-3 and 9-4 and by copying down all entries sharing the same rows with that reaction, recording the situations involved and each reaction's probability as well. This little subset of information could be shuffled into a configuration around the reaction in question, in preparation to tap its significance. That done, the behavior semanticist has before him a parcel of information that roughly corresponds to the knowledge about that act in the minds of individuals who have accumulated impressions of it through experience.

First Example

Imagine a reaction that takes place mainly in perturbing interpersonal situations. As alternatives to this reaction, aides either try to suppress the situation, try to change it, or permit it to go on. Still other reactions used by aides in those situations are to suggest entering an activity or to show no overt change in behavior. The most common of these alternatives is trying to suppress the situation. The reaction in question is qualitatively different from all of these and yet meaningfully related to them.

It is hard to say whether the reaction would spring to mind given these facts. But it is plausible that as an alternative to curbing, changing, permitting, or doing nothing about a social problem people sometimes BANTER (*u*) in such situations.

To interpret bantering, I scanned matrices 9-3 and 9-4 for *u*'s occurrence and listed its situations, along with information about all the alternative reactions, in Table 10-1 for convenient reference. Table 10-1 is actually a composite of parts of 9-3 and 9-4, with the entries rearranged. As shown, BANTERS' almost constant companions are TELLS TO STOP (*g*) and COMPELS TO STOP OR TO DO IT (*k*). PERMITS (*l*) also recurs as an alternative, and there are seven other reactions that appear with BANTERS in no more than one of its five situations.

Here is a singular property of reaction *u*: though used in five different situations, it does not appear in the same situation in both hospitals. Private aides banter with patients only when the latter make requests (situation 1), perform unusual physical gestures (18), or perform ordinarily private gestures in public (21). State aides do not. They banter when patients are in distress (11) or engage in mischief (13). The situations themselves are noteworthy. Four of the five are trying circumstances.

Table 10-1. Data for interpreting reaction u (BANTERS) [a]

Reactions of aides

Situations: A patient . . .	REFUSES *t*	FULFILLS REQUEST *a*	TEACHES OR CORRECTS *p*	REASSURES AND TRIES TO REMEDY *q*	COMPELS TO STOP OR TO DO IT *k*	TELLS TO STOP *g*	BANTERS *u*	PERMITS *l*	NO OVERT CHANGE IN BEHAVIOR *d*	GREETS *f*	SUGGESTS ENTERING ACTIVITY *i*	$\Sigma p(S)$ [b]
1 makes a request	18	94	4				2					.118 (P)
11 is in distress				20		3	3					.034 (S)
13 is making mischief for someone					8	15	10	13	6			.046 (S)
18 performs an unusual physical act						10	14	3		4	2	.033 (P)
21 performs a private act in public					4	15	2	6	6	4	2	.021 (P)
Sum of p(S)p(r)	18	94	4	20	14	43	31	16	6	4	2	

[a] Situations in which it occurs, and alternative reactions that also happen in those situations, copied from Matrices 9-3 and 9-4.
[b] P = private hospital; S = state hospital

Patients display unusual types of conduct in two of these (18 and 21). The other two are common forms of disturbance (11 and 13) (pages 124–126).

Tantalizing, harassment, mockery, and playful interference are the manifest content of bantering. The aides responding to problematic conduct in this way are not dealing with the patients severely. They are more sporting than when they try to suppress the behavior (g, k). Yet they are not as easygoing as they are when they allow the situation to continue (l and perhaps d and f). Nor are they as businesslike as when they try to reassure or change the situation (q and j). Reflecting on these alternatives, I locate bantering between the poles of suppression, forbearance, and the direct management of a challenging situation. Thus, in the face of troubling circumstances that one neither approves of, can allow, can cope with, nor will squelch, banter has the flavor of uneasily laughing away the problem. Since the most likely alternatives are telling and compelling to stop, banter may be a cover-up for disapproval or frustration. It seems to be a release for the aide who is confronted with tumult but who does not put a stop to it.

The aides may see these situations as typical of their patients' problems. Upsetting circumstances, the reluctance to oppress people already in plight, and helplessness in the face of urgency—all swirl around the use of reaction u. Suppression is an unacceptable alternative. Yet the aides are not indifferent. They feel responsible for the patients, but at the same time they are seized by impotence over what to do. Banter vents their tension obliquely. It is diversionary. Given that the most likely alternative is stopping the situation, it is also a rather tolerant move toward patients. The phrase *diverting tension* fits this connotation of reaction u.

Although it is possible to assume that diverting tension was a purpose or goal of the aides, and although it is possible to assume that this diversion was an outcome or a consequence of bantering, this interpretation of BANTERS does not rest on either of those assumptions. Maybe the aides did not aim to divert tension. Maybe tension was not diverted in the end. Whatever the conclusions reached about these unobservable matters, BANTERS can be taken to connote diverting tension according to the empirical content of its whole act—the situation, the alternative reactions, and their probabilities. Accepted on its terms, the semantic technique stands in the same relation to meaning as the syllogism does to truth. The interpretation may be valid whether or not it is true.

In this case it seems to be true. I reject the possibility that BANTERS may connote ridicule or sarcasm here, because of its alternative reactions. Other instances come to mind in which people make light of their troubles, crack jokes in the face of difficulty, and mildly tease one another to take the edge off grave occasions. It even happens in times of bereavement. Jews are supposed to grieve and recite eulogies in the days of traditional mourning after a funeral. But as an alternative to comforting and reassuring the mourners, those who gather in the house of the deceased to "sit shivah" often spend their time telling jokes. Similarly, the Irish wake, officially a solemn vigil by the body of the dead person, is often a merry scene.

Bantering does not connote diverting tension every time it is used. Where the alternative reactions differ, BANTERS' meaning will be different. In situation 1, bantering in response to a patient's request must therefore be interpreted another way. In that case the most likely alternative is FULFILLS REQUEST (a). Reaction p (TEACHES OR CORRECTS) is an alternative too, so even here u might be a defense against a vexing circumstance, perhaps a nasty or demanding tone in a patient's request. But the clear difference between the most probable alternative here and those in other sets implies that there is another connotation.

Situation 1 is commonplace. It is the most frequent in the private hospital and is also habitual in the state setting. Its content is routine and familiar. It is far less problematic than the other four situations. The most likely alternatives in situation 1 are FULFILLS REQUEST (a) and REFUSES (t). These are clearcut reactions that could bring the situation to a conclusion. So the situation is directly resolved one way or another 98 percent of the time by fulfilling or refusing (see Table 9-1). About 2 percent of the time some complication is introduced. Thus BANTERS may be understood as countering the resolution of the situation in this case. Here u's connotation may be introducing tension, or *playing*.

Again I do not assume intent or outcome. I cannot say that the aide's motive is to play, nor can I be confident that tension results. I only deduce this connotation according to behavioral alternatives. Since BANTERS occurs so rarely in situation 1, I cannot be so confident about this interpretation as I would be if it were backed up by quantitative regularity. Yet if other instances are needed to confirm it, they readily come to mind. A humdrum situation is a background to playfulness. Huizinga says that tension is a part of play. After lying on the beach in the hot sun for two hours, a boy sticks his foot out to trip his friend as the latter struggles to his feet for a swim. During the thousandth trip to the market, the husband adds an absurd item to the shopping cart, perhaps a fifty-pound bag of cat food though they have no cat, and watches for his wife's reaction. Bantering introduces excitement in dull moments and a chance for relief in tense times. These may not be its only connotations.

In this exercise one may be left with the uneasy impression that a category has explained a category, that behavior semantics is a way of establishing tautologies, and that I have achieved only a refinement of what was understood before rather than a new insight about the reaction. In so problematic an endeavor as the meaning of social conduct, one might even be generous and persuade himself that it is the best we can expect from seeking meaning in objective evidence. Not so. I use a category to give import to a category, but behavior semantics is built upon a foundation broader than the single reaction. It depends upon knowledge of reactions combined into sets. As such it is analogous to studying the nature of a chemical element as part of various molecules. Such inspection adds to understanding even though the element can be studied in other ways. Semantic analysis begins with a fieldlike consideration of behavior. The reaction is placed among other reactions according to their likelihoods in situations. Since I interpret a category in the light of its alternatives, I deal here with a type of meaning resting on the principle of relativity and not on the principle of inherence. Dewey said that "no sound . . . is a word or part of language in isolation. Any word or phrase has the meaning which it has only as a member of a constellation of related meanings." Here too, a reaction depends on its kin for its tenor, and all members of the set are reversible in the analysis. A given reaction can be treated as an alternative while one of its alternatives becomes the reaction whose significance is to be divined.

This structure of meaning is to a large extent self-supporting. But not completely so. There is a trickle of dependence on outside assumptions in a vital way. Each time I interpret one reaction I insinuate meanings for its alternatives. For example, in analyzing u I took for granted that reactions g and k could be understood as attempts to suppress behavior. I dropped hints of a similar form about all of u's alternatives. I cannot explain fully at this point where all these assumptions come from. It would require an exposition many times multiplied of the analysis demonstrated in this chapter, as well as additional argument. Words are used in the description. So the significance of verbal language intrudes. The interpreter must make assumptions about the alternatives in order to get under way with his assay of a given reaction. The assumptions come from the same type of reasoning, achieved through prior experience and learning. It may be that this pool of understanding is fortified by a mix of nominal, signal, causal, consequential, and moral meanings as well. Digging for a single connotation inevitably results in pulling at roots that are attached in a widespread network with many other offshoots of meanings, actions, and events whose underground connections one cannot apprehend at the moment.

The field definition of a meaningful event is thus not just a definition-label slapped on a category-label. Connotations are bootstrap creatures risen from sets of categories and livened by their unequal probabilities.

Second Example

Liberal use of a reaction betokens many meanings. A reaction that joins numerous situations is likely to find itself in the company of dissimilar alternatives. Its meanings therefore vary. This is the case for reaction d (SHOWS NO OVERT CHANGE IN BEHAVIOR). It is one of the most versatile in the aides' repertoire. It appears in eight different situations, four of them in both hospitals. Whereas only ten other alternatives are in sets with u (BANTERS), nineteen reactions are alternatives to d in various situations. So d occurs in nearly one-third of the situations with more than two-thirds of the reactions of the entire repertoire.

Table 10-2 contains information pertaining to d, copied from Matrices 9-3 and 9-4. I have arranged the data so that situations are clustered by how they share reactions and the reactions by whether they happen in the same situations. The array is more diffuse than that in Table 10-1. For example, whereas u (BANTERS) has g (TELLS TO STOP) as a partner in four of its five situations, no one of d's partners appears in more than three of its eight situations. Only four of the nineteen alternatives appear in as many as three situations. These are c (TELLS OR REMINDS TO DO SOMETHING), o (ASKS ASSISTANCE), b (CONVERSES), and m (BRIEFLY AGREES OR DISAGREES). Three others, g (TELLS TO STOP,) q (REASSURES AND TRIES TO REMEDY), and p (TEACHES OR CORRECTS), appear in two situations each. The remaining twelve ($s, a, n, v, j, h, i, r, f, k, u$ and l) each appear in only one situation with d. Such dispersion of alternatives declares that d does not lend itself to unitary interpretation.

By reshuffling the columns and rows of Table 10-2 to bring the numbers closer together, three main groups of alternatives are cast into relief. This tells that there are three meanings in this repertoire for SHOWS NO OVERT CHANGE IN BEHAVIOR. The dashes in the table demarcate the clusters. Of the eight situations depicted, the uppermost three in the table (5, 12, and 13) share the following reactions: m (BRIEFLY AGREES OR DISAGREES), q

(REASSURES AND TRIES TO REMEDY), and *g* (TELLS TO STOP), as well as reaction *d*. There is some overlap with the next three situations (2, 4, and 8). Reaction *m* also appears in situation 4. Reaction *b* (CONVERSES) also appears in 2 and 4. And reaction *p* (TEACHES OR CORRECTS) also appears in 8. The three uppermost situations have five reactions unique to their group. These are *q, g, k, u* and *l*.

Table 10–2. Data for interpreting reaction *d* (SHOWS NO OVERT CHANGE IN BEHAVIOR)

Reactions of Aides

Situa-tions	STIPULATES A CONDITION — s (P^b) (S)	FULFILLS REQUEST — a (S) (P)	CARES FOR OR SERVES — n (S) (P)	TELLS OR REMINDS TO DO SOMETHING — c (S) (P)	SUGGESTS ENTERING ACTIVITY — j (S) (P)	SUPERVISES ACTIVITY — h (S) (P)	PARTICIPATES FULLY — i (S) (P)	WITHDRAWS — r (S) (P)	PARTICIPATES PART — v (S) (P)	GP — f (S) (P)
13										
12										
5										
4								20 4		
8					5 5	2 23	4 9			
2				6 23					30 4	
3			16	29						
10	21 40			3						
Σ	21 40	16	38 23	5 5	2 23	4 9	20	4	30 4	

^*a*^ Situations in which it occurs, and alternative reactions that also happen in those situations, copied from Matrices 9–3 and 9–4.
^*b*^ P = private hospital; S = state hospital

The two clusters overlap so I expect the meanings of *d* to shade into each other. Nevertheless, there is enough difference in the reactions to the three topmost situations in Table 10–2 to suggest that they are a subgroup for which *d* can be interpreted differently than it can in its appearance in the other five situations. Indeed, *d* is the only reaction that the uppermost three have in common with the two lowest situations in the table (3 and 10). Therefore, the meanings of *d* in these uppermost and lowest situational clusters will assuredly differ.

Notice how free of content my comments are. I have begun to expound an act, but I have yet to say anything about the content of the reactions being compared. So far my remarks refer to the formal aspects of conduct—which reactions are grouped together in which sets, the degree of overlap between sets, what meanings are likely to be different because reactions have few alternatives in common, and so on. Still the analysis does progress toward conclusions about meanings. It is a feature of

Table 10–2. (continued)

ASKS ASSISTANCE o		CONVERSES b		SHOWS NO OVERT CHANGE IN BEHAVIOR d		BRIEFLY AGREES OR DISAGREES m		TEACHES OR CORRECTS p		REASSURES AND TRIES TO REMEDY q		TELLS TO STOP g		COMPELS TO STOP OR TO DO IT k		BANTERS u		PERMITS l	
P	S	P	S	P	S	P	S	P	S	P	S	P	S	P	S	P	S	P	S
					6								15	2		10		13	
				15	8	17	3			3									
			11	29	23	8	13	4		3		24	5						
4		57		8		16													
7	32			6	3			3											
	9	7	47	12	14														
				3															
				5															
11	41	64	58	78	54	41	16	7		6		24	20	2		10		13	

behavior semantics because it draws much from the structure of action and because semantic structure was taken into consideration in classifying (see Chapter 7, especially step F), that some of the interpretive task is accomplished in the course of systematization. Thus when I assess formal properties, I do not start from the beginning. I pay attention to the pattern of the evidence. My bearings let me say in confidence that the meaning of reaction *d* in situations 3 and 10 will differ from its meaning in situations 5, 12, and 13. Situations 3 and 10 have only one other reaction (*c*) besides *d* in common with the middle group of situations (2, 4, and 8). Noting less commonality of reactions between 3 and 10 and 2, 4, 8 on the one hand than there is between 2, 4, 8 and 5, 12, 13 on the other (the latter two clusters have three reactions—*b, m,* and *p*—in common besides *d*), I also deduce that there will be greater similarity between the latter two meanings of SHOWS NO OVERT CHANGE IN BEHAVIOR than between either of those meanings and that for reaction *d* in situations 3 and 10.

In 3 and 10, the content of the alternatives to *d* in the order of their likelihoods is FULFILLS REQUEST (*a*), TELLS OR REMINDS TO DO SOME-THING (*c*), STIPULATES A CONDITION (*s*), and CARES FOR OR SERVES (*n*). These reactions occur when patients ask permission to leave the ward or to make a telephone call (10) or when it is time for a scheduled activity (3). Under such conditions with such alternatives, SHOWS NO OVERT CHANGE IN BEHAVIOR on the part of aides does not carry pointed interpersonal signifi-cance. It rather reflects the avoidance of work, shirking or postponing what is to be done as part of the job. This is apparent both from the contexts and from what aides do otherwise in those situations. They are otherwise so engaged in fulfilling requests, telling, reminding, stipulating, caring, and serving that the absence of these reactions signifies resting or delaying work. Therefore, SHOWS NO OVERT CHANGE IN BEHAVIOR here connotes *lounging.* According to Table 10-2, this meaning applies only to the private hospital population. Reaction *d* does not occur in these situations in the state setting.

In situations 2, 4, and 8, the content of the alternatives to *d* in the order of their probabilities is CONVERSES (*b*), GREETS (*f*), BRIEFLY AGREES OR DISAGREES (*m*), ASKS ASSISTANCE (*o*), TELLS OR REMINDS TO DO SOME-THING (*c*), SUPERVISES ACTIVITY (*h*), WITHDRAWS (*r*), PARTICIPATES FULLY (*i*), SUGGESTS ENTERING ACTIVITY (*j*), PARTICIPATES PARTLY (*v*), and TEACHES OR CORRECTS (*p*). These reactions happen when an aide and a patient pass each other or meet (situation 2), a patient makes a remark or is having a conversation with an aide (4), or an aide is working on the ward and some patients are nearby (8). The acts of conversing, greeting, agreeing or disagreeing, asking assistance, telling, reminding, supervising, withdrawing, participating fully, suggesting activities, and so on strongly suggest a theme of participation with patients in these situations. The dealings are primarily of a social sort and secondarily task-oriented. Under such circumstances, with such alternatives, aides who SHOW NO OVERT CHANGE IN BEHAVIOR opt for avoiding direct positive interaction with patients. In these contact opportunities it signifies interpersonal reserve. Here *d* can be interpreted as keeping distance and being uncommunicative, or as *aloofness.*

In situations 5, 12, and 13, the content of the alternatives to *d* in the order of their likelihoods is TELLS TO STOP (g), BRIEFLY AGREES OR DISAGREES (m), PERMITS (l), CONVERSES (b), BANTERS (u), REASSURES AND TRIES TO REMEDY (q), TEACHES OR CORRECTS (p), and COMPELS TO STOP (k). Again, the most probable alternatives suggest a theme. These reactions involve trying to curb, allow, or change situations in which a patient performs an unusual verbal act (5), complains or denounces the hospital (12), or makes mischief for someone (13). I have already noted, in establishing the meaning of reaction u (BANTERS), that situation 13 is problematic. Situations 5 and 12 are also awkward and potentially embarrassing. It is understandable that aides might try to suppress or remedy or correct such behavior on the part of patients. In this context the alternative SHOWS NO OVERT CHANGE IN BEHAVIOR is very close to PERMITS (l). It allows the situation to continue. Contrasted with the sufferance of reactions m (BRIEFLY AGREES OR DISAGREES) and u (BANTERS), reaction d conveys unconcern or *indifference*. As expected, this interpretation of reaction d is closer to the meaning of aloofness accorded it in the preceding three situations than to the connotation of lounging settled on it in situations 3 and 10. There is more overlap in the reaction sets and in the meaning of the two situational clusters 2-4-8 and 5-12-13.

So reaction d (SHOWS NO OVERT CHANGE IN BEHAVIOR) can mean lounging, aloofness, or indifference. These interpretations are rounded and filled out by also considering reaction d in each act-whole. The spread of d's occurrence and the several clusters of alternative reactions that are found with it in different situations lead to connotations ranging from postponement of work through interpersonal reserve to ignoring patients.

Table 10-2 tells us that there are three meanings to d in the private setting and but two in the state institution. One could interpret this reaction using the data of one population alone; that is, by sorting out the information of Table 10-2 according to each setting. Somewhat different interpretations might then be established. The two interpretations of d attributed to the state hospital would hold. But those two interpretations—aloofness and indifference—may merge in the private hospital because of the different situations involved.

I originally introduced the reaction of SHOWS NO OVERT CHANGE IN BEHAVIOR by following the principle of considering all possibilities. It was to serve in a behavioral scheme as the zero serves in arithmetic. Here we see how richly it can be endowed with meaning. And this does not exhaust its connotations. If a white student and a black student pass each other in the corridor of a newly desegregated public school, reaction d on the part of the white may connote the onset of interracial peace if its probable alternative was a form of harassment. In another case, by considering it against its plausible alternatives, a famous detective in literature once used the reaction to infer a characteristic of the criminal he sought. In the case of "Silver Blaze" Sherlock Holmes remarked on "the curious incident of the dog in the night-time." Inspector Gregory challenged this by saying that the dog had done nothing during the night of the crime—it had not even barked. Holmes replied, "That was the curious incident," and went on to conclude that the criminal must have been someone familiar to the dog.

These exercises demonstrate the possibilities of the method. The event is less than the significance bestowed on it. Instead of losing individuality, a reaction gains a connotation from its participation in the whole act. Thus madness in behavior does not erupt, it converges. Happiness is not created, it is assembled. Freedom is not the privilege of a specified action but the presence of alternatives. The connotation is formed by the web of the whole.

It is true that the categories are partly defined by the aides. Step D in the classification (see Chapter 7) is the framing of behavior units according to participants' testimony. Undoubtedly the aides announced units, *actemes,* that were meaningful to them, just as phonemes are units of speech that the linguist uses based on differential recognition of sounds by native speakers. But while aides may have had meanings in mind, my use of the categories at that point was denotative. I assembled categories into sets of alternatives according to the field records, not according to aides' interpretations. .

All the reaction categories in the case study are amenable to the kind of analysis made for u and d. The more different reactions per situation and the more widely dispersed among situations they are, the more numerous the connotations possible and the less firmly is any one connotation attached to an act category. Thus reaction d (SHOWS NO OVERT CHANGE IN BEHAVIOR) has more connotations than u (BANTERS). Reaction g (TELLS TO STOP) also happens in many situations (see Matrices 9-3 and 9-4), but its partners are so consistently and predominantly reactions k (COMPELS TO STOP OR TO DO IT) and l (PERMITS) that g probably has a unitary meaning. Not so for reactions j and b. While j (SUGGESTS ENTERING ACTIVITY) occurs in about the same number of situations as g, its reaction alternatives are clustered into two distinct groups. This can be discerned in 9-3 and 9-4. Hence j will probably be interpreted in two ways. Reaction b

(CONVERSES) is also a candidate for multiple connotations. It appears in a number of situations with varied alternatives. I will establish these several meanings in the following chapter as I make an interpretive comparison of the two groups of aides.

Connotations are more abstract than conduct. They refer to themes found in act patterns rather than in single acts. Aloofness, for example, is not in itself behavioral. It may apply to different conduct in different settings.

The method also shows how the number of meanings carried in behavior can be larger than the number of different reactions used. I found three separate connotations for SHOWS NO OVERT CHANGE IN BEHAVIOR and two different ones for BANTERS. Therefore, the twenty-four reactions in the repertoire will yield more than twenty-four meanings.

Complementary and Coupled Distributions

A dimension I referred to in Chapter 5 and then used in interpreting u and d is the degree to which reactions are grouped together in situational sets. For example, I remarked that since BANTERS (u) had different alternatives in situation 1, its meaning would diverge in that case from its connotation elsewhere. In this section I will show how this dimension helps interpret reactions that are similar in appearance.

This is a formal basis for meaning. It does not consider the content of the reactions (after observing that they are similar) but rather their dispersion in a repertoire. Modern linguistics also relies on formal criteria for meanings. That language and behavior should both have structural grounds for their semantics should not be surprising, since speech is a part of interpersonal behavior.

While different from the reaction being considered, an *alternative* is not always an opposite. It is simply an act having membership in a set larger than one. Those in the sets that include reactions u (BANTERS) and d (SHOWS NO OVERT CHANGE IN BEHAVIOR) may be opposites to them, may be substitutes for them, may differ only in degree, or may be unlike without being contrary. All are possible.

A distribution of two or more alternatives in a repertoire is *complementary* if the reactions are similar in appearance but occur in different situations. Similar reactions so distributed are likely to have the same meaning.

This is the case, for example, for reactions d (SHOWS NO OVERT CHANGE

IN BEHAVIOR), *e* (LEAVES THEM TO THEMSELVES), and *r* (WITHDRAWS), whose distributions appear in Table 10-3 (copied from Matrices 9-3 and 9-4). In the private hospital at least one of the three occurs in each of twelve situations, but in ten of those situations no more than one of the types shows itself. It is a nearly perfect complementary distribution. The situations in which two of these reactions occur vary according to whether or not aides and patients are actively in contact. These are situations 4 (A patient makes a remark or is having a conversation with an aide) and 6 (Patients and aides are at recreation together). One can only withdraw if

Table 10–3. **Complementary distribution of reactions *d* (SHOWS NO OVERT CHANGE IN BEHAVIOR), *e* (LEAVES THEM TO THEMSELVES), and *r* (WITHDRAWS)**

| | *Reactions* | | | | | |
| | *Private Hospital* | | | *State Hospital* | | |
Situations	*d*	*e*	*r*	*d*	*e*	*r*
2	12			14		
3	3					
4	8		20			8
5	29			23		
6		9	7			2
7		12			20	
8	6			3		
9		30			31	
10	5					
12	15			8		
13				6		
14		3			10	
23			3			
Σ	78	54	30	54	61	10

there is contact. If not already engaged, he may be aloof (*d* in 4, as analyzed in the preceding section) or leave the patients to themselves (*e* in 6). So the reactions are complementary if this distinction is made within these situations. In the state hospital the complementarity among *d, e,* and *r* is perfect. Only one of the three reactions is found in each of ten different situations there. No two ever happen together.

In classifying, I distinguished among the three categories *d, e,* and *r* while acknowledging that they appeared similar. The relation between d and e was also reflected in somewhat complementary field records made by the observers. Because these three reactions are all forms of disengagement from or not seizing contact opportunities with patients, they seem to be substitutes for one another in different situations.

What about the different meanings demonstrated for d? There is no contradiction here. These are different types of inferences. If there is any doubt about meaningful substitutability among $d, e,$ and r it would refer to those situations for which the alternatives occur in only one hospital, namely 3, 10, 13, and 23. Indeed, the meaning of d in situations 3 and 10 is markedly unlike its other connotations. The meaning of a reaction is given by the alternatives in the sets, but there is also utility in looking at its formal distribution when interpreting it.

In general, the more that similar alternatives are distributed separately across situations, the more likely that they are meaningful substitutes for one another. Their use parallels the way synonyms are used in speech.

The *coupled* distribution is opposite of complementary. It is the degree to which two or more similar reactions are found together throughout. Coupled distributions tip off differences. Superficially the reactions' differences are in degree. Had such gradations in categories been compressed in classifying, the roster of reactions would not have been so sensitive to behavioral differences among people. Personal differences are sometimes quantitative, and if these reactions differ in degree of the same meaning, coupling may reflect variations among different individuals in the same situation.

Here is the significance of the dimension. Similar reactions in complementary distribution may mean the same thing, be substitutes for one another, and reflect variations in the same person's conduct across different situations. Similar reactions in coupled distribution probably differ to some degree in meaning, are not substitutes, and reflect variations among different individuals in the same situation.

These distinctions apply best at the extremes of coupling and complementarity. But acts do not align themselves neatly at opposite poles of the dimension. They come variously sorted. To show how the distributions can occur on a graded scale, I scanned Matrices 9-3 and 9-4 and selected several clusters of similar-appearing reactions. They are presented in Table 10-4. From left to right the parcels of alternatives show a progression from a perfect complementary distribution (b and i) to a perfect coupled one (r with v).

Reactions b (CONVERSES) and i (PARTICIPATES FULLY) are qualitatively similar. Participating fully almost always includes conversing with others; both reactions involve a high rate of interaction, and in both the aides' and patients' actions are the same. Just as speech is a subset of all behavior, b could be considered a subcategory of i. These reactions also form a perfect complementary distribution in both populations, which implies that they are substitutes for one another and may be interpreted in the same way.

Reactions f (GREETS), m (BRIEFLY AGREES OR DISAGREES), and v (PARTICIPATES PARTLY) form an almost perfect complementary distribution. Only in situation 4 (A patient makes a remark or is having a conversation with an aide) does a coupling appear (between m and v). It implies that for the most part the three reactions may substitute for one another and have the same connotation. In situation 4 the two reactions differ in degree, for in one alternative the aide responds scantily with gestures of agreement or disagreement (m), and in the other he only listens (v). Whether the two reactions will be distinguished in seeking the meaning of aides' conduct in situation 4 will depend on the assessment of the other alternatives in the set. But since reaction m is four times as likely as v in that situation in both populations, the complementarity of the distribution predominates. It would be a mistake to think that similar reactions in complementary distribution are the result of poor classification that imposed artificial distinctions upon essentially the same conduct. Reactions f, m, and v have noticeably different properties. Those are the primary criteria of classification. Acts may differ overtly and mean the same thing.

Reactions c (TELLS OR REMINDS TO DO SOMETHING), h (SUPERVISES ACTIVITY), j (SUGGESTS ENTERING ACTIVITY), and p (TEACHES OR CORRECTS) are somewhat similar. They all focus on eliciting a different type of conduct from what is happening. Their distribution is mostly complementary in both populations. One or more of them occur in seventeen situations, and in only four situations (6, 7, 8, and 9) do any two of them happen together. For the most part these reactions may possess similar connotations and be substitutes for one another. Again, whether distinctions should be made in the situations where these reactions are coupled will depend on an examination of the alternatives in the sets.

Reactions g (TELLS TO STOP) and k (COMPELS TO STOP OR TO DO IT) are found in nine different situations in the state hospital, and in six situations they occur together. In the private hospital they happen in eight different situations and are members of the same set in three. So they are

Table 10–4. Some complementary, partially coupled, and coupled distributions

Reactions

Situations	Private Hospital													State Hospital												
	b	i	f	m	v	j	h	p	c	g	k	r	v	b	i	f	m	v	j	h	p	c	g	k	r	v
1	7							4						47		42					12					
2			30						6					3								23				
3	57								29					25								78				
4				16	4							20	4	11			8	2							8	2
5				8				5		24							13				4		5			
6		36			6	4						7	6		19	16		7	7		15				2	7
7		3	10			4	10								15				10	16						
8		4				5	2								9				5	23						
9	4													7					19	2						
10									3		2											3				
11	8																						3	8		
12				17																			15	2		
13			3														3									
14																14				8			7	12		
15										11	6															
16						9	27												3	19						
17											7								3					14		
18			4			2				10									6				4	3		
19						14																				
20	3							12		15	8													3		
21										1	4												6	2		
22											3												7	5		
23												3			4							3				
24		9							11																	
25	2													2												
Σ	81	52	47	41	10	38	39	21	49	61	30	30	10	95	47	72	24	9	53	68	31	107	47	49	10	9

coupled on half of the occasions. In Chapter 7 I remarked on differences between these alternatives. They diverge in the amount of force incorporated in suppressing or removing a situation. The prospects for interpreting them are muddled by the fact that reaction k has two guises, compelling to stop and compelling to do something. The latter expression of k pertains in situations 11 (A patient is in distress) and 17 (A patient delays or resists doing a required activity). One might decide that it is worth distinguishing between the two forms of k and place aside the evidence for situations 11 and 17 where k takes the form COMPELS TO DO IT. The result of this weeding would be seven situations, with g and k (COMPELS TO STOP) coupled in five of them.

Since g and k are mainly coupled now, the same alternative reactions appear in their sets. Sameness in alternatives implies similar meanings. But because they are coupled, g and k cannot be substitutes for one another. Hence they must have connotations that differ in degree, and they probably reflect the behavior of different people in the same situation.

The right-hand lot in Table 10-4 is a small one consisting of r (WITHDRAWS) and v (PARTICIPATES PARTLY). Although v occurs in only two situations, whenever it appears r appears with it. Now there happens to be an almost perfect complementary distribution among f, m, and v and a nearly perfect complementary distribution among d, e, and r (Table 10-3). That is, v and r have affinities for manifestly different reactions. The probabilities confirm this disjunction too. Reactions m, v, and r occur in situation 4 (A patient makes a remark or is having a conversation with an aide) in both settings. In both settings, r's likelihood is about the same as that for m. In situation 6 (Patients and aides are at recreation together) in the private hospital, r's probability is close to that of v. Equiprobable reactions in the same situation are definitely not complementary. On the other hand, where m and v appear in the same situation they have substantially different likelihoods, a feature of complementary reactions, so that these two may be substitutes for one another. This pattern suggests that the coupling of v and r reflects acts of different individuals having somewhat different meanings for them. The small number of instances leaves this analysis inconclusive.

Looking at such distributions emphasizes the location of acts among others. Its import applies only to overtly similar reactions, and it would be risky to conclude substitutability or difference from a mere distribution alone. As such, the technique can augment any method that addresses itself primarily to content categories in deciding about same or different meanings.

Situational Semantics

So far I have applied the interpretive technique only to reactions. It can also be used to understand situations. The behavior table does not tell what comes before a situation except to mention those conditions—hospital setting, positions of the persons—that are part of the enduring milieu. But the table does provide a type of helpful information. It tells the reactions to each situation. These are following clues. They are what G. H. Mead implied by saying that the significance of an event is to be found in the response to it. "This implies a definition of meaning—that it is an indicated reaction which the object may call out. When we find that we have adjusted ourselves to a comprehensive set of reactions toward an object we feel that the meaning of the object is ours." This is a clear reference to the act-whole. A situation's meaning would be conveyed by the set of reactions to it.

Each reaction appears only in a select group of situations. It bestows a connection among those group members. In that way it implies a difference between those situations and others not having the reaction. The situations sharing the same reactions are likely to have salient features in common and to be construed in the same way.

Matrices 9-3 and 9-4 can be used to locate such ensembles. Each vertical column in each matrix shows the aggregates of situations that have a reaction in common in that act-population. In every repertoire there may be little families of situations sharing the same reactions as offspring and having only distant kinship with other families whose offspring are different sets of reactions. Here are examples of interpretations using this technique:

1. If the meaning of a situation can be established by noting its reactions and also by remarking on those that do not join in, a careful combing of Matrices 9-3 and 9-4 would separate the repertoire into three main subgroups. A group composed of situations 5, 11, 12, 13, 15, 17, 18, 19, 20, 21, and 22 shares several or most of their reactions. Even without knowing their qualitative natures I would be justified, according to the principle that common reactions muster situations having common meanings, in assuming that they have a similar connotation. That bunch would differ from another consisting of situations 2, 4, 6, 7, 8, and 9 and also

from a third group containing 1, 3, 10, and 14. I will anticipate some connotations for these clusters. They can be labeled respectively problematic, open-ended interpersonal, and routine task-centered. There is some evidence to follow in support of these meanings, and I will elaborate these interpretations in Chapter 11.

2. Reaction d (SHOWS NO OVERT CHANGE IN BEHAVIOR) occurred in eight situations, but its alternative reactions were more selectively dispersed. The aides' responses of reassuring and remedying, quelling, or relieving tension take place in only three of those eight situations, 5, 12, and 13. These reactions are q (REASSURES AND TRIES TO REMEDY), g (TELLS TO STOP), k (COMPELS TO STOP OR TO DO IT), u (BANTERS), and l (PERMITS) (see Table 10-2). Such reactions strongly imply that those situations are problematic.

It follows that the other situations, whose reactions differ, are not problematic. Situations 3 and 10, for example, followed as they are by a (FULFILLS REQUEST), c (TELLS OR REMINDS TO DO SOMETHING), s (STIPULATES A CONDITION), and n (CARES FOR OR SERVES), and from which reactions for squelching or correcting conduct or for various kinds of informal sociability are excluded, seem predominantly task-centered occasions. Conversely, a review of the reactions that are found almost exclusively in situations 2, 4, and 8, namely b (CONVERSES), f (GREETS), i (PARTICIPATES FULLY), v (PARTICIPATES PARTLY), r (WITHDRAWS), o (ASKS ASSISTANCE), j (SUGGESTS ENTERING ACTIVITY), and h (SUPERVISES ACTIVITY), leads to the conclusion that these situations are preeminently open-ended opportunities for personal interaction.

3. Reaction u (BANTERS) means diverting tension in four of the five situations in which it occurs. Bantering is situationally selective in the two settings. That is, aides do not banter in the same situations in both hospitals (see Table 10-1). Since bantering happens in different situations in the two hospitals, to the extent that reaction u gives connotation to the situations it implies that different situations have the same meaning for aides in the two settings.

Bantering connotes diverting tension, an attempt at relief from vexing matters. Therefore, aides in the two hospitals are tense about different affairs. Private aides become uneasy when their patients make unusual physical gestures or perform a private act in public (see Figure 7-2). They are mostly bothered by their patients' uncommon upsets. State aides are troubled by patients in distress or patients making mischief. They are mostly bothered by their patients' common tumults. No doubt both groups of aides are upset and baffled by other actions of patients as well. But their bantering in these situations implies that these are special problems. How come? Why do different proceedings aggravate the aides in the different hospitals? I will answer these questions in Chapter 13.

Scientific and Lay Understandings

This presentation is at best a partial account of the way laymen establish meanings. I deal solely with the aspect called connotation and do not discuss other aspects, such as nominal, signal, causal, consequential, and moral meanings. The man on the street is not so restricted. He freely resorts to inferences about another's motives, to knowledge of where certain conduct leads, and to what he likes in settling on the significance of an act. Even if my technique were a fair illustration, it does not tell how a person ties connotation to other kinds of meaning.

Behavior semantics gets at meanings based on knowledge of actions. Yet there is a difference between the conclusions reached by researchers and by laymen even within this form. The researcher is equipped with statistical methods and uses a probability sample. He follows rules that remain consistent during his survey and carries out estimations fitted to his explicit assumptions about populations of acts. He takes formal account of complementary and coupled distributions. He performs a neat dissection on the connotation of an act, using transition matrices. Findings of his repeated surveys stand a good chance of being compatible.

The layman employs a more rudimentary version of the technique. His sample of behavior is governed by fortunes that shape his interpersonal opportunities. His classification of events will be erratic because he changes the rules now and then. While he knows that each situation and reaction he confronts is drawn from a set of alternatives, his estimate of their probabilities is contrived from feelings as well as from information strewn in memory. He gives priority to events that are personally important. He does not wait until all the evidence is arranged before he starts interpreting conduct. Just as he falls short of the grammarian in using correct speech, he cannot match the behavior semanticist in systematic interpretations.

We might expect laymen to fare badly in sharing meanings with one another. Their handicaps seem so severe. They have incongruous knowledge because each one's experience is a biased sample. People from divergent backgrounds and upbringing, ages, sexes, occupations, and places of residence put together idiosyncratic act-wholes. Then they process their knowledge sloppily.

The prospects for misunderstanding would be enormous if there were not a big redeeming circumstance. The same categories of conduct are found in many social relationships. Those acts take place on numerous occasions and in far more sets than a determined researcher can deliberately tap and record. Laymen effortlessly accumulate and register all their experiences in their daily rounds. They use this broad-based knowledge in interpreting. The wider base of evidence, the looser symbolic constructions, and the diffused interpretations—all increase the chances for overlap. There is a region of sharing, not a point, in human understanding.

Besides, ordinary folk believe they understand one another because of objective evidence. If the other person's *reaction* fulfills anticipations, his neighbor thinks he comprehends. That is because the first person (who performs the situational behavior, being stimulated by it) imagines a set of probable alternative responses. When he observes that the other's overt conduct is one of the set he evoked mentally, he takes it as sharing meaning.

If the reaction has a high probability, he would be very confident. But since the entire set is in mind, even a less likely alternative would still signal understanding. Spending time with someone and being exposed to situation after situation in which unlikely reactions are employed leaves one with a feeling that here is a person with a basically different outlook from one's own. If the reaction put forth had zero likelihood in that situation, he believes the other person missed the message. Suppose one person brings news of the death of a world-famous leader, and another reacts by saying "Feldspar." The first will suspect a communicative failure. Of course, he might decide that his listener is dissembling, because of other knowledge. This is a valid condition. But it is a complication beyond the scope of connotational meaning. I speak here only of observable clues.

Observable conduct is primary. One type of disconcerting experience for many of us is a relationship with an estimable person whose behavior suddenly ends the myth of sharing. Between good people, it can take some time to happen. The sheer decency of their outlooks and their courteous moods guide them to do predictable nice things for one another. It makes each feel understood, that communication is perfect. One day a simple act reveals a different state of affairs. It does not have to be harmful. Just unexpected. This reaction gives the clue that the other has been thinking along different lines. This creature is no soul mate after all, but a separate person with a distinct logic and feeling. His reactions happened to match one's own so often that an aura of mutual understanding emerged.

This is different from another case in which the reaction is neither desired nor gratifying, yet it connotes shared understanding. Suppose a student whispers to his neighbor during an examination, "I don't know these answers, let me see your paper." If the other student should growl hoarsely, "Leave me alone, you cheat!" he shows a type of reaction likely to be in the set of alternatives. The would-be cheater knows this and believes his message was understood.

Different situations have different numbers of alternatives in their sets, so they allow wider or narrower regions of mutuality. If a man asks what time it is, he does not expect many different reactions. He would feel something was wrong if in return he heard a monologue on the nature of time. If, however, one person speaks to another about love, a large number of reactions including a monologue could be taken to connote understanding. Sometimes a girl is irritated with her boy friend because he keeps insisting on a single-reaction meaning of love.

11

Meaningful Comparisons

⟞⟋⟍

Likeness and difference can be established on several grounds. If one asks how the behavior of the two aide groups is alike and how it diverges, certain comparisons are implied by the structure of acts. The tests should deal with situations, reactions, their probabilities, and meaningful interpretations. In this chapter I will present seven comparisons referring to these aspects of conduct. The first few are primarily quantitative. The remainder are principally qualitative. The quantitative comparisons have lessons beyond their specific findings. One (the second comparison) shows how choice of calculation can affect the outcomes. Another (the third) shows how numbers by themselves can reveal characteristics of behavior. Both numbers and words can be meaningful. It happens that the third and fourth comparisons give hints to the findings of the interpretive analyses that follow them.

Comparison 1: Correlations Between Situations

How alike are the situations encountered by aides? All situations listed in the behavior table (except 26, A patient smiles and his false tooth drops out) happen in both settings. The correlation between rates of occurrence is .66 between the two populations. It is statistically significant, yet low enough to tell of differences in proportions of types of contacts that aides have with patients. Some types of differences are mentioned in Chapter 9.

Comparison 2: Correlations Between Reactions Using Different Baselines

Students of a social scene can be as selective as they wish. They may fix only on dramatic events or on acts they deem to be most vital to mankind. However, such attention will overlook other evidence in the same way that certain information will not be collected if certain questions are not asked. It is therefore instructive to review the implications of different degrees of selectivity in comparing social conduct. I will use the same measurement, the correlation coefficient, in each of the following five examples, but I will apply it in each instance to a different portion of the population of acts. It turns out that the correlation between the two groups is statistically significant ($p < .001$) in all five cases.

1. Sometimes reactions of individuals are matched while situational contexts are ignored. If this were done for the aide groups, the correlation between probabilities of reactions, $\Sigma \, p(r)$, given in Matrices 9-3 and 9-4 would yield a coefficient of .72, declaring a moderate amount of similarity between the two.

2. It is sounder to refer to situations as baselines against which reactions would be compared. The behavior tables permit this step. I correlated the probabilities of all reactions to all situations (all numbers in the cells in Matrices 9-3 and 9-4) and found the coefficient moved up to .75.

3. Even more similarity is disclosed if the probabilities of all acts, simple or compound, are compared. This is the most natural basis for comparison since it deals with full, intact representations of observable events. The value of the coefficient, calculated from the entries for $p(S)p(R)$ in Table 9-1, is .78.

4. A stronger correlation is suggested if modal behavior alone is taken into account and less frequent actions ignored. One form of the mode is the most probable reaction in each situation after acts have been decomposed into reaction components. For example, the modal reaction in situation 1 for both hospitals is *a,* and this refers to its appearance in acts 1-*a* and 1-*p*-*a*. A comparison of modal reactions from Matrices 9-3 and 9-4 yields a coefficient of .81.

5. The strongest correlation is asserted if only modal acts are compared. The modal act is the most likely response, simple or compound, indicated

by the figures in the p(R) columns for each situation in Table 9-1. For example, the modal act in situation 1 in both hospitals is 1-*a* (the appearance of reaction *a* in act 1-*p-a* is not considered). Where a discrepancy existed between the modal acts in the two hospitals, I chose the reaction that occurs more often in the situation, summing each reaction across hospitals and taking the one of higher frequency. In seven situations this procedure resulted in the choice of one hospital's mode four times and the other hospital's mode three times. The correlation between modal acts is .83.

Do aides in both hospitals behave similarly toward patients? The correlations say yes, regardless of which of the five perspectives one applies. The similarity varies according to the emphasis given to situational contexts and to the most frequent acts. In any case the resemblance is strong enough to vouch for the two populations being versions of the same repertoire.

This handful of comparisons shows how different knowledge can be generated by selective attention. To focus on only the most frequent actions may result in depicting groups as more similar than they are throughout. To compare only reactions without considering contexts may result in understating the similarity between groups.

The nature of the difference between aides in the two institutions is revealed by the fact that their behavior with patients is more alike if compared within situations than if those contexts are overlooked. Apparently the two groups differ from one another mildly but in the same way in situation after situation. The accumulation of these mild disparities erodes the overall similarity between them.

Comparison 3: Variety in Reactions

Table 9-2 shows that state hospital aides combine reactions into compound acts much more than do private aides. This prompts a question about which group shows more behavioral diversity overall. Whatever the answer, of course, it will not imply that each individual aide in that setting exhibits more variety in his conduct than any aide in the other hospital.

When acts are decomposed, as in Matrices 9-3 and 9-4, eighty-two cells in Matrix 9-3 (private hospital) have probabilities other than zero, whereas in Matrix 9-4 (state hospital) there are eighty-six such cells. This crude tally can be refined by dividing it by the number of situations in the population. Applied to the private hospital, this measurement is $82 \div 26 = 3.15$, where 82 is the number of different acts (r) and 26 is the number of different situations. For the state hospital it is $86 \div 25 = 3.44$. The average variety of acts, simple (r) or compound (R), is another form of this measure. There are on the average 3.35 different acts per situation in the private hospital and 3.96 per situation in the state setting.

Another useful measure of variety in behavior is the average number of equiprobable acts per situation (where two or more acts are equiprobable if their p(R)s are within .005 of one another). This measure considers the relative frequency of reactions as well as the different types used. Its denominator is the number of situations in the population, and its numerator is the total number of acts tied in probabilities.

In the private hospital there are seven situations (4, 7, 11, 14, 15, 19, and 22) having two alternatives tied in probability and two situations (1 and 20) in which three alternatives are equiprobable (see Table 9-1). By this formula the private aides show a $20 \div 26 = .77$ average of equiprobable acts per situation, where 26 is the number of different situations and 20 is the sum of the number of tied reactions (R). In the state setting there are eight situations (3, 5, 7, 11, 12, 13 [two pairs], 17, and 22 [two pairs]) in which two alternatives are equally likely, two situations (8 and 14) having three ties each, one (18) having four equiprobable reactions, and one (5) in which five alternatives are tied. So the average of equiprobable acts is $35 \div 25 = 1.40$ per situation for that population. More state aides' reactions have the same likelihoods, an average of 1.40 equiprobable acts compared to only .77 in the private institution.

These measures show that the aide repertoire with patients is generally more restricted in the private hospital. The state group shows more diverse and complex conduct. I will discuss the import of this difference in Chapter 13.

Comparison 4: Troubling Situations

This comparison comes from the main interpretation of reaction u (BANTERS) as diverting tension. Since this bantering takes place in different situations in each hospital, it implies that different situations are tension-producing for the two groups of aides. Private aides are bothered by patients who make unusual physical gestures or who perform ordinarily private acts in public. State aides are bothered by patients who show ordinary forms of distress or who make mischief. I will also discuss the significance of this in Chapter 13.

This string of comparisons still does not satisfy a commanding question about behavioral similarity and difference. We want more than enumerations. We want understanding. Is the conduct of aides toward patients meaningfully equivalent in the two hospitals? Correlation coefficients by themselves do not tell. If the two act-populations are versions of the same repertoire, in what ways are they versions rather than exact copies of each other?

In the remainder of this chapter I will attempt meaningful interpretations in order to answer this question. I will be concerned with connotations of acts and will not explain what causes them. Describing and understanding behavior at this stage will be the background for my try, in Chapters 13 and 14, to uncover the causes at work.

Although I plan to compare the total relationship and will consider all reactions in the repertoire, I can gain precision by dealing with a portion of the act-population at one time. In this way fewer situations are involved. The dispersion of reactions among situations is more limited. Particular meanings will be less obscured by the welter of potential connotations in an entire repertoire. So I will study little ensembles of whole acts. In the course of proposing that situations which share the same reactions have meanings in common, I located three coherent ensembles. Their themes are open-ended interpersonal opportunities, problematic situations, and routine task-centered contacts. In Chapter 10 I also carried out some interpretations of situations and of reactions. Here I shall refer to those instances and extend them. I will not report all details of my assessments, but I will outline the grounds for them enough to show how they follow the reasoning offered in the preceding chapter.

After deciding on meanings in an ensemble, I will compare the probabilities of those acts in the two populations. In doing so I will accept as worthy of note any form of meaningful conduct that would occur less than once in five times ($p < .20$) by chance. This cutoff point may not be stringent enough for readers accustomed to significance levels for which the chance happening would be less than once in twenty times ($p < .05$) or less than once in a hundred times ($p < .01$) in order to accept the findings.

The reasons for my more liberal criterion are the following. Many projects in social research focus on a single test or on a few tests, so the level of statistical significance for each test becomes critical to the entire investigation. In my analysis I will not only interpret each finding by itself but also as part of a pattern. A pattern of seven findings will be reported here, and over two dozen more will be reported in Chapter 13. Some are not so statistically significant as others. But they are theoretically eminent by virtue of their participation in the pattern. One would be foolish to dwell enthusiastically on an outcome that is statistically very significant but flanked by several contradictory findings. Similarly, it would be unwise to ignore an outcome having a chance probability of less than once in five times ($p < .20$) if it is meaningfully compatible with a set of findings at more stringent levels of significance. In evaluating a set of findings, I will consider the pattern confirming an idea or the lack of such a configuration. Moreover, my meaningful comparisons will treat sets of dependent and non-mutually exclusive types of events. The theoretical probability for such sets is smaller (hence more likely to be statistically significant) than the sum of the probabilities of the separate types of events. Finally, my comparisons are exploratory. I am open to whatever can be learned from them. It would be wasteful to overlook a suggestive finding that accompanies other findings just because its particular outcome is likely more than once in twenty but less than once in five times ($.05 < p < .20$) by chance. Social conduct is enigmatic enough to warrant attention to every clue.

Comparison 5: Open-ended Interpersonal Opportunities

One flock of situations has occasions for informal contacts between patients and aides as its manifest content. They pass each other in the corridors or meet on the hospital grounds (2). Contact opportunities arise at recreation, such as playing indoor or outdoor games (6) or at parties and picnics (7), or in the context of work, as when aides are engaged in ward tasks and patients are nearby (8). There are also inactive circumstances when aides and patients are on the wards and the former are free of immediate chores (9). There is also that universal social give-and-take, conversation, oftentimes initiated by patients (4). These six situations make up 33.8 percent of the private hospital act-population and 44.2 percent of the state hospital act-population. Are there meaningful contrasts in the conduct of the two aide groups in these situations?

It is simpler to interpret elementary reactions rather than single and compound acts in populations where so few compound acts appear. These situations contain a limited number of elementary reactions—thirteen in all. They are dispersed in a way that permits subjecting them to the technique of behavior semantics.

Most of these reactions appear several times among the sets, and most of them are in complementary or coupled distribution. The trio d (SHOWS NO OVERT CHANGE IN BEHAVIOR), e (LEAVES THEM TO THEMSELVES), and r (WITHDRAWS) is in complementary distribution throughout the population, as in these six situations. Reaction r is coupled with d in situation 4 and with e in situation 6 in the private hospital, but these couplings reflect varieties of the situations rather than differences between the reactions. If the aide is already engaged in conversation or recreation with patients, he withdraws (r). If he is given the opportunity to participate, he leaves them to themselves (e).

Groups of other alternatives suggest that $d, e,$ and r comprise a meaningful trio. Specifically, reactions v (PARTICIPATES PARTLY), m (BRIEFLY AGREES OR DISAGREES), and f (GREETS) form another almost perfect complementary distribution (see Table 10-4). And v is always coupled with r.

The contrasts between these two trios and interpretations already made help establish their meanings, interpretations that justify rendering r along with d and e. Of the three possible meanings for reaction d that I established from analyzing its dispersion among alternatives throughout the population, the one that fits best here is that of *aloofness*. These six situations do not focus on schedules or services. They are not centered on manifestations of illness. Nor are they chiefly problematic or rowdy. Here aides may interact with patients, but they are not obliged to do so because of routine duty or in order to stop trouble. The situations are informal and do not call for specific conduct by aides. The alternatives in three of these situations (2, 4, and 8) were the very ones I used to establish that d connotes interpersonal reserve. Here the connotation is extended by the fact that the same patterns of alternatives appear in situations 6, 7, and 9. They imply that e and r signify avoidance and escape from dealing with patients and that the three reactions are variants of aloofness.

This interpretation is buttressed by the content and qualities of the alternatives. One alternative trio is the aforementioned $f, m,$ and v. In the same situations these reactions include at least some positive interaction with patients. Instead of overlooking or retreating from opportunities, $f, v,$ and m betoken mild fraternization. Greeting upon meeting (2-f), playing the game (6-v), and murmuring comments in conversation (4-m) stand in contrast to aloofness in these contexts. Yet this trio is not full-fledged sociability. These gestures reflect courtesy and doing the decent thing rather than treating patients as chums. An apt term for this pattern is *amenity*, a manner found in smooth and pleasant social intercourse.

The alternatives that help fix the meaning of f, m, and v as amenity in these situations are b (CONVERSES) and i (PARTICIPATES FULLY). This pair is in perfect complementary distribution. Reaction b appears in 2, 4, and 9 while i occurs in 6, 7, and 8. As alternatives they are acts of fellowship, such as stopping to chat upon meeting (2-b), singing and dancing with patients at parties (7-i), and so on. The camaraderie of these acts is affirmed by their contrast to the two above-mentioned trios, and here reactions b and i mean *friendliness*.

Of the other five reactions in these sets, four of them, c (TELLS OR REMINDS TO DO SOMETHING), j (SUGGESTS ENTERING ACTIVITY), h (SUPERVISES ACTIVITY), and p (TEACHES OR CORRECTS), have been identified in a mostly complementary and partially coupled distribution (Table 10-4). Here they are more often coupled than not. Although this coupling implies that they are not substitutes for one another, they appear to be gradations of a meaningful dimension that reflect individual differences or situational variation. I chose to interpret them together in the light of the other alternatives already considered. The situations are commonplace, neither narrowly focused nor expressly problematic. In those contexts, the acts of reminding a patient to keep a doctor's appointment (2-c), bidding patients to enter into recreation (6-j, 7-j, 8-j, 9-j), supervising their movements (7-h and 8-h), and correcting their play (6-p) are a composite of superintendency that is conspicuous in a relationship like that of a camp counselor with his campers. He activates and guides his boys. The actions also resemble those of a mother who tells her children to make their beds (2-c), to move elsewhere so that she may clean a room (8-h), and what television program they may watch (9-h) and who tries to involve them in activities if they are just sitting around ("Why don't you go out and play?") (6-j, 8-j, and 9-j). Authority is expressed, control is exerted, but it is more regulatory than dominating. Because of the partly coupled distribution, the meaning of this cluster is broader than those already interpreted. As an alternative to aloofness, amenity, and friendliness in these situations, the c-h-j-p quartet connotes *directiveness* on the part of the aides.

Reaction o (ASKS ASSISTANCE) remains. Considering situation 8 (An aide is working on the ward and some patients are nearby), some may think this reaction is another form of supervision, of getting patients to do work, and that it therefore belongs with the reactions meaning directiveness. But although o is more likely to occur in situation 8, it makes its appearance in situations 2 and 4 as well. Assistance can be emotional, financial, physical, and so on. The specific content of reaction o furthers this impression. Although an aide may be forceful in enlisting patients when he is working on the ward (8-*o*), it need not mean he is bossy. Patients know that favors can be garnered from aides if they help them in their work. The exchange is rarely manipulative skullduggery on the part of either aide or patient. It is a common type of reciprocity. Youngsters know they can win favors from their parents by washing the supper dishes or mowing the lawn. Parents and children often bargain explicitly about such assistance when permission to stay out late is at stake. Taking into account the three situations in which *o* is enacted, and its alternatives, this reaction is not directiveness. It is relying upon the other for help. Since the aide appeals to the patient for information (2-*o*), for advice and sympathy (4-*o*), and for help with chores (8-*o*), I interpreted reaction *o* as signifying *dependence*.

Table 11-1 contains information extracted from Matrices 9-3 and 9-4 for these reactions in these situations. The presence of connotations in this ensemble can be directly compared as proportions by setting the events from each population equal to 1.000. The two rows immediately below the data give the relative proportions of the grouped reactions occurring in the ensemble, and they are followed by the results of tests of the significance of difference between members of each pair of proportions. These show some statistically significant and meaningful differences between the two populations.

Aides in the private hospital are much more aloof with patients than are aides in the state hospital. The latter, on the other hand, are far more directive with patients. The private aide is likely to avoid interaction with patients, either by not initiating contacts (reactions *d* and *e*) or by not sustaining them (*r*). He does not usually ask patients to help him, nor does he often tell, remind, teach, correct, supervise, or encourage his patients to enter into activities (*c, j, h, p*). It is curious that the private aide should be about equally aloof and friendly toward patients. It seems to be a contradiction, but it is easily explained. I will postpone the explanation because the accounting itself discloses something fundamental about act-populations—a property whose nature I will expound in Chapter 13. In that discussion I will deal with this aloofness-sociability contradiction in the behavior of private hospital aides.

Given the same choices in the same situations, the state hospital aide does not often avoid interaction with patients. He is more likely to be directive, both inviting them to engage in certain activities and telling them how to engage in those activities, and he is likely to be as friendly as he is directive. There is no significant difference in friendliness between the two aide groups.

The population of acts in the private hospital is roundly 257 (see Table 9-1), while at the state hospital it is roundly 280. The greater directorship in the latter population confirms a finding about human interaction reported by Borgatta and Bales. Individuals who interact at a higher rate than others also provide more orientation, opinions, and suggestions to others. More acts are contained in the state hospital population, and greater directiveness in conduct is found there as well.

A clear trend, though not statistically significant, adds to the contrast between the aloof aides and the directive ones. The latter also appear to be more dependent upon patients (see *o* in Table 11-1). State aides dominate their patients, but they also call upon them for help. The private aides, on the other hand, keep more apart from patients and neither direct nor depend on them very much.

It has been common in studies of behavior to define themes of action as opposites in use. One either dominates or submits. One either loves ("expresses positive feelings") or hates (". . . negative feelings"), and so on. That orientation still persists here and there in analyses of behavior. Perhaps it hangs on because it is convenient to treat people as pure types. But a categorical outlook does not reflect the way people actually behave. Such extremist thinking permits the formulation of simple and encompassing hypotheses about the nature of social relationships. "You wouldn't do that to me if you loved me!" the child exclaims, to which the parent replies, "I'm punishing you *because* I love you!" Children are not alone in misinterpreting other's actions. Parents declare "Good little boys don't do that!" when it is obvious that good little boys do. Findings of a study by Bales and Strodtbeck indirectly corrected this misconception. They found that people participating in discussion groups moved through a series of phases in the course of resolving a problem. In one phase they both gave *and* asked for many opinions and directions; in a later phase they expressed both positive *and* negative feelings. The supposed opposites occur mutually in the course of interaction in problem-solving groups, and mutual directiveness and dependence also characterize the relationship between the state hospital's aides and patients.

I realize that I am inquiring into differences between two populations that are alike. According to the correlations reported in comparison 2, the two are pale but distinct images of one another. With this in mind it is understandable that some differences may show up as trends and not be

Table 11-1. Fifth comparison of behavior in the two settings

Reactions:

		Aloofness						Amenity						Friendliness			
		SHOWS NO OVERT CHANGE IN BEHAVIOR		LEAVES THEM TO THEMSELVES		WITHDRAWS		PARTICIPATES PARTLY		BRIEFLY AGREES OR DISAGREES		GREETS		CONVERSES		PARTICIPATES FULLY	
		d		e		r		v		m		f		b		i	
		P^a	S	P	S	P	S	P	S	P	S	P	S	P	S	P	S
Situa-	2	12	14									30	42	7	47		
tions	4	8				20	8	4	2	16	8			57	25		
	6			9		7	2	6	7							36	19
	7			12	20							10	16			3	15
	8	6	3													4	9
	9			30	31									4	7		
	Σ	26	17	51	51	27	10	10	9	16	8	40	58	68	79	43	43

	Aloofness	Amenity	Friendliness
Private	.308	.195	.328
State	.176	.170	.276
Z^b	2.23	.47	.81
	p < .03		

^{a}P = private hospital; S = state hospital.

^{b}Two-tailed test.

^{c}Data not ascertained in the private hospital is 3 percent and in the state hospital .7 percent. This would not affect the outcome where the private hospital shows the larger proportion. I

Table 11-1. (continued)

	Directiveness			Dependence		
TELLS OR REMINDS TO DO SOMETHING	SUPERVISES ACTIVITY	SUGGESTS ENTERING ACTIVITY	TEACHES OR CORRECTS	ASKS ASSISTANCE	NOT ASCERTAINED	
c	h	j	p	o	NA	Σ
P S	P S	P S	P S	P S	P S	P S
6 23				9	8 3	63 138
				4		109 43
		4 7	5 15		2	69 50
	10 16	4 10				39 77
	2 23	5 5	3	7 32		24 75
	2	19				34 59
6 23	12 41	13 41	5 18	11 41	10 3	338 442
	.106			.033	.030^c	= 1.000
	.278			.093	.007	= 1.000
	3.02			1.72		
	p < .01			p < .09		

rechecked the tests for c-h-j-p and for o, assigning each hospital's amount of error (NA) to its proportions. The difference between the two groups on Dependence is then at the .34 level of significance, and for Directiveness it remains beyond the .01 level.

statistically significant. I will accept such trends as meaningful but not decisive in themselves and will further investigate the two act-populations. There may be additional trends as well as clear differences. This added information will constitute a pattern and afford a broader base for drawing conclusions.

Comparison 6: Problematic Situations

Given that private aides are reserved with patients and that state aides unreservedly supervise patients, what else characterizes the relationships? Another subset whose situations share reactions is that consisting of numbers 5, 11, 12, 13, 15, 17, 18, 19, 20, 21, and 22. They include common forms of distress (11), rowdiness (13), and complaining (12) on the part of patients, uncommon forms of verbal (5) and physical (18) gestures, performing ordinarily private acts in public (21), and violating regular hospital schedules (17) and boundaries (15).

These occasions are not the familiar and easy contact opportunities of everyday life. But they are important in the aide-patient relationship. Some of them embody the crux of the patient's condition—emotional stress and suffering and instances of bizarre conduct. Here grief, disorientation, and incapacity are disclosed. If there is a difference between the two groups of aides in reacting to these situations, it will bespeak differences in their therapeutic efforts.

The eleven situations comprise 31.6 percent of the population in the private hospital and 26.7 percent of that in the state hospital. That is, about 81 and 75 acts respectively are referred to in these two subpopulations. Fourteen different reactions follow these situations. The range of their occurrence is shown in Table 11-2.

Some of the interpretations for this comparison have already been carried out. My analysis of u (BANTERS) considered its appearance in four of these situations (11, 12, 18, and 21). The core of its meaning is diverting tension when its alternatives are d (SHOWS NO OVERT CHANGE IN BEHAVIOR), l (PERMITS), g (TELLS TO STOP), and k (COMPELS TO STOP OR TO DO IT) (Table 10-1). One of the three meanings inferred for reaction d, that of indifference, is based on its appearance in situations 5, 12, and 13 (Table 10-2).

Applying these understandings, I grouped d (SHOWS NO OVERT CHANGE IN BEHAVIOR), l (PERMITS), and x (PERMITS UNDER A CONDITION) as signifying *indifference* in these situations. Except for d with l in situation 13 in the state hospital, the three are in complementary distribution. These reactions connote indifference because of such alternatives as *u* and *m* (BRIEFLY AGREES OR DISAGREES), to which I gave the connotation *sufferance*. The passive aspect of *m* led me to this rendering. This refinement between two kinds of allowing did not affect the population comparisons. Whether the five reactions are treated in the two above-mentioned groups or taken together, the proportions of occurrence are obviously similar.

Reactions *g* (TELLS TO STOP) and *k* (COMPELS TO STOP OR TO DO IT) appear in coupled distribution. Although these convey a difference in degree, I kept them together for reasons already given in Chapter 10. In these situations, contrasted with indifference, sufferance, and other themes, *g* and *k* connote *prohibition* that ranges from stern admonishment to forcible restraint. I did make a distinction, however, between compelling to stop and compelling to do something. The latter is not purely a move to suppress the patient's behavior but to change it. In situation 11 (A patient is in distress), the aide compels a drunk patient to stay awake in order to prevent him from lapsing into a coma. In situation 17 (A patient delays or resists doing a required activity), patients are compelled to get out of bed or to eat. These seem different from the policing actions of catching a wandering patient and leading him back to his group (15-*k*) or preventing a prankster from going further (13-*k*). The disparity is between curbing an activity and *redirecting* it. The latter connotation applies to reaction *k* in situations 11 and 17 and to reactions *j* (SUGGESTS ENTERING ACTIVITY) and *p* (TEACHES OR CORRECTS), which also occur in these situations. Reactions *j* and *p* meant directiveness in the first comparison (Table 11-1). Their connotation changes somewhat in aligning them here with instances of *k* (COMPELS TO DO IT).

As usual, such a grouping of alternatives and development of intepretation will be affected by the remaining acts to be understood. There are two other reactions that go further than the mere redirection of patients' behavior in coping with these problem situations. Instances of caring for patients (*n*) or reassuring and trying to remedy matters (*q*) differ from redirecting because they are overt attempts to solve the problem itself rather than merely to substitute another situation for it. For example, upon seeing a patient walking about naked, an aide helped him dress (21-*n*). (Let me be specific about how to understand act 21-*n*-*k*. The aide saw a patient undressed. He secured his clothes and dressed him. Then the patient began undressing himself and the aide made him stop. The probability for this compound act was apportioned between the two reactions

Table 11-2. Sixth comparison of behavior in the two settings

Reactions: (Situations)	SHOWS NO OVERT CHANGE IN BEHAVIOR (d) P[a]	S	PERMITS (l) P	S	PERMITS UNDER A CONDITION (x) P	S	BRIEFLY AGREES OR DISAGREES (m) P	S	BANTERS (u) P	S	TELLS TO STOP (g) P	S	COMPELS TO STOP (k)[b] P	S
(Indifference)							(Sufferance)				(Prohibition)			
S 5	29	23					8	13			24	5		
i 11										3		3		
t 12	15	8					17	3						
u 13		6	15	13						10		15		2
a 15				5	7						11	7	6	12
t 17			2	9										
i 18			3	2					14		10	4		3
o 19			4	9										
n 20			3										8	3
s 21									2		15	6	4	2
22						2					1	7	3	5
Σ	44	37	27	38	7	2	25	16	16	13	61	47	21	27
Private				.247						.130		.259		
State				.288						.109		.277		
Z^d				.59						.40		.26		

[a] P = private hospital; S = state hospital.
[b] In situations 13, 15, 18, 20, 21, and 22.
[c] In situations 11 and 17.
[d] Two-tailed test.
[e] If data not ascertained (NA) is assigned to Help theme for private hospital aides

Table 11-2. (continued)

		Redirection					Help				Communication						Σ	
SUGGESTS ENTERING ACTIVITY		TEACHES OR CORRECTS		COMPELS TO DO IT		CARES FOR OR SERVES		REASSURES AND TRIES TO REMEDY		GREETS		CONVERSES		ASKS WHAT IS THE MATTER		NOT ASCERTAINED			
j		p		k[c]		n		q		f		b		w		NA			
P	S	P	S	P	S	P	S	P	S	P	S	P	S	P	S	P	S	P	S
			4						3			11				4		65	59
				2	8			20	20				8					30	34
									3							18		50	14
																		15	46
																		24	24
9	3			7	14											18		18	26
2	3									4								33	12
14	6													5		4		27	15
		12											3	3				29	3
																		21	10
						2			5						5			4	24
25	12	12	4	9	22	2		20	31	4		11	11	8	5	26		316	267
		.146						.063				.073				.082[e]		= 1.000	
		.142						.124				.060						= 1.000	
		.07						1.33				.33							
								p < .19											

(see Table 11–1, footnote c), there is no significant difference between the two groups.

by the method of decomposition described in Chapter 9.) When a patient complained about some condition of life in the hospital, an aide tried to correct the condition (12-*q*). When a patient was crying and upset, an aide did not merely stop the crying or distract the patient but tried to soothe him and made suggestions about what might be done (11-*q*). These attempts to improve situations in ways directly relevant to their problematic character signify *helping*.

The challenges to fathoming acts are like those in classification. There is room for disagreement about interpretation just as there is about categorization. It is easy to be doubtful about specific decisions if they are considered by themselves. But heeding the entire ensemble affects one's perspective. Bearing in mind every alternative in these situations, you can plausibly allocate the reactions discussed in the preceding paragraphs to the motifs of prohibition, redirection, and help.

The other reactions, *b* (CONVERSES), *f* (GREETS), and *w* (ASKS WHAT IS THE MATTER), that occur in the situations form a meaningful group. It contrasts with the connotations of other clusters while having its own overt properties. These involve utilizing sensory access to patients, yet they provide no clue that the situation is thereby being changed, improved, worsened, or even permitted to continue. Reaction *w* is often used as a therapeutic gesture. To interpret it so here would require assuming that beneficial consequences follow from such queries, but no information about its consequences is available in this study. In other studies the evidence for its clinical effectiveness is mixed with evidence for the clinical effectiveness of psychotherapy in general. That, in turn, is an inconclusive matter at present and lends no support to the assumption that asking someone what is the matter is in itself helpful. Accordingly, I classed *w* with *b* and *f* and interpreted them as *communication*. The vagueness of these three reactions is significant in contrast to other alternatives. Aides are confronted with the pangs of mental disorder, the everyday aggravations, and the annoyances of life in an institution. In times of perplexity many aides may find indifference or sufferance or prohibition or redirection or their efforts to help inadequate. They do not know what to do but they are concerned. Instead of immediately seizing upon a positive line of action when they are uncertain, they grope toward it through communicating with the patients. Notwithstanding social scientists' and pollsters' repeated conclusions that men often use speech to conceal their thoughts, unsophisticated people may talk to one another in the belief that it opens man to man.

Table 11-2 shows no statistically significant differences between the two groups in their reactions to patients in problematic situations. A trend appears in one instance. State hospital aides have a somewhat greater disposition to help patients (p < .19). The large error factor for the private hospital, resulting from loss of some field notes after their contents were classified as situation 12, would undermine anything more than a mild significance accorded this trend by itself. However, it joins a pattern for state aides who are more directive and dependent and for private aides who are more aloof. Perhaps it will be buttressed when further findings are unearthed.

Comparison 7: Routine Task-Centered Contacts

The two comparisons have so far dealt with 65.4 percent of the act-population at the private hospital and with 70.9 percent of that at the state hospital. The bunchings I have given situations are not the only plausible assortment. For example, situation 3 (It is time for a scheduled activity) has four reactions in common with situation 2 (An aide and a patient pass each other or meet). However, the low probability of b (CONVERSES) in situation 3, which reaction appears only in the state setting, and the high probability of n (CARES FOR OR SERVES) in 3 while being absent from 2, as well as the qualitative content of situation 3, led me to exclude 3 from the fifth comparison. It does have a suitable place in a quartet of situations that also includes 1 (A patient requests an item or service or information), 10 (A patient asks to be let off the ward or to use the telephone), and 14 (Patients are eating in the dining room). These are routine occasions for contact opportunities between aides and patients. They comprise 25.6 percent of the act-population in the private institution and 25.8 percent of the population in the state institution. However, the reactions are not so thoroughly shared among these situations. In the fifth comparison (Table 11-1) thirteen reactions occurred in both hospitals in those situations, and there were no alternatives that were part of only one population. In the sixth comparison only two reactions (f and n in Table 11-2) out of fourteen were not found in both populations. In contrast, there are five reactions, b (CONVERSES), d (SHOWS NO OVERT CHANGE IN BEHAVIOR), h (SUPERVISES ACTIVITY), o (ASKS ASSISTANCE), and u (BANTERS) out of the thirteen occurring in these four situations that are part of one but not both populations. Such selectivity implies differences. It also makes the consolidation of categories harder and the interpretation of meaning flimsier. By virtue of their distributions I settled on interpretations for four clusters of reactions and left the others (two of which are found in only one population) undefined.

Again I was able to use my earlier analysis of reaction d (SHOWS NO OVERT CHANGE IN BEHAVIOR) as a keystone. In situations 3 and 10 I interpreted this conduct as resting or postponing work in idle moments of routine affairs, rather than as the aloofness or indifference that it meant in other contexts. Reaction e (LEAVES THEM TO THEMSELVES), which appears instead of d in situation 14, can be construed in the same way. I labeled the meaning of both reactions as *lounging*.

That connotation is buttressed by the fact that the most likely alternatives are a (FULFILLS REQUEST) and n (CARES FOR OR SERVES). These reactions have slightly different implications in the several situations. Reaction a is used when patients initiate a request (situations 1 and 10). Reaction n in situation 14 refers mainly to waiting on tables while patients are dining, whereas in situation 3 it refers mainly to helping feeble and incompetent persons get cleaned and dressed. In situations 1, 10, and 14 the actions of opening doors, providing needed articles, and bringing food trays to tables are so much the conduct of a valet in attendance that I separated the caring-for aspect of n in situation 3 and interpreted n in situation 14 along with a as connoting *service* to patients.

Reactions c (TELLS OR REMINDS TO DO SOMETHING), h (SUPERVISES ACTIVITY), p (TEACHES OR CORRECTS), and s (STIPULATES A CONDITION) again appear to be directive. In these contexts, even more than in the first ensemble studied (Table 11-1), such actions have the quality of assuming responsibility for the details of daily existence for people who live in an institution. With reaction j (SUGGESTS ENTERING ACTIVITY) missing from the quartet that appeared in the first comparison, and s manifest in its place, these alternatives connote more regulative than activating behavior, and in comparison with the tenor of lounging and service I took them to mean *supervision*.

Against the themes of lounging, service, and supervision, b (CONVERSES) and f (GREETS) bespeak infusing a personal tone in routine contexts. I construed such actions on the part of aides to reflect their *sociability* with patients. I use the word *sociable* here rather than the more powerful import of the word *friendly*, because f (GREETS) had been considered an amenity in the fifth comparison and was not grouped with b in Table 11-1. The two meanings are close.

The remaining reactions, o (ASKS ASSISTANCE), t (REFUSES), and u

(BANTERS), were not shared across situations, and I treated them as residual alternatives in this comparison.

Table 11-3 contains the array of pertinent data. It reveals two significant differences between the act-populations as well as a trend. The strong findings are that the private hospital aides provide more service to their patients, while—as might be expected from the pattern already unearthed—the state hospital aides provide more supervision.

The trend shown in Table 11-3 is pertinent in the light of the other trends that are present. State hospital aides, who in the fifth comparison were more prone to depend on patients and in the sixth comparison showed a tendency to help patients in trouble, here show a greater proclivity than their private hospital counterparts to be sociable toward patients. More about these trends soon.

Recapitulation

In all, 91 percent of the private hospital act-population and 96.7 percent of the state population have been compared in the three ensembles. I have stayed close to the evidence in carrying out the semantic analysis, relying on neither bold inferences nor auxiliary information from the survey that was not included in the behavior table. While other themes are woven into these relationships, as are other potential meanings of the aides' behavior, this analysis permits two general conclusions to be drawn about the act-populations.

First, there is a repertoire for psychiatric aides with patients that appears in different settings. The significant correlations found between the two populations of acts (comparison 2) testify to the similarity between them. It is clear from comparisons 5, 6, and 7 that private hospital aides are not without sociability or concern or directiveness in their dealings with patients. Nor are state aides exempt from aloofness or from giving service. Some situations not included in the comparisons, such as 16 (Some patients are on their way from one place to another), 24 (Someone comes to the ward for a patient), and 25 (A new patient is on the ward), are ones in which only one reaction was used, the same in both hospitals. The uniformity of conduct in these situations adds to the resemblance between the two populations of acts.

Second, given a repertoire found in many settings, there can be significant qualitative differences among its local act-populations. People in different institutions make different choices among the options available to

Table 11-3. Seventh comparison of behavior in the two settings

Reaction categories (with column letters):

Lounging: *d* = SHOWS NO OVERT CHANGE IN BEHAVIOR; *e* = LEAVES THEM TO THEMSELVES; *n*[b] = CARES FOR OR SERVES

Service: *a* = FULFILLS REQUEST

Supervision: *c* = TELLS OR REMINDS TO DO SOMETHING; *h* = SUPERVISES ACTIVITY; *p* = TEACHES OR CORRECTS; *s* = STIPULATES A CONDITION

		d P[a]	*d* S	*e* P	*e* S	*n*[b] P	*n* S	*a* P	*a* S	*c* P	*c* S	*h* P	*h* S	*p* P	*p* S	*s* P	*s* S
Situa-	1							94	74					4	12		
tions	3	3								29	78						
	10	5						40	8	3	3					21	5
	14			3	10	15	5					8					
	Σ	8		3	10	15	5	134	82	32	81	8		4	12	21	5
Private				.043					.582					.223			
State				.039					.337					.411			
	Z[d]			.12					2.88					2.38			
									p < .01					p < .02			

[a] P = private hospital; S = state hospital.
[b] In situation 14.
[c] In situation 3.
[d] Two-tailed test.

Table 11-3. (continued)

Sociability

GREETS		CONVERSES		REFUSES		ASKS ASSISTANCE		BANTERS		CARES FOR OR SERVES		Σ	
f		*b*		*t*		*o*		*u*		*n^c*		Σ	
P	S	P	S	P	S	P	S	P	S	P	S	P	S
				18	14			2				118	100
			3				4			16	24	48	109
												69	16
3	10											21	33
3	10		3	18	14	4		2		16	24	256	258
	.012				.070				.008		.062	= 1.000	
	.050				.054		.016				.093	= 1.000	
	1.29												
	$p < .20$												

them in the same situations. So a dualism of similar-yet-different may be manifest between instances of a repertoire. Had individuals been studied rather than social positions, the result could have taken this form. Individuals are similar yet different, enabling us to understand them in general while appreciating their personal qualities.

In the case studied here, private hospital aides have a decided edge in aloofness toward patients and in providing services for them. State hospital aides, on the other hand, surpass in supervising and in asking for assistance. However, the superintendency of state hospital aides is not unrelenting authoritarianism. Instead it is imbued with care and personal involvement. The three trends of dependence, help, and sociability reveal this. While they are not statistically significant and might not signify much if treated individually, the three are telling in the overall pattern of findings.

The parental tone of the state hospital aides' relationship with patients is caught in situation 1 as well as anywhere. The ratio of fulfilling or refusing patients' requests is the same in both hospitals. The slight difference in the probabilities is due to the state aides' not bantering with patients (u) and their clearly greater penchant for TEACHES OR CORRECTS (p)—trying to get the patients to ask nicely. Another reaction that expresses the quality of the state aides' relationship with patients is o (ASKS ASSISTANCE). The state aide asks one patient where another patient is ($2\text{-}o$), asks a patient to tell others that it is time for an activity ($3\text{-}o$), and asks patients nearby to help him in his housework ($8\text{-}o$). The private hospital aide is less involved in housework on the ward. Situation 8 (An aide is working on the ward and some patients are nearby) happens one-third as often in the private hospital. In the private hospital, aside from situation 8, assistance was sought on only one other occasion, when an aide began telling a patient of his own troubles ($4\text{-}b\text{-}o$). In situation after situation the state aides appear more like mothers or camp counselors than like bossy guards. Their relationship with patients contains an ample amount of reciprocity.

In fact the keeper-of-the-keys aspect of guarding is more applicable in the private hospital. Situation 10 (A patient asks to be let off the ward) undoubtedly occurs four times more often there because more of its wards are kept locked (see Table 6-1, footnote a). While the state hospital aide sometimes gives up being a sentinel, the private aide never does entirely. Compare their reactions to situation 15 (A patient is not where he is supposed to be) in Table 9-1. Overall, state aides compel patients more than do their private hospital counterparts (4.9 percent versus 3.0 percent), but they are also more permissive (3.8 percent versus 2.7 percent).

(See Matrices 9-3 and 9-4 for these comparisons.) The bulk of the excess in state aides' use of reaction k (COMPELS) occurs in situations 11 (A patient is in distress) and 17 (A patient delays or resists doing a required activity), in which they compel patients *to do* something. The majority of the private aides' use of reaction k is to compel patients *to stop doing* something. Overall, private aides exhibit more than twice as much spoken prohibition (g) as permissiveness (l). In the state hospital, permitting a situation to continue (l) is almost as likely as telling patients to stop (g).

The cumulative impression gleaned from these analyses is that the private hospital aides are *aloof servants* and that the state hospital aides are *involved directors*.

One might suppose that someone could tell this just by observing with intelligence and sensitivity for a brief period, without having to analyze so many types of behavior. Did I need so many categories? Did I have to go to such lengths to discover that aides in the private hospital are aloof and that aides in the state hospital are directive? These connotations match what one can recognize informally because my analysis demonstrates the empirical base of everyday understandings.

People do not observe aloofness or involvement. They note concrete behavior and initially categorize it according to their own scheme for denoting acts. In this way they award nominal meaning. Then they interpret what they perceive. They may appraise the event according to values they hold and norms to which they subscribe, thus pronouncing moral meaning. They may also render causal or consequential meanings if they infer the event's impetus or effects. They may also draw conclusions about connotations—such as aloofness or involvement, directiveness or servanthood—by considering the situation and the reaction and its possible alternatives. Such connotations are not rooted in the behavior observed but in a mental organization of the observer's experience.

If I had not been concerned with developing a method for the systematic study of behavior, if I had dispensed with explicating behavior semantics and demonstrating its applications, and if I could have foretold that the meaningful issue in this social relationship was to be aloof servanthood versus involved directorship—instead of love and hate, trust and mistrust, influence and impotence, esteem and disfavor, or any other theme of current interest—I might have more briskly dispatched this interpretation. But this semantic procedure would still be undercurrent, as it is in all symbolic understandings.

In the past, when mind was equated with the central nervous system, it was sometimes claimed that humans have an enormous capacity to think but that they hardly make use of their brains. That claim may have overlooked how one thinks about interpersonal acts. The review of an entire repertoire, its ensembles of act-wholes with their sets of alternatives and the probable sequences of behavior, is a mental exercise of great scope and agility. The more complex the act, the more fully occupied is one's central nervous system in grasping its significance. More of the brain is used than heretofore believed. The layman seizes meanings so fast and implicitly that his discernment is taken for granted. The social scientist plods along explicitly and requires ten chapters to portray even one relationship out of the profusion in society.

12

Nonverbal Messages

∽✏∾

People use such words as personal, full, and deep when they speak of social intimacy. They also believe that a minimum rate of contact with another person is needed to sustain psychological closeness. From this comes the maxim "Out of sight, out of mind." In Chapter 2 I proposed that different kinds of sensory stimulation were to be found in different social relationships. The sensation of intimacy in an encounter is not the same as that of formality. Intimate acts enlist more receptors, especially those that only work effectively near the body. Using a proximal mode is crossing a threshold in a relationship. Even the complexity of messages increases with physical nearness. More receptors come into play. More elaborate communications can be received. In this chapter I will review the elements of such communication in general. Then I will turn to the case study and let it tell us more.

Forms of Sensory Communication

Several popular works on nonverbal communication have made their appearance recently. They deal mainly with body gestures related to courtship and to territoriality. These works have two flaws. One is the persistent and familiar mistake of assuming inherent meaning. We are told, for example, that the pose of crossed legs means a tendency to repel sexual advances. The other flaw is incompleteness. There is much nonverbal communication on other topics, which if taken into account would balance the perspective about these gestures.

The sensations of social encounters are treated as well in the literature of social science. Different writers emphasize various kinds of channel use, and because so much attention is otherwise paid to auditory stimulation, discussions of sensory communication stress the other modes: vision, smell, touch, pressure, temperature, and taste. Among the attempts to develop systematic descriptions of nonvocal gestures are those by Birdwhistell, by Hall, and by Hutchinson.

Hall treats this "silent language" through its equivalent dimension of physical distance between people. He distinguishes between the distance receptors and the immediate receptors and refers to *public distance, social distance, personal distance,* and *intimate distance.* (1966) He says that interpersonal behavior becomes more intimate abruptly as the border between a farther and a nearer spatial zone is crossed. These zones would be delineated more precisely, however, by the quantumlike increase in communication made possible by moving within range of sense organs that can only be used at close quarters. The essence of interpersonal space is the degree of access to the receptors that it allows.

As in speech, humans can produce an enormous variety of nonverbal actions, yet few of them are regularly performed in any culture. There are variations among different groups too. In Ghana and in Punjab adult men who are friends hold hands in public or walk with arms about each other's shoulders. In the United States they do not. Hall says that North Americans avoid bodily contact with strangers and reserve touching for moments of intimacy. He observes that Latin Americans having a conversation stand near one another while North Americans converse at one remove. "As a consequence, they think we are distant or cold, withdrawn and unfriendly. We, on the other hand, are constantly accusing them of breathing down our necks, crowding us, and spraying our faces." (1959)

Attempts at influence also vary among cultures. Expectations and demands can be conveyed through subtle excitation of receptors in otherwise innocent discourse, as when the person holds the other's eyes in his gaze or lays his hand gently on the other's shoulder. In the United States, applying influence is often overt and direct, with unequivocal and categorical speech, and also often includes resort to physical coercion. In Japan it is usually indirect. The Japanese convey negation by forgetting, vagueness, postponing, avoiding, overlooking, hesitating and thinking, and being noncommittal. (Vogel)

Different groups within a culture also maintain typical interpersonal distances. Rosenthal found that in the course of laboratory experiments in psychology, male and female experimenters leaned toward female subjects to the same degree. But when the subjects were males, female experimenters did not lean as close as did male experimenters. Yet women are apparently heavier users of distance receptors for they maintain more eye contact than do men, both in a group of the same sex (Exline) and in an interview situation even if the interviewer is of the opposite sex. (Exline, Gray, and Schuette) In an experiment in which he studied pairs of men and women, Rubin found that women spent much more time looking at men than men spent looking at women.

Even social loneliness is more fully brought home by sensory components of the mood. A stranger feels most alone when he is physically close to other people whom he does not know rather than when he is with only his familiar self for company. The larger the number of persons congregated, the less opportunity anyone has to be in proximity to all others. To be sure, in a crowd we are nearer to our neighbors than we may be during a backyard picnic. But the ratio of general proximal access is reduced. The larger the number in the group, the smaller the chance for multiple stimulation from all to all. Though one may fall under the sway of the crowd through a flooding of stimulation, the experience is more that of slavery to the mass than intimacy among individuals. Even father, mother, and child cannot achieve the physical intimacy possible when only two of the three attempt it. With touch, pressure, temperature, smell, and taste a common part of such relationships, one person inevitably gets in the way of the other two.

Impaired sense organs also interfere with opportunities for social ties. Such cases include blindness, deafness, loss of limbs, and even the common cold. The lessened capacity will restrict chances for communication. Just how this blocks social life depends on which sense receptor is faulty. It hinders the aspect of a relationship primarily linked to that mode. If one is blind, he cannot interact with others out of earshot. He is therefore deprived of the most universal and casual contacts. Within hearing range he can engage others. Though loss of sight robs him of opportunities to establish new contacts, it does not rob him of the capacity for intimacy. Deaf people, on the other hand, though able to engage in more casual initial contacts cannot provide the needed auditory access. With speech from others given no entrance, it is more difficult for a deaf person to develop the friendships a blind person can achieve. The deaf must rely on a greatly constricted circle of friends, many of whom are also deaf or who know sign language.

When made aware of an impairment in another person, some people become so uneasy that they constrict the scope of interaction possible. Some people feel freer in the presence of others who are sense-handicapped. The ugly find themselves comfortable with the blind. The person with a colostomy may feel more secure in the presence of someone with a heavy cold. Other people compensate for one mode's deficiency by providing more stimulation to another mode. They speak louder than usual to the blind. They employ more gestures, head noddings, and exaggerated lip movements with the deaf.

Imagine a situation in which adults accustomed to rely on interaction with one another through visual cues are suddenly forced to do without the services of their eyes. The above-mentioned tendency to compensate suggests that when they find themselves without visual access they would resort more to hearing, touch, and the proximally effective modes. This was demonstrated by a natural experiment on November 9, 1965. That evening, the major portion of the populated region of northeast United States was subjected to a blackout for about five to ten hours because of a widespread electric power failure. People stranded together started talking to one another and became friends. Many couples who were together when suddenly deprived of their visual access to each other (and also deprived of such diversions as the evening television programs) went to bed earlier. They came into greater proximity. They could still hear one another and feel one another. Many of them copulated in the course of the evening. Evidence for this was given in the form of a sudden, unseasonal jump in the birth rate in that region of the country almost exactly nine months later.

Messages of Aloofness and Involvement

Now that the two aide-patient relationships have been distinguished as aloof servanthood and involved directorship, I will examine the role of sensory experience in such patterns. Having planned to check the connection between social intimacy and sensory utilization, I classified the stimulation of receptors in the course of systematizing the field records.

Since private aides are more aloof, they should utilize sensory access less often. The surpassing directiveness of state hospital aides should be shown by more utilization. Their greater involvement with patients should also reveal itself in greater use of more proximal modes even when the same reactions are compared between the two groups. However, intimacy does not imply a constant high level of stimulation. It implies a cumulatively higher level than manifest in an aloof relationship and the use of more channels in acts expressing closeness.

What is greater sensory utilization? It is a larger number of receptors stimulated more often in interaction. To measure it I employed three tests in this order of priority: (1) At least some stimulation has to impinge upon a receptor. The failure to deliver stimulation to any mode is non-usage. (2) The more receptors stimulated, the greater the use of access. In a comparison of two instances of a reaction, the one showing more modes stimulated discloses greater use. Variety takes precedence over frequency; the larger variety of channels employed does not necessarily imply greater level of use. (3) Given an equal number of channels stimulated, the higher the total frequency of use, the greater the sensory stimulation.

Table 12-1 gives the stimulation patterns for all reactions. For each receptor stimulated in a reaction, I calculated a separate fraction. It is the number of times that channel was used divided by the number of times that reaction occurred in a forty-hour period.

Different channels are not necessarily used in combination. For example, there may be an event in which the sight mode is stimulated but not the hearing mode, and another instance in which auditory stimulation takes place without visual stimulation. The latter happened when an aide who was sweeping in the day room grumbled loudly that he wished people would stop putting their cigarette butts in the flower pots (act 8-*p*). Even patients who didn't see him could hear him. Every time reaction *p* (TEACHES OR CORRECTS) occurred in the state hospital the hearing channel was stimulated, so the fraction for it is 1.000. The fraction reporting sight stimulation for reaction *p* in the state hospital is .920 because of act 8-*p* just mentioned. The same pattern of using the auditory more than the visual channel occurred in the private hospital for reaction *c* (TELLS OR REMINDS TO DO SOMETHING). Its fractions are .961 and .763 respectively. Here too aides called out to patients who could not see the aides but who were within earshot.

On the other hand, although receptors are measured separately in Table 12-1 because they were not necessarily used in combination, several receptors *can* be stimulated simultaneously in an act and usually they were. REFUSALS (*t*) always entailed delivery of the message both visually and audibly, as indicated by the entries of 1.000 for both channels in both populations of acts.

If two modes turn out to have equal fractions less than 1.000, reflecting equal usage, it does not imply that they are always stimulated together but

Table 12-1. Sensory stimulation in reactions[a]

Reactions		Private Hospital							State Hospital							
		SIGHT	HEARING	TOUCH	PRESSURE	TEMPERATURE	SMELL	TASTE	NONE	SIGHT	HEARING	TOUCH	PRESSURE	TEMPERATURE	SMELL	TASTE	NONE
All acts[b]		812	762	48	48	17	9		115	861	837	131	95	28	13	2	104
FULFILLS REQUEST	a	1.000	678	14						1.000	749	157	33				
CONVERSES	b	1.000	1.000	45	45					978	1.000						
TELLS, REMINDS TO DO 'THING	c	763	961	25						981	945	120	27				
NO OVERT CHANGE IN BEHAVIOR	d	281	82						719	139	124						825
LEAVES THEM TO THEMSELVES	e	58	58						883								1.000
GREETS	f	1.000	1.000	189		68				1.000	925	118	105	105	31	31	
TELLS TO STOP	g	743	936	31	128					828	1.000	39	130				
SUPERVISES ACTIVITY	h	1.000	767							1.000	926	130	130				
PARTICIPATES FULLY	i	1.000	1.000							937	956	87	44	44			
SUGGESTS ENTERING ACTIVITY	j	1.000	1.000							1.000	1.000	148	93	55			
COMPELS TO STOP OR TO DO IT	k	1.000	945	321	501	273	91			1.000	772	624	704	124	62		
PERMITS	l	773	658						113	748	778						148
BRIEFLY AGREES OR DISAGREES	m	846	903							886	1.000						
CARES FOR OR SERVES	n	1.000	939	182	182		61			1.000	1.000	910	639	243			

Table 12-1. (continued)

ASKS ASSISTANCE	o	1.000	1.000					934	1.000			
TEACHES OR CORRECTS	p	1.000	1.000	93				920	1.000	112	56	
REASSURES & TRIES TO REMEDY	q	1.000	1.000	324	432	216	108	1.000	1.000	192	192	128	64
WITHDRAWS	r	808	711			96		1.000	1.000			
STIPULATES A CONDITION	s	828	1.000					589	1.000			
REFUSES	t	1.000	1.000					1.000	1.000			
BANTERS	u	732	1.000					1.000	1.000	159	159	
PARTICIPATES PARTLY	v	1.000		794	294			1.000			206	
ASKS WHAT IS THE MATTER	w	1.000	1.000					1.000	1.000			
PERMITS UNDER A CONDITION	x	500	500					1.000				

[a]Calculated only for known acts and reactions; excluded Not Ascertained category equals 6.4% of acts in private hospital and .8% of acts in state hospital. All fractions in table are given to three places, with decimal points and left-hand zeroes omitted.

[b]This row adjusted for compound acts. In these figures a given sensory mode is counted only once per act even if there were two or more reactions in which that mode was stimulated (page 137).

that they are used in equal proportions during times that the reaction takes place. Table 12-1 shows that no receptors were stimulated 88.3 percent of the times reaction e (LEAVES THEM TO THEMSELVES) was used in the private hospital. Of the remaining occasions, vision and hearing were affected equally but never together. If they had been stimulated together, each fraction would be .167 instead of .058.

Table 12-1 yields information for the three criteria of sensory use. Criterion (1) can be checked by noting whether the None cell for a reaction is less than 1.000 or blank. If it is, at least some stimulation impinged upon a receptor. For criterion (2) one may note how many of the seven other cells for the reaction have entries other than zero and compare the tallies for the two hospitals. The measure of the level of sensory stimulation (3) is the sum of the fractions (except in the None cell) for a reaction in an act-population.

As shown by the summary in the topmost row, aides in the two hospitals have styles of sensory use that parallel the difference already discerned in the two relationships. State hospital aides show greater overall utilization of patients' receptors than do their private hospital counterparts.

I cannot unqualifiedly say that this greater stimulation of more proximal modes confirms the idea of a direct relation between sensory and social intimacy. People of different socioeconomic backgrounds vary in their sensory use. In our culture use of proximal channels in day-to-day social relationships is connected to social class position. It is more characteristic of patients and aides in the state hospital. Patients in the private hospital come from higher classes, and different ways of developing and maintaining intimacy are employed in their subculture. In a survey of mental illness among different social classes, Hollingshead and Redlich found that affluent psychiatric patients usually undergo verbal psychotherapy as a form of treatment while poorer psychiatric patients are subjected to physical therapies and interventions. This pattern of the types of treatment received by persons of certain classes typifies the subcultural difference in the stimulation of receptors.

Before evaluating the proposition about sensory use and intimacy, let us review the information in Table 12-1 more fully. To the extent that aides in both hospitals perform the same reactions, do they also show the same scope of sensory stimulation? For most reactions it is easy to learn which of the two groups took more advantage of access. Reaction k is an example of a tie between the two groups according to criterion (2), the number of different channels. Applying criterion (3) and summing usage across all modes discloses that the state aides deliver more stimulation when compelling patients to stop or to do something. That is, those who are more directive also stimulate more. This supports the idea that transmission of information is essential to interpersonal regulation.

The comparison for reaction g (TELLS TO STOP) is an instance in which the order of priority among the criteria makes a difference. Private aides stimulate more receptors. They would be credited with greater utilization even though their frequency of channel use across all modes is slightly lower.

The data show that particular sensory channels tend to be employed in particular reactions. It is obvious for sight and hearing, but both groups of aides utilize the other modes similarly as well. Smell is stimulated in reactions k, n, and q in both hospitals and in no other reactions except for greeting (f, when embracing) in the state hospital. Reactions f, k, n, and q generally entail stimulation of more modalities than do other reactions. The use of touch differs somewhat, however. It is likely to occur in reactions a, f, g, k, n, p, and q in both populations. But private hospital aides alone employ touch in reactions b and d while only state hospital aides touch in reactions c, h, and i.

Something unexpected is disclosed here. In keeping with my original notion of intimacy, I would have expected reactions d (SHOWS NO OVERT CHANGE IN BEHAVIOR) and e (LEAVES THEM TO THEMSELVES) and r (WITHDRAWS) to be credited with little use of any modes. They are often distancing acts that keep aides and patients apart. Yet except for e at the state hospital, sense channels are stimulated when reactions d and e occur. Indeed, there is more use of receptors for these reactions in the private hospital.

It is possible to stimulate receptors in the course of showing no overt change in behavior. It happened when an aide whistled while he continued to work (act 8-d, page 137). Patients nearby heard him even though he did not address them. Once during the performance of reaction d at the private hospital, even touching took place. An aide brushed by a patient who had begun to speak to him. Brushing by someone without changing stride, especially if that person is speaking to the passer, is the essence of ignoring that person. It is like continuing a normal conversation with a friend while his parents engage in a loud and abusive argument in the next room. In that context it conveys being ignorant of distractions.

Redundancy for Emphasis and Clarity

People who do not want to be interrupted often convey an air of being very busy at whatever they are doing. As the boss passes by, employees impart absorption in their work by producing noise and visual gestures as signs of activity and showing no overt change in behavior. So reactions d and e can involve excitation of receptors. The aides who use more channels in these reactions are those in the private hospital, who deliver less stimulation overall.

This gives a significantly broader function to sensory communication in social life. The employees who convey being involved in work when the boss is near and the private hospital aides who convey aloofness show that receptor stimulation is not exclusively related to intimacy or directiveness. It is usually greater in intimate relationships. But even for the message of aloofness more sense modes will be used in transmitting the meaning. We know that receptor capacities are not independent of each other. Acts affect combinations of channels, and inputs from all are merged in perception. People gesture and touch one another in transmitting messages emphatically. They make stronger claims, communicate more clearly, when using several modes at once. And people perceive gestures and touch and sound in combination when "listening" to one another. This is affirmed by the findings in Table 12-1, which also tell us that *aloofness, indifference, and unawareness may be conveyed emphatically by stimulating more receptors.*

Other familiar practices verify this idea. The subway rider postures in a way that signals absorption in his newspaper when a drunk pesters him on the train. This lack of behavior change is remarkable, for under ordinary circumstances a commuter will glance up and around him at each station stop or pause periodically by looking away from his book. If two men are talking and there is an embarrassing episode nearby, one may feign unawareness by fixing his gaze on his companion's face, whereas under more relaxed conditions he tends to look about. Another instance, which applies to e (LEAVES THEM TO THEMSELVES), is the girl who conveys indifference to a boy whom she likes by boisterously engrossing herself with others in his presence when she is not receiving attention from him.

An act transmitted through several sense channels contains redundant elements. Redundancy is sometimes thought of as superfluity. In information theory it is the part of the message that can be eliminated without losing essential information. The idea also fits social conduct. Surely one can speak to another without seeing him, one can gesture without touching, and so on. There is redundancy both in sending and receiving acts. But redundancy is excessive only when it is part of a unitary message transmitted through perfectly clear channels to a completely accurate receiver. This is rarely the case in human interaction.

If some receptors are not engaged by another's action, they are open to alien signals. Simultaneous prodding of other receptors can adulterate a message sent through the sound channel. It is harder, for example, for an employee to persuade his coworker to leave before completing his tasks if at the same time the coworker spies his foreman beyond the friend's shoulder. This opens the prospect that additional or contradictory messages may be delivered through behavior that travels over several channels. Language is more than speech. I will never forget the camp counselor who laid his hand on my shoulder and spoke to me sweetly in front of the other campers when I had prolonged my rest period and arrived late for afternoon sports, meanwhile brutally pinching my collarbone.

If there is interference while sending a message or if the receiver is imperfect, then redundancy may be helpful rather than superfluous. Employing several channels to convey a single message results in a higher signal-to-noise ratio. This is a safeguard. The message is more fully sent. At the other end, reception is more reliable. An imperfect receiver is able to gather enough information to recognize the message. The service of redundancy in sensory communication is the same as in spoken language. Ambiguity is checked and the message is clearer. All statements gain in clarity and force by being sent and received over multiple channels—even messages of aloofness.

The man trying to seem undistracted when bothered by a drunk on the subway may even rattle the pages of his newspaper as he turns them, conveying more positively that he is absorbed in reading. When a woman riding on a bus realizes that a man next to her is attempting to become familiar, say by sitting close enough for their knees to touch, the woman often makes a distinct sound as she shifts position to establish more distance between them. It emphasizes the significance of her moving apart. There need be no conscious intent on the part of the actor to use more information channels. People habitually do so.

The technique is exemplified in the interaction between a motorist and a hitchhiker. If the driver will not make a pickup, he will usually show no overt change in behavior, watching the road and avoiding eye contact. The matter is more ticklish if the hitchhiker is near a traffic light and making his appeal to drivers as they stop. If the driver does not give him a ride, he sometimes sits staring stonily ahead waiting for the light to turn green. But sometimes he performs a series of activities that imply attention elsewhere. He readjusts the rear-view mirror, turns on the radio, leans over to get something from the glove compartment, and so on.

If the hitchhiker chooses not to accept an offer of a ride, he also shows an increase in the variety and strength of cues that communicate the negative decision. It is not rare for a hitchhiker to refuse a ride. Occasionally he feels that the car was moving too slowly as it approached him and that waiting some minutes longer would be worth it if he has a long way to go. Girls who hitchhike are wary of over-eager drivers or of situations they judge dangerous, and they refuse these offers. (Often they cannot articulate what they rely on to come to such decisions.) When refusing a ride the hitchhiker involves himself in doing nothing, looking everywhere but at the interested driver, whistling abstractedly, pacing back and forth studying the turf, scratching his back, adjusting his rucksack, and so on.

This process may explain the findings in an experiment by Rosenthal and Jacobson, who showed that expectations about others' conduct could be conveyed to them in subtle ways. For example, students from whom teachers expected superior academic performance did indeed perform better, even though the students were randomly selected and this outcome was simply suggested to the teachers at the beginning of the school year. How did the teachers communicate their expectations? Perhaps by using more sensory modes and more proximal modes in conveying *the same ostensible message* to those students. For example, a teacher may call upon a student to speak in class and may then take a stance gazing at the ceiling with hands clasped behind his back as he listens to the recital. Or he might engage the student with his eyes as well as ears and even approach close enough to lay a hand on the pupil's shoulder.

What of social intimacy? If someone is more involved with another, he is more likely to be physically close to the other. People who are spatially closer have more opportunities deliberately and accidentally to stimulate more receptors, especially those receptors that operate proximally. There is greater opportunity to send (and therefore to receive) a complex signal. Remember too that mind works partly outside the body, as in the feedback routes that run between the motor and sensory equipment of the person. Interaction in proximity results in a more comprehensive participation by another person in those external portions of mind. Thus multiple channel use, especially when more than sight and hearing are affected, results in the partners in interaction experiencing the relationship with more merged minds. Such an interpersonal state can be intimacy of the type we call friendship, or of the mixed dominating and affectionate type that is found in most relations between parent and child, or of the primary controlling and somewhat helpful sociable type found in the relationship between aides and patients in the state hospital.

In the preceding chapter I called attention to a difference between the caring for and the service portions of reaction n. Upon reexamining the original field records, I found that when patients were eating in the dining room (situation 14) private hospital aides acted only as waiters. At the state hospital, however, the aides undertook a more direct caring activity in that situation. They fed those patients who did not eat on their own. Yet both types of action were cast into the single category in the course of classification. I tallied the stimulation of receptors for all n reactions in situation 14 and found a different employment of sensory modes in those acts:

	Private Hospital	State Hospital
	Sight/Hearing/Touch	Sight/Hearing/Touch
Acts 14-n and 14-n-f:	1.000 .800 ...	1.000 1.000 1.000

These data reflect my interpretation that in the private hospital aides acted as servants. They used only visual gestures and sound. In the state hospital, reaction n always represented acts of feeding patients and included touching as well as speaking and gesturing.

This suggests that considerations of sensory use could be helpful in classifying acts. It would call for some distinctions where I deemphasized them, as in reaction n. It would have helped clinch the case for keeping the two categories of CARES FOR and SERVES separate. I now believe that my policy of closely adhering to the category sizes provided by the aides in their testimony, which persuaded me to leave some categories coupled (e.g., n, q), should be amended. If a check on sensory use shows differences between distinguishable-though-similar reactions, it would be wiser to establish categories that separate the types (notwithstanding the testimony of informants who are members of the subculture) and to classify those reactions as compound acts if the two types do occur together according to the field records. It is not a matter of objective evidence taking precedence over subjective testimony. One could always assemble categories into compound acts if it were appropriate. But the refinement would be sensitive to nuances in behavior that turn out to be meaningful.

All sensory forms are shown to partake in social relationships. A study of talk alone would not afford an understanding of those aspects in which sound is not used. In the private hospital, aides utilize the auditory mode in only 76.2 percent of their contact opportunities with patients (Table 12-1). So sound transmission is missing from 23.8 percent of the acts that comprise that population. In the state hospital, the aides affect patients' hearing in 83.7 percent of their acts, leaving 16.3 percent of their conduct without audible communication. If, for example, one relied on analyses of tape-recorded conversations to study interpersonal behavior, and if the relationship studied is like that of aides with patients in the private hospital, one would have to be satisfied with knowledge of a little more than three-quarters of it and would be forced to concede ignorance about the remaining quarter. If the population studied from audio tapes is like that found in the state hospital, one would do somewhat better, but knowledge of one-sixth of the acts would still be denied. Sampling biases of these magnitudes are intolerable in a discipline aiming to make quantitative statements.

More than sampling accuracy is involved. Sensory capacities provide limits to complexity in acts. There are only so many channels with just so much room. No interpersonal message will be fully conveyed to another person if it exceeds in scope and depth his ability to receive it. Finally, the nonverbal components ensure meaningful behavior, for they clarify messages and underscore both intimacy and distance.

13

Act-Populations as Systems

Scientific economy dictates that when there are equally plausible ways of explaining a phenomenon an edge is to be accorded the neater one, the one that has fewer variables and fewer assumptions to defend or the one that accounts for more different events than do others. So before investigating other influences I will consider how much of the action reported can be explained by behavior itself.

This does not necessarily simplify the job. A law of conservation of explanation is in force. If the version relies on fewer variables, it may have to use them in more complex statements. Complexity and abstraction are shifted from categories of the subject matter to premises that join the categories to one another. This resembles the relation of advanced forms of mathematics to more primitive forms. Boolean algebra, for example, is a general language in which complex statements can be developed about a variable which is so simple that it has only two possible states, yes and not-yes. The equations employed in Boolean algebra take onto themselves the elaboration that in other schemes are spread among many variables.

With the use of this approach in interpersonal conduct, some of the explanation can be reduced to a behavioral account. This would redress a long-standing neglect. Some students are so committed to the view that interpersonal behavior occurs in the service of something else—for example, an individual or an institution—that they fail to appreciate the extent to which behavior governs itself. To be sure, the account may be insufficient. Factors beyond interpersonal events influence acts. In stressing behavior's role in causing behavior, I do not intend to ignore contributions of other agents. Several processes combine to produce social conduct. There may be several ways of arriving at the same result. It is not necessary that all determinants perform all the time. It is also an oversimplification to give heavy emphasis to one aspect and relegate others to subsidiary roles, as if one factor is primary and all others are merely its conditioners or contingencies. A cause is integral. Lesser influences no more deserve the label of contingency in a general explanation than does a single auspice merit the designation of main cause because we study it and understand it best. The point is well made by Hardin. "When we think in terms of systems, we see that a fundamental misconception is embedded in the popular term 'side-effects' . . . This phrase means roughly 'effects which I hadn't foreseen, or don't want to think about.' As concerns the basic mechanism, side-effects no more deserve the adjective 'side' than does the 'principal' effect. It is hard to think in terms of systems, and we eagerly warp our language to protect ourselves from the necessity of doing so."

Whatever portion of the findings can be explained by variables already known leaves less to be solved in other ways. I shall devote this chapter to causal contributions made by behavior and will treat the influence exerted by other factors in the next chapter.

I wish to explain the meaningful differences between the two act-populations. A number of behavioral connotations led me to identify themes of aloof servanthood for private aides and involved directorship on the part of state aides. Private aides less often seize opportunities to inter-act with patients. They withdraw from patients more often. State aides superintend patients more. Even though they use compulsion more, they are also more permissive. State aides perform more compound acts and show more variety in conduct than do private aides. This is not due to individual differences based on numbers, for about the same number of aides were observed in each hospital. The two aide groups differ in the occasions on which they try to divert tensions by bantering, which suggests that different types of patients' conduct aggravate them. There is another curiosity. Although state aides are more involved with patients, situations 4 (A patient makes a remark or is having a conversation with an aide) and 23 (Patients invite an aide who is not busy to join them in recreation) happen more often in the private hospital. All these findings warrant a coherent explanation.

Self-Regulation

Behavior itself is a prime shaper of conduct because a population of acts is systemic. A system is an entity made up of parts that are related to one another. Relatives, as we know, provide opportunities and constraints. They affect one another to the extent that they are in active contact. I described one form of mutual influence in behavior as feedback. The timing and content of a person's output can become, through a channel outside the body, an input that affects his further conduct. A similar process happens in interpersonal behavior. One action affects the probability of another. The latter in turn influences the chances of the first happening again. Though it does not explain all that goes on in a social relationship, this self-regulation does account for some of the patterns.

1. Situations select reactions.

The behavior table shows that a situation has a certain likelihood and, given the situation, that reactions have distinct probabilities of following it. There is a pool of twenty-four reactions, yet only a few of them appear in any given situation. The situation must therefore exert some influence upon conduct. If a reaction assumes a specific probability for that situation and another probability in another situation, the reaction is to that extent determined by the situation. This is not a strong explanatory claim. It is essentially descriptive. Yet in the history of science there has been a progressive abandonment of the wish to make strong explanatory claims and an acceptance of descriptive propositions which hold so consistently that they in time acquire the status of laws. The word *law* is imprecise here. It insinuates some forceful governing process, whereas it is no more than a very reliable descriptive statement. Perhaps it was used by men to soften their frustration in being unable to grasp the *why's* of their subject matter or to reach back successfully to first causes.

The behavior of the people in the situation guides the selection of a subgroup of reactions from among those possible. If this boundary condition should change, then the subset of possibilities would change too. Consider situation 3 (It is time for a scheduled activity). The subset of reactions evoked by it includes c (TELLS OR REMINDS TO DO SOMETHING), n (CARES FOR OR SERVES), o (ASKS ASSISTANCE), b (CONVERSES), and d (SHOWS NO OVERT CHANGE IN BEHAVIOR). Suppose a patient delays or resists doing the activity at that time. This can transform situation 3 into situation 17 (A patient delays or resists doing a required activity). With this shift of situation, the above-mentioned subset of reactions acquires a zero probability of occurring. Instead, three other reactions, k (COMPELS TO DO IT), j (SUGGESTS ENTERING ACTIVITY), and l (PERMITS), become the only ones with probabilities other than zero. A change in the situation is enough to engender a move from one subset of reactions to another for all aides.

If two act-populations differ in the likelihoods of certain situations, the likelihoods of certain reactions will be affected. We know that the probabilities for the situations confronting aides in the two hospitals correlate .66. This leaves room for differences. One of the most marked differences can be found in a group of five situations that have something in common. They are numbers 1 (A patient requests . . .), 4 (A patient makes a remark or is having a conversation . . .), 10 (A patient asks to be let off the ward or to make a phone call), 12 (A patient complains or denounces the hospital), and 23 (Patients invite an aide who is not busy to join them in recreation). In these situations *the patients carry the initiative to the aides*. Portions of other situations fit here too, but the size of each portion is hard to determine and I will discuss only the five mentioned. In these situations patients make demands upon aides. Situations 1 and 10 reflect dependence upon aides for services imposed by the nature of institutions in which entrances, exits, and access to supplies are controlled by the staff. Situations 4 and 23 show the patients' interest in sharing informal activities with aides. Patients in the private hospital make much more of these overtures. The situations are more than twice as likely there ($\Sigma p(S) = .364$) as in the state hospital ($\Sigma p(S) = .177$). In other words, whereas the state aides are more likely than private aides *to make demands upon patients,* private hospital patients are more likely than state hospital patients *to make demands upon aides.* That is why certain reactions such as fulfilling requests (*a*) occur more in the private hospital. They are called out more often by situations in that institution.

This will help explain the finding that private hospital aides provide much more service to patients (Table 11-3) and that private hospital aides seem equally aloof and friendly toward patients. The amount of friendliness shown by private hospital aides in the face of their aloofness is noteworthy in connection with the findings of Table 11-1. The largest single contribution to that friendliness rating is made by reaction *b* (CONVERSES) in situation 4 (A patient makes a remark or is having a conversation with an aide). Since situation 4 is one in which the patient often takes the initiative in interacting, it appears that the private hospital patients *pull companionship out of their aides.* It is not given as readily in other situations. Those aides are aloof until patients draw them into conversation.

This influence upon chatter is corroborated by findings of a separate series of studies dealing with the duration of speech elicited from respondents in many types of interviews and from astronauts by ground staff members during manned space flights. The results strongly imply that the duration of the questioner's utterance is itself the most influential variable. The researchers (Matarazzo *et al.*) are not particularly satisfied with this result. They seek to analyze it into some aspect of the interviewer style, such as asking open-ended questions, but fail to identify any other correlate. Ray and Webb studied the transcripts of President Kennedy's regular news conferences to determine whether this so-called speech duration effect operated when more than two persons were involved in an interview. They too found a positive relation between the length of reporters' questions and the length of the President's answers. People can be drawn into conversation by directing conversation at them. And they will talk longer if their partners speak longer in asking them questions.

My emphasis on an objective explanation for behavior does not slight its meaningful cast. Situations determine reactions but not through a mindless mechanism. Comprehension is present. One interprets and understands the situation to which he responds. I have shown in Chapter 10 that we do not have to peer into the murky realms of mood and intention in order to grasp the tenor of an act. We review situations experienced and alternative reactions observed. In demonstrating the method of behavior semantics, I did not make all meanings of all acts explicit. Some situations and reactions are widely experienced in everyday life. An individual has and uses an understanding of acts based on his broad participation in society. So even if I had tried to interpret the aide repertoire thoroughly, it would represent only a morsel of the connotations associated with some acts. One of the reasons certain acts take place is that they are meaningful reactions to meaningful situations.

Since reactions only come up in certain situations, a reaction's likelihood depends on the occurrence of particular situations. Anything that influences a given situation to occur contributes to the occurrence of certain reactions. One can therefore reduce the likelihood of a reaction if he can prevent the situations that elicit it. Or he can enhance the reaction's probability by promoting the situation. The situation, however, is not in itself sufficient to decide which alternative of its set will be used.

It is a bold step to declare that what has been found related in temporal order is a cause followed by an effect. Situation and reaction may both be caused by a third factor and be independent of each other. Yet it is customary to accept timely associations (that is, that the probability of a reaction is influenced by the immediately preceding events) as a tentative explanation of the phenomenon even while allowing that the account may be revised.

2. Reactions determine situations.

We know there is a feedback control of conduct for a single individual. His own behavior (for example, speaking) provides evidence that he uses for continuing action along one course rather than another. The influence of this echoing process also applies to the course of social interaction.

The principle developed in the preceding section identifies a reverberating influence in populations of acts. In a social encounter, one person's reaction becomes situation for another. Aides' reactions become situations for patients. Consequently, the reactions of aides affect the occurrence of patients' situations. It happens because acts are hatched from contact opportunities, and they use up time as they are performed.

The beginning of the act is sensory access, a chance to reach another person through his receptors. Understandably, once someone seizes the opportunity, the sense channels are occupied and access to those persons abates for the duration of the interchange. Excepting occasional intrusions and distractions, other situations do not occur for the parties involved as long as their episode lasts.

There is also an upper limit to the number of acts in a population. Behavior takes time. The duration of the populations studied here is forty hours. So there cannot be more acts than the ones which used up the allotted time. Any reaction using up more time than average will simultaneously reduce the amount of time to be used in other ways. I have no direct information about durations of the reactions in this repertoire. Yet certain categories of conduct imply more prolonged contacts while others typify briefer contacts, according to general experience. Still other reactions tend to vary and are hard to gauge consistently.

Short-duration reactions use up less of an act-population's total time. They thereby leave more room for other kinds of situations to occur. Reactions m (BRIEFLY AGREES OR DISAGREES), r (WITHDRAWS), and t (REFUSES) seem customarily short in duration. Such reactions, and non-initiating ones like d (SHOWS NO OVERT CHANGE IN BEHAVIOR), by not maintaining contact for long or not utilizing contact when in sensory access, have similar effects on the likelihood of certain situations. They enhance conditions for new encounters. The aide is available again sooner. On the other hand, reactions h (SUPERVISES ACTIVITY), i (PARTICIPATES FULLY), and q (REASSURES AND TRIES TO REMEDY) are relatively prolonged in each instance of use. These postpone the occasions for new encounters.

In a comparison of the two groups, the longer reactions *h, i,* and *q* make up 11.5 percent of the private hospital population and 14.6 percent of the state hospital population. Contrarily, relatively brief reactions (*m, r, t*) comprise 8.9 percent and 4.8 percent of those populations respectively. Long-duration reactions happen more in the state setting, and briefer reactions take place more in the private setting. This fits the findings reported in Chapter 11. State aides spend more time with their patients.

If one utilizes contact opportunities briefly, he quickly regains the chance to interact with someone else. Avoiding a contact opportunity leaves one immediately free for another. Since contact opportunities are affected in this way (the less they are seized, the more new ones are available), it is possible to raise the probability of a situation not only directly but also by not performing reactions that take oneself out of circulation.

I will now explain the greater probability of situations 4 (A patient makes a remark or is having a conversation with an aide) and 23 (Patients invite an aide who is not busy to join them in recreation) in the private hospital. Private aides utilize fewer contact opportunities with patients than do state aides in situations 2 (An aide and a patient pass or meet), 8 (An aide is working on the ward and some patients are nearby), and 9 (Patients are in the day room and the aide is not engaged in ward work). The state hospital aide is more likely to seize opportunities afforded by situations 2 or 8 or 9. Having utilized the opportunities, the state aides make overtures from patients unnecessary. The private aide, by more often leaving patients to themselves on these occasions, leaves room for patients to make advances. In the absence of competing acts, other acts can take place. In a milieu where people initiate contacts less often, an opening is provided that others may fill. Private hospital patients engage in the same acts toward their *aides*—initiating conversations (situation 4) and inviting them to enter an activity (23)—that state aides undertake with their *patients*. The difference between act 2-*b* and act 4-*b* is often a matter of who began the conversation. The self-regulating character of the population is exposed in the way state aides inhibit situations 4 and 23 by reacting to other situations. Thus aides' reactions affect the kinds of situations likely to confront them.

It is a common belief that although characteristics of a social group can be recognized, they are said to be ultimately reducible to the actions of the individuals who compose them. Why stop there? Are not persons ultimately reducible to the actions of the molecules that compose them? No use is made of molecular terminology when a person is described. We recognize this reduction as unsuitable because it calls for abandoning the terms and postulates of a certain level of organization among phenomena. Instead, we employ ideas and propositions that refer to an entire behaving system. Similarly, in this account of interpersonal behavior as a system, I have not referred to individual feelings or beliefs or decisions. Instead, I have shown how situations and reactions tell on one another, jostle their likelihoods and durations, and how patterns emerge from the contingencies of conduct itself. Acts in the interpersonal arena have their own system. Its influence on behavior will be overlooked if the events are treated only as the products of individuals.

This discussion brought out another distinction between a situation and a stimulus. Reactions have an influence on situations, while in classical theory a response does not determine a stimulus.

Interacting Populations

Something puts initiative for friendliness in the hands of aides at the state hospital and leaves it in the hands of patients at the private hospital. It is revealed by extending the principles of self-regulation to include additional populations of acts. An organization has a network of social relationships linking a number of positions. Each incumbent of a position partakes of several relationships. If acts affect acts, the distribution of influence will obtain across all acts that happen, not only for those of a single relationship. In the natural condition, rather than in the case I isolated for convenience in study, situations and reactions would refer to those for all persons in the setting within sensory access—nurses, social workers, psychiatrists, psychologists, clinical trainees, visitors, and recreational therapists—as well as for aides. With this enlargement we can see that human density will add to the regulation of behavior by behavior. Its effect is noticeable in many circumstances.

A simple case is that of people walking along the street. Each individual is subject to the boundary conditions of other persons in his vicinity. If no one is near him, he is the sole establisher of his trajectory and speed. Then as he moves into an area where more people are walking, he responds to their positions and speeds, and his own movement becomes restricted and governed by their movements. Each of us can remember times we were in a hurry and became increasingly impatient with others around us who were ambulating unconcernedly. Herman and Gardels, reviewing patterns of automobile traffic, report the same kind of collective effect exerted on a driver by the traffic around him, resulting in his adjusting the speed and trajectory of his vehicle to the movements of cars in his immediate environment. Likening traffic flow to the kinetic theory of gases, they write: "Beginning with a situation of light traffic, it is clear that a driver will do as he wishes—presumably within the limits of the law. But as the traffic concentration goes up, more and more restrictions are imposed on the driver. He must subjugate his wishes to what he can do safely—or to what he can do at all. The theory predicts that at some critical concentration there will be a transition from individual flow to collective flow, in which traffic moves in a rather gelled state. In that state every driver is doing what is forced on the community by the properties of this peculiar kind of fluid."

Borgatta and Bales found a similar collective flow in groups. They saw different interaction rates among individuals and wondered whether participation in a group created influences that could override personal behavior dispositions. Accordingly, they assembled in discussion groups persons with similar styles of interpersonal action. They found that when only persons who are characteristically "high participators" compose a group, they depress each other's activity. On the other hand, in groups composed only of "low participators" some individuals tend to seize interaction opportunities more when others utilize fewer of them. The researchers concluded that while the characteristic rates of individuals may be affected by their personal makeup, a competitive situation exists among the rates in a group. The higher one person's activity, the more another's rate is impeded. In the absence of such competition individuals tend toward their maximum rates.

So an entire field of behavior is mutually regulative. The actions of one person are affected by the conduct of others at hand. The dispersion of behavior in an assemblage depends on the number of people involved. Two is company, three is a crowd. At the beginning of the twentieth century, Simmel more formally differentiated between two-person groups and three-person groups. Dyads and triads, he said, were prototypes on both sides of a critical transition point at which a self-regulating relationship is supplemented in regulation by the presence of other populations of acts: "Where three elements, A, B, C, constitute a community, there is added to the immediate relationship which exists, for example, between A and B, the immediate relationship which they gain by their common relation to C.

. . . There is no relationship so complete between three that each individual may not, under certain circumstances, be regarded by the other two as an intruder. . . ."

In several places I returned to the theme introduced in Chapter 2, how individuals are dependent on their sensory environment. In Chapter 12 I reviewed the obstacles of personal sensory impairment to relations with others. In the immediately preceding section I recounted how utilizing some contact opportunities prevents other ones from arising. The principle of mutual exclusion has its sensory component too. If A utilizes the channels to B, C cannot do so at that time. So A cuts off access to B by C.

This condition further explains the establishment of probabilities for certain situations in the hospitals. Some situations will be less likely as a result of competition posed by the presence of other act-populations, namely those involving patients in relationships with persons in positions other than that of aides. The probabilities of contact opportunities in one population depend on the probabilities of those situations in accompanying populations. Since any factor depressing the likelihood of a situation also curbs the chances for certain reactions (those that are used in that situation), the density afforded by the presence of people in other social positions will affect the aides' behavior with patients. Let us look at the mechanism more closely.

Competing act-populations arise from a condition of *relational density,* which is the number of different social positions in which incumbents have direct access to one another. It refers to both numbers of positions and the presence of incumbents. Above a certain level relational density spurs competition for access to a certain group. In the case at hand, the aides' access to patients is affected by social contacts between patients and others. If other staff members interact with patients, the latter are taken out of circulation. They become less available to aides. Of the two aide groups, therefore, the group in the hospital that has greater relational density will be the group that is more constrained in its contacts with patients.

The private hospital places a full treatment team on every ward. Psychiatrists, psychologists, social workers, nurses, and recreational therapists abound. Aides comprise about 30 percent of the treatment staff. The hospital is also a major teaching institution, a training unit of a large medical school, a practicum for students from psychology and social work departments of nearby universities, and the hospital has its own school of psychiatric nursing. There are always interns, residents, field work students, and trainees present acquiring supervised practical experience in psychotherapy. On the other hand, the state hospital has fewer clinical personnel. Only a skeleton crew of professionals staffs it. There are also fewer trainees because of the lack of professionals to supervise them. Nurses too are in short supply, and aides make up about 70 percent of the total treatment staff.

Therefore, the private hospital should constrain its aides more. Relational density would affect such opportunities as situations 2 (An aide and a patient pass each other or meet) and 9 (Patients are in the day room and the aide is not engaged in ward work) in that setting. Patients who pass or meet aides are likely to be accompanied by another staff member, and few patients are likely to be sitting alone on the ward.

Why the restriction of certain acts? The presence of others may constrain them, but this does not explain the quality of aloof servanthood among aides in the private institution. To describe more fully the influence on aides' behavior, I will provide some information about the conduct of other staff members. We did not systematically record what other staff members do in the presence of aides, whether or not patients were around, so I must proceed along this line based on my informal observations.

Behind the regulative mechanism just described there is a forceful struggle over privileged situations with patients, ones that are excluded from other relationships. It coincides with the nature of the treatment technology receiving primary emphasis in the private hospital—psychotherapy. Psychotherapy as practiced by the private hospital's professionals entails the establishment of *transference,* that is, a shifting of the patient's feelings and outlooks so that they become oriented toward the therapist. It is common for people to project crucial attitudes toward persons of significance to them. The therapist utilizes this transference in treatment. If he can help the patient resolve these issues with respect to their own relationship, the patient may be able to apply the constructive solutions to alliances he develops with other persons. In order to crystallize the transference, the clinician seeks a personal bond, involving trust and intimacy, with the patient. It is important that it be exclusive and that others do not enter into close personal relations as well. If the patient had alternative opportunities to concentrate his feelings and energies, this condition would detract from the therapeutic bond and the intensity of the transference would be weakened. So clinicians guard their relationships with patients jealously. At the same time, there are only two hundred patients in this private hospital. Considering the number of professional staff members and clinical trainees, the supply of patients approaches scarcity.

This meager supply fosters competition among staff members for treatment opportunities. It results, not surprisingly, in the powerful ones winning. The hospital treatment hierarchy consists, from the top down, of psychiatrist, psychologist, social worker, nurse, recreational counselor, and lastly aide. The higher the position of the staff member, the more he succeeds in reserving privileges of intimacy with patients for himself. The range of actions for aides is correspondingly circumscribed. They are explicitly discouraged from personal involvement with patients and are instructed to avoid certain kinds of situations because the nurse or psychiatric resident working with certain patients fears competition in transference. If an aide is observed engaged in friendly exchange with a patient who has received attention from a clinical trainee, the trainee gets upset. He complains and insists "That's *my* patient" and enjoins the aide about further intimacy. Consequently, when patients invite an aide who is not busy to join them in recreation or for coffee (situation 23), aides in the private hospital tend to hesitate and STIPULATE A CONDITION (s) before accepting or to WITHDRAW altogether (r) more often than to PARTICIPATE FULLY (i).

Here is the reason why private aides are tense about unusual disturbances (page 208). Patients who perform unusual physical gestures or who do an ordinarily private act in public are manifesting conduct associated with mental illness. Aides might try to help if they could, but they are prohibited from dealing with derangements in a helpful manner. To do so might bring criticism from other staff members who see those disturbances as therapeutic opportunities vital to their own work. Low in status, aides are left to do what others in the hospital hierarchy do not reserve for themselves. The outcome is a more restricted and aloof relation with patients. The private hospital aide becomes largely concerned with serving them, escorting them to and from activities, and providing the interstices of a social life within the hospital when called upon to do so by the patients.

Whereas the professional treatment staff's presence in the private hospital results in limited involvement for those aides with their patients, the low relational density in the state hospital permits a wider range and a greater variety of behavior for its aides. In the state setting therapists are scarce, not patients. There are many inmates at hand. Almost no one but aides and some nurses are regularly on the wards. Instances of competition for access are therefore rare. Higher-ranking staff members in the state institution do not ordinarily object if an aide becomes friendly with a patient or if the aide performs activities that would otherwise go unperformed. Given that there is little competition for access to patients and that other social relation-ships do not pivot on the factor of transference, the state aides widen their repertoire. They assume more discretion over the lives of their patients.

Two illustrations of this are the following: act 3-c (see Table 9-1) includes instances of aides handing out medicines to patients. This act rarely happens in the private hospital (we observed it once there). In the state hospital aides assume duties customarily reserved for nurses, and act 3-c is almost three times more frequent in that setting. This shows how a repertoire enlarges when another relationship is not occupied. The second example, of state aides moving into the uninhabited territory of therapists, is even more graphic. Situation 5 (A patient performs an unusual verbal act) happens with nearly equal frequency in both hospitals. The private aides' reactions show that they interpret this as conduct to be quelled or ignored. State aides react in many ways that imply they perceive unusual verbalisms as a province of their own treatment responsibility (see Table 9-1). Increased concern as well as greater power is reflected in state aides' involved directorship. They care for patients in the way that parents, camp counselors, and child guardians care for their charges, with a blend of solicitude, inexpertness, and schoolmasterism.

In this context the state aides are more vexed by obvious distress and by aggravations to other patients. It is revealed not only in their pattern of bantering (u) in situations 11 and 13, but also by the fact that when a patient hits another patient the state aide is likely to reassure the one who was struck as well as deal with the attacker (see act 22-q-w in Table 9-1). The absence of competing populations helps explain the greater scope and involvement of state aides compared to private aides.

This account of the division of labor applies to other hospitals. It applies wherever similar conditions of relational density exist. An individual's repertoire depends not only on what kind of a person he is and what he commits himself to do in an organization but also on interpersonal con-tingencies. If there are many others, there will be competition and his scope and variety of conduct will be curbed. There are many cases of trying to maintain dominion over a particular work sphere. Competition and border skirmishes are a pervasive and familiar part of the evolution of today's occupations and professions. The craft guilds of Western Europe during the Middle Ages strove to prevent encroachment by persons living outside a locality and to reserve for the indigenous artisans the privilege of regulat-ing their own workmanship and prices. Contemporary arguments over who has the right to perform certain work, such as jurisdictional disputes among labor unions, are aimed at marking out territories in which certain groups will have exclusive access to jobs for their members and rights for collective bargaining. Professional groups, too, claim rule over certain areas of work because of exclusive expertise.

If there is low relational density, the range of one's repertoire will enlarge. The absence of incumbents from social positions can blur the division of labor in directions of both more and less skilled tasks performed. For example, if there are few persons in subordinate positions in an ongoing enterprise, the boss will be observed doing many things. The engineer who does not have a secretary sharpens his own pencils, empties his wastebasket, cleans his desk, and types his correspondence. In the same way, if there is no doctor at a dispensary in a small town, the nurse or pharmacist will medicate. Discussing the role of the nurse in a hospital, Hughes observed that "her place in the division of labor is essentially that of doing in a responsible way whatever necessary things are in danger of not being done at all." This includes assuming the physician's command and making decisions when he is not present, thereby exceeding her level of authority and perhaps straining beyond her level of expertise. She also sometimes checks the laundry and sweeps the floor when the personnel responsible for these tasks are not on duty. In the household, the breadth of a mother's population of acts with her children is more restricted when their father is regularly present. The scope of her relationship with the children expands when he is away for more than a few days.

Behavior choices are meaningful under conditions of high and low relational density. When people in two or more social positions respond to the same situation, the person who acts first offers an interpretation. The next to act offers an alternative, and so on. Each reaction is a stroke of significance. All reactions together are the bearings for fixing a connotation to any one reaction. Learning the *probabilities* of the elements in the set, a person adds to the meaningful surround that he will be aware of in the moment he acts. He can guess how his conduct will be interpreted because he knows what others are likely to do in the situation.

External Mind Processes

A question about the findings of the case study can be raised that fits this account of the division of labor. The idea of relational density is that it spurs competition for privileged social relationships. Powerful persons win and reserve favored situations with others for themselves. Consequently, weaker individuals assume more residual liaisons. If continual communication enters into the regulation of behavior, would private hospital aides forget the injunctions of the clinical staff against becoming personal with patients when those clinicians are *absent?*

The answer is implied by the nature of mind having channels outside the central nervous system. The explanation of mind-determined behavior would also consider its outside processes and not refer only to learned rules and other internal states of individuals. Since behavior is regulated by surrounding influences as well, heeding admonitions about conduct will be tempered by immediate conditions of the milieu.

This idea was also broached by Durkheim in his treatment of this topic. His account of the origin of the division of labor in society begins with "more individuals sufficiently in contact to be able to act and react upon one another." Then, "The closer functions come to one another . . . the more points of contact they have; the more, consequently, are they exposed to conflict. As in this case they satisfy similar needs by different means, they inevitably seek to curtail the other's development." The competition among them reaches a point at which some who are losing the fight begin to differentiate themselves, usually by specializing in functions that more successful competitors had not claimed. Here they can subsist. ". . . the vanquished can maintain themselves only by concentrating their efforts upon a part of the total function they fulfilled up to then." Durkheim summarized this process by saying, "The division of labor varies in direct ratio with the volume and density of societies, and, if it progresses in a continuous manner in the course of social development, it is because societies become regularly denser and generally more voluminous." Durkheim also suggested that the outcome cannot be decreed according to a preconceived plan. Because of this, he declared that the specializations that develop must be in constant communication during the time they persist. Recently this factor of constant communication has been reasserted in an account of organizational behavior as an expression of a *negotiated order.* Strauss and his colleagues describe the hospital as a milieu in which adjustments among the relationships are "continually being established, renewed, reviewed, revoked, revised." Among people in various positions they see daily negotiations maintaining, reappraising, and changing social arrangements in the organization.

To explain the process, I will cite a pure case that happened during an experiment several decades ago. The researchers, Lippitt and White, believed that the climate of leadership for a group would affect the behavior and experiences of its members. They undertook to compare the possible effects of three leadership styles, described briefly as *autocratic, democratic,* and *laissez-faire.* The experiment began with the establishment of some clubs for eleven-year-old children, each having an adult leader who assumed one or another of the three leadership styles. A measure of productive activity was used, and the researchers found that during a period of time when the laissez-faire adult was out of the meeting room, that group's productivity—which had been the lowest of all groups—rose markedly. The authors reported this finding conscientiously without being able to explain it. They wrote, "The apparent increase in group productive time with the laissez-faire leader out of the room may or may not be a meaningful result. Two or three times it was noted that when the adult left, one of the boys exerted a more powerful leadership and achieved a more coordinated group activity than when the relatively passive adult was present." Clearly, if one believes that established leadership can be preserved by memory, the mere absence of the adult for a short period of time should not be enough to dispel the effect of his influence. And if one continues to accept the formal definition of the situation as the group's having a laissez-faire leader, the increase in productive activity for the group may be hard to comprehend. In actuality, with the adult gone there was room for someone else to expand the scope of his behavior toward his pals, and he did. One of the boys replaced laissez-faire leadership for that group by some more forceful kind during the adult's absence. Since *the leadership climate actually changed,* the increase in productivity is understandable in the light of the original hypothesis: leadership styles influence conduct of group members. The finding is easier to interpret if one makes a behavioral assessment of leadership rather than hewing to the researchers' formal designation.

The relative power of immediacy versus rule depends on the length of time a given social relationship has been in effect. This experiment was a short-lived affair for its participants. Over a longer period the memory of the leader would last longer in his absence. Yet if the experiment had been carried out so that there were a series of club meetings with an established pattern of the laissez-faire leader being absent for a part of the time, there would also be a different pattern of leadership consistently in effect during his absence.

In the case of the private hospital aides, where social relationships have been in existence day in and day out, the influences on behavior are similar. While acts of clinicians affect aides' conduct, I do not say that they physically elbow aides out of the way from patients or that their incessant presence holds aides in check. The clinicians are absent from the wards at times, and still the aides obey them to some extent because the aides have learned and adjusted to their superiors in a context. That context includes the same patients, the light of day, and the furnishings of the ward (as well as the presence of other staff members). Even when clinicians are absent these other familiar features remain. The patients do not change into Ifugao tribesmen. There is no replacement of corridors and ward rooms by the kraals of the veldt. Nor does it suddenly get dark with Antarctic winds blowing outside. Inasmuch as cues remain, some of the influence remains. A milieu relevant to a specific performance can evoke the disposition for that performance.

Rules, however, are not self-perpetuating. Norms have a potency that lingers beyond the instant of delivery, but norms wane and will vanish if not regularly rejuvenated. They deteriorate without the external cues that maintain them. Although clinicians need not guard the territory of their relationship with patients ubiquitously, it does matter that their presence *is deemed probable*. No matter how well a norm is learned, no matter how strong conscience is believed to be, the power of an injunction depends on the probability of its being enforced.

Private hospital clinicians have a high probability of being present at certain times and of being absent at other times. If relational density has immediate influence, then when the density subsides the restrictions on aides should dwindle as well. At those times private hospital aides should become more like state aides in their conduct toward patients. This hypothesis can be tested.

A Test of the Hypothesis

There are two main time periods during the week in the private hospital. One of them corresponds to the times and days that most professionals and clinical students are present on the wards and hospital grounds. This period is *weekdays,* encompassing Mondays through Fridays from seven o'clock in the morning till five in the afternoon, and Saturdays from seven in the morning till one o'clock in the afternoon. (While few are present as early as seven in the morning, many clinicians arrive about eight o'clock. Our time unit of observation covering their arrival began at seven. Many of them work a half day on Saturdays.) This fifty-six-hour period is matched by another of the same length that spans the remaining waking hours. *Evenings and weekends* covers Mondays through Fridays from five in the afternoon to eleven o'clock in the evening, Saturdays from one in the afternoon until eleven in the evening, and all day Sunday—from seven in the morning till eleven at night. Clinicians are rarely present during this period. For comparison purposes the same breakdown can be made for the state hospital.

If the hypothesis were applied to the two populations of acts, I would deduce greater behavioral differences between the two time periods for the private hospital aides than for the state hospital aides, for there is greater difference in relational density between the two time periods in the private setting. State aides, because of the sparseness of staff in other positions at their institution, should show less fluctuation in their round-the-clock conduct toward patients. I concede that I do not know exactly how many of the aides work on permanent shifts and how many rotate from one shift to another in the course of their employment. But in both hospitals few aides are permitted to work on the day shift permanently. About two-thirds of the aides in each institution shuttled between day and evening shift work during the period of this study. Therefore, I will speak of the actions of one group of aides working at different times.

I can develop a number of specific predictions in the framework of this general idea. Having studied fifteen meaningful behavior patterns and reported the findings in Tables 11-1, 11-2, and 11-3, I reviewed each aide group for each of these patterns, for both weekdays and for evenings and weekends. As many as sixty distinct comparative predictions can be generated. Upon making this review, I deduced thirty-one of them. I did not commit myself for the remaining twenty-nine because I could find little relevance to the hypothesis for them. (For example, since the friendliness of private hospital aides is largely evoked by efforts on the part of patients, the density-hierarchy hypothesis does not bear as directly on this connotation of aides' behavior.)

Comparison five refers to situations 2, 4, 6, 7, 8, and 9 (see Table 11-1), in which contact opportunities with patients arise in conditions that are not closely linked to life in mental hospitals. The situations are neither problematic and expressive of disturbed states in patients (which are the bases for the sixth comparison) nor the routine circumstances of institutional existence (like time schedules, locked doors, and communal dining halls, that are the bases of the seventh comparison). Instead, these situations are found in many repertoires. In this respect they are more ambiguous grounds for developing predictions since other more universal factors may pertain to them. Nevertheless, some implications seem clear from the hypothesis and from the nature of psychotherapeutic treatment: (1) The private hospital aides should be more aloof toward patients while the professionals and student clinicians are present; that is, on weekdays. With the latter absent on evenings and weekends, the private hospital aides should then be less aloof toward patients. By the same token, when other staff members are present these others will attempt to activate and guide patients. (2) So private hospital aides will show less directiveness on weekdays and more on evenings and weekends when responsibility for patients is left mainly to them. (3) It follows too that if the private aides were to become dependent upon patients it should happen at a time when others are not around to compete with them—on evenings and weekends.

The state hospital aides, comparing weekdays with evenings and weekends, should show about the same amount of (4) aloofness, (5) dependence, and (6) directiveness around the clock.

Comparing private and state aides on weekdays only, it follows from the propositions and from knowledge of differences between the two groups that (7) the private aides will show more aloofness. At that time in the private hospital, other staff members compete for patients. In the state hospital, the weekday period of activity therapies and the sparseness of professionals and clinical students should result in relatively less aloofness than shown by private aides. For these reasons, on weekdays, state aides also will be (8) more directive and (9) more dependent than their private hospital counterparts.

The disparities in denseness of hierarchy between the two hospital settings fade out on evenings and weekends. Since the differences found between the populations are based on these disparities, they too should dissolve and the two groups will show about the same (10) aloofness, (11) directiveness, and (12) dependence toward patients during those hours.

Predictions for situations involved in the sixth comparison (see Table 11-2) are easy to make. These cases are the foci of treatment activity in the mental hospital. It follows from the arguments about relational density that private hospital aides should differ in their conduct toward patients in the two time periods. They should behave more like therapists when other therapists are absent. On weekdays, while professionals and clinical students are around, these aides should be (13) more indifferent toward patients in problem situations. However, in the sparse milieu of evenings and weekends, as they respond to situations in which patients are troubled, those aides should become (14) more helpful. There is no reason for the private aides to be more (15) redirective or (16) prohibitive toward patients in one time period or the other, for these themes are not central to their competition with clinicians, and I assume that these will be about the same in the two periods. (17) The state aides should not alter their help-fulness toward patients throughout the week. In a comparison of the two groups of aides in the two time periods, it follows from the hypothesis that (18) the state hospital aides would be more helpful on weekdays, but (19) on evenings and weekends private hospital aides should be as helpful as state aides.

The seventh comparison also provides ground for predictions. These routine situations (see Table 11-3) are not involved in the competition between aides and clinicians. This should be reflected by no difference in the private hospital aides' (20) sociability, (21) supervision, and (22) service in the two time periods. State hospital aides should also show about the same amount of (23) sociability, (24) supervision, and (25) service at both times.

For different time periods, predictions for the two aide groups follow from reasons already offered. The sharp disparities between the two groups concerning the amount of service and supervision provided, with the lack of any implication from the principle of relational density for distinguishing these situations between times of the week, suggest that the private hospital aides will give more service on both (26) weekdays and (27) evenings and weekends and that the state aides will be more supervisory on both (28) weekdays and (29) evenings and weekends. As for sociability, the state aide should be (30) more sociable on weekdays, whereas (31) on eve-nings and weekends the two groups should be alike since the differences in relational density and hierarchy dissolve at those times.

Overall, private aides should behave more like state aides on evenings and weekends when the clinicians are not present, and the state aides should remain the same around the clock. The opposite of these patterns would deny the relational density hypothesis. If the private aides behave the same way during both time periods and state aides act differently between the two periods, the hypothesis would be clearly rejected and the principle of mind as partly environment-dependent would be called into question.

The results of tests of the difference between proportions for the thirty-one predictions are given in Figure 13-1. We know that the two groups are similar in general. Since differences between them or between the two time periods may be mild, I have again responded to trends. I cite a difference wherever the test of significance indicates that it would occur fewer than one out of five times by chance (p < .20).

The hypothesis fares well. The tests show that private aides do vary more between weekdays and evenings and weekends than do state aides. Of the thirty-one specific predictions, twenty-one are confirmed and ten are not confirmed.

The correctness of predictions from the hypothesis varied among the three groups of comparisons (grouped by the themes set forth in Tables 11-1, 11-2, and 11-3).

The predictions related to Table 11-3 (numbers 20 to 31) were generally supported, except that no difference in sociability appeared between private and state aides on weekdays (30). The overall difference in sociability is faint (see Table 11-3). Apparently it is equally dispersed throughout the week. Another predictive failure in this group of comparisons was that private aides are slightly more supervisory on weekdays than they are on evenings and weekends (21). This latter outcome may be explained by the fact that situation 10 (A patient asks to be let off the ward or to make a telephone call) happened far more often in the private hospital, and comings and goings from the wards take place mostly during the daytime there. In this situation the aide on a locked ward often STIPU-LATES A CONDITION (s), such as asking the patient to sign a ledger kept for the purpose of knowing where patients are, as he unlocks the door. This contribution to the tally of the private aides' supervision weighed in the difference.

Finding this disparity in the time periods for situation 10, I investigated all the cases. For if a prediction failure could be explained away by timely happenings of situations, then successful predictions might be due to such unevenness too. It turns out that some other situations also take place selectively in the time periods. However, their implications for behavior differ depending on the comparison, and I will report the relevant time-tables as I review each set of findings.

The outcomes of predictions related to Table 11-1 (numbers 1 to 12) yielded supporting evidence and a handful of surprises as well. Private aides tend to be somewhat more directive on evenings and weekends than they are on weekdays, as expected (2). When private aides are compared with state aides, the latter are more directive on weekdays (8), and the two groups are about the same on evenings and weekends (11). The state aides

Figure 13–1. Outcomes of predictions based on relational density hypothesis

Predictions	Outcomes	
	As Predicted	*Not as Predicted*
1—Private more aloof weekdays than eves/weekends		Eves/ends more, p < .01
2—Private more directive eves/weekends than weekdays	p < .17	No difference
3—Private more dependent eves/weekends than weekdays		Eves/ends more, p < .02
4—State equally aloof weekdays and eves/weekends	No difference	
5—State equally dependent weekdays and eves/weekends	No difference	
6—State equally directive weekdays and eves/weekends	No difference	No difference
7—On weekdays, private more aloof than state		No difference
8—On weekdays, state more directive than private	p < .02	
9—On weekdays, state more dependent than private		No difference
10—On eves/weekends, private and state equally aloof		Private more, p < .14
11—On eves/weekends, private and state equally directive	No difference	
12—On eves/weekends, private and state equally dependent		State more, p < .08
13—Private more indifferent weekdays than eves/weekends	p < .01	No difference
14—Private more helpful eves/weekends than weekdays	No difference	
15—Private equally redirective weekdays and eves/weekends	No difference	
16—Private equally prohibitive weekdays and eves/weekends	No difference	
17—State equally helpful weekdays and eves/weekends	No difference	
18—On weekdays, state more helpful than private	p < .12	
19—On eves/weekends, private and state equally helpful	No difference	

Figure 13-1. (continued)

20—Private equally sociable weekdays and eves/weekends	No difference	
21—Private equally supervisory weekdays and eves/weekends		Weekdays more, p < .20
22—Private equally serving weekdays and eves/weekends	No difference	
23—State equally sociable weekdays and eves/weekends	No difference	
24—State equally supervisory weekdays and eves/weekends	No difference	
25—State equally serving weekdays and eves/weekends	No difference	
26—On weekdays, private more serving than state	p < .05	
27—On eves/weekends, private more serving than state	p < .01	
28—On weekdays, state more supervisory than private	p < .13	
29—On eves/weekends, state more supervisory than private	p < .03	
30—On weekdays, state more sociable than private		No difference
31—On eves/weekends, private and state equally sociable	No difference	

are equally dependent (5) and equally directive (6) in the two time periods, as predicted. As for private aides, they did not differ in dependence between the two periods as expected (3), but they were no less dependent on patients than were state aides on weekdays (9). A disparity in amount of dependence between the two groups is shown in a trend for state aides to display more dependence than do private aides on evenings and weekends (12). The findings for aloofness also deny my predictions. The state aides are unexpectedly more aloof on evenings and weekends than they are on weekdays (4), and the private aides mirror this greater aloofness on evenings and weekends (1), which is opposite my prediction based on the hypothesis. I expected the two groups not to differ in aloofness on evenings and weekends, but the private aides are more aloof then (10). I expected private aides to be more aloof than state aides on weekdays, but there is no difference between the groups at that time (7).

Here are two patterns concerning dependence and aloofness that are contrary to the hypothesis. The only difference in dependent behavior is that on evenings and weekends state aides depend on patients more than do private aides. All my predictions for aloofness were contradicted. It is mainly an evening and weekend phenomenon in both settings. At that time private aides are more aloof than state aides; the two groups do not differ on weekdays with respect to this theme.

There are other plausible explanations for these outcomes. As the day wears on, aides may be less energetic and less willing to engage with others. Aides may be less interested in contacts with patients of widely different class backgrounds, which is the case in the private institution. Two situations in which aides are aloof occur more often on weekdays in the state hospital but happen evenly in the private setting. These are situations 2 (A patient and an aide pass each other or meet) and 4 (A patient makes a remark or is having a conversation with an aide). Perhaps they are more common on weekdays in the state hospital because tranquilizers are dispensed more liberally there. State hospital patients get sleepier sooner in the evening. Behavior is shaped by biochemical factors, such as fatigue and drugs, and by attitudes toward others of different social classes, as well as by the presence or absence of people in certain organizational positions.

The findings related to Table 11-2 (numbers 13 to 19) support the four most important predictions based on the hypothesis. They are 14, 17, 18, and 19. All have to do with aides helping patients in trouble. As expected, state aides are more helpful than are private aides on weekdays (18), and the two groups are alike on evenings and weekends (19). While state aides are equally helpful during both time periods (17), private aides are more helpful toward patients on evenings and weekends than they are on weekdays (14) when other staff members are around. The expectations that private hospital aides would be about equally redirective (15) and equally prohibitive (16) throughout the week are also confirmed. The prediction for more indifference in the private aides' behavior on weekdays versus evenings and weekends (13) was not borne out. It is about the same in the two time periods. Indifference does not represent the treatment relationship as much as help does, for it is expressed in situations involving institutionally required activities and optional activities as well as those involving disturbed or distressed patients. Maybe clinicians exert less pressure on aides in the private hospital with respect to this theme.

The situations analyzed for predictions 13 through 19 are distributed fairly equally between weekdays and evenings and weekends in the state hospital. In the private hospital, however, two unusual forms of conduct—situations 5 (A patient performs an unusual verbal act) and 18 (A patient performs an unusual physical act)—happen significantly more often on weekdays. This is a surprising finding. In another essay I have discussed the reasons for interpreting it as a reverse placebo effect. Clinicians are present mainly on weekdays and these situations seem to be based on the psychotherapeutic ritual in which clinicians elicit manifestations of illness in trying to deal with them. The distribution of the other problematic situations was not biased in favor of one of the time periods.

The outcomes of this entire thirty-one-part test, like the timetable found for unusual acts of patients in the private hospital, generally confirm the idea that behavior is regulated by behavior.

Implication

By substantiating the influence of the environmental part of mind, I do not reject what is already well understood about other causes of conduct such as inner urges and attitudes. These also exert influence. But behavior is shaped by the external portion of mind as well. It was fruitful to check the association between types of conduct and times of the day and week. My test results support Durkheim's belief that maintaining a division of labor requires continuing contact among the parties. It supports Strauss and his colleagues' impression of a continually adapting organizational order. Learned conduct is sustained by day-to-day experience. Rules are not internalized and followed once and for all.

The sketch of self-regulating populations also sits well with these findings. All accord a little more power to environment and sensations than yesterday's ratings of their causal roles. We need not assume that whatever a person does will always be explained by his personal history and internal states. He decides in his mind how he will react, and part of that mind is in the environment. Interpersonal situations have their say.

PART FOUR

Further Topics

14

Linkage to Organizations and Individuals

There are several appealing routes along which one might continue to explore interpersonal behavior. Much remains to be surveyed. Yet as the possibilities multiply, the chances of doing them justice in a single book diminish. Accordingly, I have chosen to discuss three topics briefly in Part Four to suggest how the ideas and methods already presented may be extended. There are other important topics outstanding. However, these three follow naturally from the preceding material, and I offer them as overtures to further study.

Can interpersonal behavior be used to portray and explain everything that takes place in human experience? Is the act the elementary constituent of other entities like a person or society? The question may be put the other way. Of what is a person or an institution or a society composed? Are these pure aggregates of actions, coupled to one another and amplified? The reductionist view harbors the premise that one or a few basic components are the building blocks of all social phenomena. If so, then events involving single individuals, groups of individuals, and societies would be describable and explainable in the same terms.

A number of writers have declared that society emerges from observable interactions among individuals. Included here are Simmel, Blau, Mead, and Homans. Wynne-Edwards claims that "society is no more and no less than the organization necessary for the staging of conventional competition."

Although I believe that much can be explained using the variables of interpersonal behavior, I am wary of the "nothing but" declarations put forth. In describing and explaining society, one should be able to account

279

for the nation-state, technology, war, human hierarchies according to esteem, the nature of cities, advertisements, power kilowatts per person, community political power, crime, codes of law, the tax structure, music of an era, and stockpiles of objects in museums. Some of these items are more amenable than others to behavioral accounts. Interpersonal behavior cannot be used to explain all of them because it requires sensory access among people. Some of these phenomena may depend on human actions but are not interpersonal conduct because they do not fit its definition (page 15). How far can one move away from events when people are in sensory access and still claim that the matter is reducible to interpersonal behavior? Actions between people often lead to decisions that work on nonhuman parts of the environment and that affect people by their consequences much later. For example, the overgrazing and overplanting of prairies by one generation resulted in erosion and dust bowls in the land for a later generation. Consequently it affected the economic strength of the region, the vocational drift from farming to migrant work, and so on. To try to describe all this according to acts of people is to ignore the interaction between human and nonhuman systems and to reduce the latter to triviality in an unbalanced equation.

In the same way, because interpersonal behavior requires sensory access, I cannot accept the view that organizations are merely interactions of individuals. People in organizations do not always have access to one another, yet their conduct is part of the organizational process. For example, they often work alone to collect information from documents and to plan budgets, and they communicate with other departments by written memo. The organizational process also brings humans into contact with nonhuman objects, as in the surveillance of grounds and property, the maintenance of buildings, and the operation and servicing of machines. In these respects the organizational system is not reducible to interpersonal action.

As for social conduct's being sufficient to explain everything about individuals, remember that organic aging is a biological process. It affects everyone regardless of the differences in interpersonal lives. Death has more leverage over social relationships than social relationships have over death. In life the individual is important as a decision-maker. Some acts of artistic creation such as painting, sculpture, literature, and design are rarely interpersonal, while performance of dance, drama, and music usually are. Creative work often takes place during a span of sensory inaccessibility, when other people's prosaic assessments and dull ideas cannot slow the flywheel of concentration.

Such aspects of human activity put a heavy strain upon explanations based only on interpersonal behavior. Claims that "an individual is a phase of society and society is a phase of individual existence" may at best state a relationship in the way that bread is a phase of atoms and atoms a phase of bread. Much enters into each level that is different from the principles and data of the other level. Each level entails a particular organization of its own components. Explanatory principles at one level often have limited applicability. A cook need not know the laws of chemical combination in order to prepare a lamb stew. Its succulence or flavor is not reducible to the chemistry of the contents. Nor can a chemist who is cognizant of how rosemary and salt act on turnips by such knowledge alone turn out an acceptable stew. Similarly, an architect designing a building deals with variables and concepts other than the properties of subatomic particles of which his materials are composed. A physicist familiar with those properties is not necessarily able to draft a nice house.

The same principle fits social acts. For example, the hypothesis of relational density and hierarchy, in spite of its fair predictive power, did not anticipate the timetables of all meaningful actions. Some of the pattern is affected by processes at other levels. If so, it is useful to think of a connectedness between interpersonal behavior and parts of other systems. The fullest explanation of acts will rest on a set of principles that variously depends on processes from several of these systems.

The study of social conduct should be based on a dual program. See how much can be accounted for by populations as systems. One can establish their boundaries, measure them, and then confine research to them. By focusing on their self-regulating features, one can explain a great deal in terms of behavior itself and need not attend to processes in other systems. We have not yet determined how much can be managed by such variables and propositions alone. Until we have thoroughly explored the possibilities using the first few principles, we will not know how much will be left unexplained and what inquiries into other processes will be in order.

Still, the causal equation is complex. Assuredly, interpersonal conduct cannot explain all about a population of acts. That population is an *open system*. It permits entry of information and energy from outside its boundaries and also permits information and energy to leave its realm. Bertalanffy developed this idea to explain the difference between the trend to randomness in thermodynamic systems (which are closed and self-contained) and the trend to progressively more complex order in living things. By studying the way populations are connected with other systems, we can learn more. Scan the borders to note what factors link up with the behavior system. For each factor discovered, ask under what conditions it crosses the threshold and how it influences behavior when it does.

I will trace some linkages between two of these other systems (ideological, social, biological, chemical, and so on) and populations of acts. I choose these two because they are relevant to actions between people occupying social positions. The two systems are the *organization* in which a social position is found and the *individual* who fills the position. I will not discuss their natures in full but will demonstrate how behavior, while self-regulating, is linked to them and how their forces join to produce the behavior patterns found in the case study. It entails identifying the particular couplings between those systems and social conduct, where organizational and individual factors directly affect situations and reactions.

Organizational Contributions

In this section I will review some elements that combine to promote differences in the division of labor in organizations. From the behavioral standpoint, division of labor is an attribute already familiar to us—the restriction of variety in different act-populations. The greater the extent to which situations and reactions are not shared across the repertoires of an organization, the greater the division of labor. Each repertoire is unlike the others. From the organizational standpoint, division of labor is the apportionment of functions and responsibility and authority among a set of social positions. The more heterogeneous and profuse the apportionments, the greater the division of labor (or specialization) in the system. Influential conditions include the operating technology of the organization, its formal plan for functioning, its power hierarchy, and the actual relational density of people filling its positions. These factors will be discussed here one at a time, although the process has a simultaneous character.

Hospitals bring to bear a variety of skills and techniques selected in appropriate combination and sequence to treat each individual. Both institutions in this case study explicitly make provision for psychotherapy in their policies of service to patients. Both hospitals also emphasize the principle of constructive dealings with patients by all staff members who meet them at any time. The name of this principle, *therapeutic community,* is often invoked in the private hospital. Its administrators and supervisors say that the aide is a member of the treatment team. No one in that setting favors detachment in aides, in principle. But the two types of therapy are incompatible. Psychotherapy relies on transference, which reserves the nub of treatment for a one-to-one relationship. The program for a therapeutic community promotes many healing relationships for patients. This contradiction between exclusive and communal forms of assistance is a reason for competition.

That alone does not afford a basis for concluding that aides will end up with residual repertoires if they compete with professionals. The differential power of the positions decides this. In organizations this is conferred in advance. It stems from conscious planning in which authority is distributed according to ability and training. Weber described such a design, in which the division of labor is fitted to the system's goals and in which the conduct of each person in the system is based on his competence for the particular function designated by his position. Typical of this organizational form, he wrote, is a hierarchy in which "each lower office is under the control and supervision of a higher one," who holds authority because of his superior skills. Weber explained that commands or rules will be obeyed by individuals because they perceive it in their own best interest to do so and because they believe that the rules and social arrangements are legitimate. That is, individuals have attitudes supporting those rules and arrangements even if they are not actively involved or directly affected by all of them. The hospital stresses expertise, following rules, and submitting to higher echelons. For both the private and the state institution there are formal organization charts on which the positions, including those of professional clinicians, are arranged hierarchically.

However, the contradiction in treatment technology that spurs competition and the power hierarchy for persons with different roles in treatment that resolves the competition is still not sufficient to account for the differences between the two hospitals. What is missing is an explanation of the disparities in relational density in the two settings. The hierarchy is represented by social positions with unequal power, in that way deciding who will fail to reserve certain kinds of conduct for themselves. Density is represented by the presence of others who will compete for access to patients. The outcome of competition rests on both of these conditions. Hierarchy needs the friction of density to spark competition and exertion of power. Density needs a hierarchy to help decide who will win which behavioral preserve.

Relational density depends on there being incumbents in the positions in the hierarchy. This is influenced by organizational hiring practices, by the budget allocated to fill the designated positions on the organizational plan, and by the status of the institutions in the community. The budget for the state hospital, for example, may be planned by another agency and decided by appropriations made by the legislature in the state capital months in advance of the time that authorization for expenditures is given to the director of the hospital in another city. The several steps may be connected by documents sent through the mail between members of different agencies who do not have sensory access to one another. So these steps constitute organizational action that infiltrates to affect hiring practices in a given setting.

In the private hospital the various positions requiring training in clinical skills are fully staffed with incumbents. In addition, that institution houses a small number of patients. The combination of a fully staffed organization and a high staff-patient ratio provides the density that brings on competition. Acting from their advantageous position, the professionals lay claim to a realm because of special training and treatment necessity, and from which they exclude others. The competition is most severely felt by aspiring student clinicians (in psychiatry, psychology, and social work) whose expertise is emergent and tentative. Their desire for acceptance by their superiors incites stronger feelings of imperiled status when aides are friendly with patients and triggers energetic territorial defense. They are vigilant about maintaining jurisdiction. An aide who reacts to patients in a way resembling a clinician is seen to be a personal threat as well as a meddler in the psychotherapy program. The clinicians win, and the private hospital aides are channeled into their fraction of the division of labor.

In the state institution the force of the formal plan is sapped by scanty recruitment of professionals to its rolls. A lean budget is often cited as the cause of meager services in public institutions for the mentally ill. But many such hospitals have unfilled positions awaiting qualified applicants. Croog refers to the parallel between a hospital's interpersonal environment and the social, political, religious, and economic segments of society from which its clients come. "The relative prestige of a hospital and the type of financial support it receives are related to its being identified with a particular segment or stratum of the community. This identification, in turn, has implications for the staffing of the institution at various occupational levels. The most prestigious and respected hospitals in a community may have relatively less difficulty than low status institutions in attracting trustees, staff physicians, volunteer workers, and salaried employees." Whatever the reason, the failure to hire people for all the boxes on the organization chart results in a pattern of light density in the state setting. If others are not present to monitor the aides' performance, then the plan for them to behave a certain way cannot be fulfilled. There is also an ample supply of patients at the state hospital. Even if there were more clinical personnel, there might not be the scarcity of patients that calls forth competition. The combined sparseness of other personnel and the multitude of patients in the state hospital results in a low relational density and a low staff-patient ratio. The aides expand their repertoires, assume more responsibility for patients, and compensate to some extent for the shortage of clinicians. The result is a population of acts that blurs the division of labor.

So men formally plan organizations, and these plans are modified by contingencies that sometimes lead to more constraint and sometimes to more opportunities. The organizational factors mentioned here do not calcify into a stable scheme. They are dynamic, and the division of labor depends on the continued interaction of organizational and behavioral conditions. If any of these variables are changed, the population of acts would be different. Moreover, the outcome does not stem from a unified purpose controlling the several factors. It results from a combination of separately made decisions.

Imagine a setting in which a hierarchy does not exist but where there is density, few patients, and a contradiction in treatment principles. The outcome could be the abandonment of the transference principle and reliance instead on the therapeutic community program. Imagine a setting in which the hierarchy occurs along with density but where no contradictions in treatment exist. If the psychotherapeutic regime were the main form of treatment, division of labor might be more extreme than that found in the private hospital. Perhaps the classical stereotype of aides as guards would fit here. Imagine circumstances as they are in the private hospital as far as budget, hiring practices, hierarchy, and relational density are concerned; if there were five times as many patients, there would be less competition for access and maybe less aloofness and more scope in the aides' act-population.

None of the variables, or any lesser combination of them, is sufficient to explain the different outcomes between private and state hospital aides. The variables interact. Treatment technology is linked to the principle of rational competence on which the power hierarchy of the organization is based. The hierarchical structure is a design that hiring practices can either fulfill or leave as an unused script. Staff size in turn becomes utilizable according to a particular pool of patients. If that pool of patients is large, it could give rise to a staff-patient ratio that makes a psychotherapeutic program unfeasible and could compel a different type, of treatment that may be irrelevant to professional competence . . . and the circle of influence continues.

Individual Contributions

In the preceding section I suggested how social structure affects the aides' contact opportunities in the different hospitals and influences their behavior. It does not explain all. It does not account for the varying reactions to the same situation in the same institutions.

Private hospital aides were told what was expected of them. That is, they were told what they were not supposed to do. This inhibited them and narrowed their relationship with patients. Rules of exclusion are common in organizations and in society. Such rules leave room for differences in behavior. Leeway is given in many situations, and variety in reactions occurs. The rules, therefore, along with organizational processes, do not in themselves explain the varied reactions found in whole acts. Some of this variation, as I suggested in Chapter 13, is due to social and biological conditions at different times of the day and week.

Perhaps aides differentiate situations beyond the descriptions provided in Table 9-1. The varied reactions could also be due to finer distinctions made by aides than were made by me. One can always wonder if my classification of situations blurred distinctions that participants make in interacting. The distinctions could be based on information not available to observers, such as personal attributes of patients or past experiences with them. Differences among persons in the other position of the relationship become differences in the properties of the situation. It is an unresolved question whether this refined definition of situation is objective and overlooked (making the classification faulty) or created by the participants (making them the remodelers of the same objective scene).

People are as prone to overlook distinctions as to pay attention to them. If they do refine their perceptions of situations, it is as likely to be *something about themselves that affects the perception* as it is about the others whom they contact. In this section I will show how the sets of alternative reactions are due to personal differences that express individuality of aides.

The behavior table is not a description of a person's conduct but a description of a repertoire. It is not deducible from an individual's performance without losing or distorting qualities and quantities that are significant in the social position. It would be wrong to assume that each individual has all the traits of the population to which he contributes. Variety in the population of acts for a type of social relationship almost always exceeds that displayed by an individual. There may well be some involved, directive, and helpful aides working in the private hospital. There may be some unhelpful and aloof aides employed in the state institution.

Each person participates in and contributes to various repertoires by virtue of his having several social positions in his life condition. He may be student, parent, citizen, and customer in the course of his day. One reason for the ease of moving from one social position to another is that many situations confronted in one position are met in others (page 122). There is usually an overlap, or even perfect repetition, of the set of alternatives to the similar situations. For example, a female aide may also be a mother. As part of that repertoire, situation 14 may be stated as follows: While children are eating lunch, the mother cares for or serves (n), leaves the children to themselves (e), greets them (f), supervises the activity—perhaps to prevent skirmishes among her brood or to ensure that all drink their milk (h), or some combination of these.

The population-of-acts idea could be applied to a single individual. It would be the collection of all interpersonal conduct associated with him. We would study him in all his positions and note the reactions he chooses from the sets that usually follow the situations he confronts. He could then be described by a profile of situations and his likely reactions. It would be compatible with the description of a repertoire.

Each person takes up a style of conduct that can be traced in the repertoire. (Novelty is possible too, as I will note in the following chapter.) While his reactions will not be identical for all situations, he will show a coherent pattern. In his different relationships he will tend to employ certain reactions across many situations at higher probabilities than are credited to those reactions in the repertoires. That is, each individual will be narrower in his own conduct than the full scope of reactions seen in those situations. People in social positions in this way have an opposite effect on repertoires than the impact of relational density and positional hierarchy. The latter factors result in a restriction in variety of conduct within each act-population and differences among the organization's collection of repertoires. That is the division of labor. The individual contributes to differences *within* each act-population, while at the same time showing less variety in behavior across the several repertoires that he uses in all spheres of his own life. Because of this, and because personalities are different, alternativeness is found in the population of acts. It is due to the aggregate of contributions by different individuals.

A certain mechanism results in more uniformity in an individual's behavior than the various situations he confronts seem to demand. He is affected by his prejudices, aspirations, opinions, beliefs, motives, drives, needs, and impulses. All these appear in or are converted to bodily form to affect his definition of a situation.

The connection between an idea and movement was the basis of a crude "ideo-motor" hypothesis of behavior at the turn of the century. Several writers found significance in the muscle states and postural orientations that exist along with thought and prior to an overt reaction to a situation. Cooley wrote that "the idea of an action is itself a motive to that action and tends intrinsically to produce it unless something intervenes." Watson wrote that thinking involved the whole body and the incipient posturing (if not the movements) of various muscles. Allport reviewed the contributions of several researchers whose work suggested a connection between muscle tension and perception. A connection between ideas and muscle activity was also made by Freud, who suggested that physical symptoms were transformations of feelings of danger.

An individual's body cannot help but become part of the field he perceives. His perception will therefore be affected by his body's condition as well as by stimuli from others in his milieu. Suppose he anticipates a particular event. He shifts his eyes to where it should happen or inclines his head in the direction of the expected sound. He also prepares to react to what he expects. Both his gross movement and his incipient reaction create specific dispersions of muscle tone in his body. These tension levels in his musculature are monitored and join his mind along with sensations. There the situation is defined from a combination of all this information. Therefore, as his belief or motive becomes a tendency to act, this readiness helps categorize an interpersonal situation in a certain way.

Exuberance, passion, lassitude, and all other moods have bodily accompaniments. All are self-stimulating because they influence muscle tone. An ideology can dominate expectancy. The power of a premise is rendered in anticipation. The angry man is prepared to react to gestures toward him as if they were aggressive; the relaxed person underperceives tension in others. The strengths of people's drives and beliefs also fluctuate. So do the perspectives they harbor based on their membership in different social groups. This fluctuating relevance plays waveringly upon impressions. The stronger the belief, feeling, or motive, the more powerful the influence on somatic states and the more directly will the perception be colored by it. Sometimes an anticipation or urge may be so strong that the covert preparedness becomes overt. As a gesture it then contributes to the situation and affects other people's behavior. Friendliness begets friendliness. Sullenness begets antagonism. If the other person unwittingly cooperates by reacting with the anticipated conduct, he calls forth the performance of the full pattern whose initial movement helped shape his conduct in the first place. Here is a particular effect of reactions on the occurrence of situations.

This contribution of muscle tension and sensorimotor feedback to the recognition of situations and meanings shows that perception is not mainly cognitive or mainly behavioristic. Mind is inhabited by representatives of muscle tones and flowing juices along with symbols. One cannot explain perception, individual experience, or intelligent decision-making without including all these components.

Here are two systems, one organismic-biological and confined to the effective reaches of its sensory apparatus, the other interpersonal and found in contacts among individuals as occupants of social positions. In action the two interpenetrate. One cannot trace a boundary between them that preserves the domain of each separate and intact any easier than Shylock could collect his pound of flesh without a jot of blood.

15

Stability and Change

The same format used to portray stable practices should also be able to describe changes in patterns of conduct. It should enable us to locate both conservative eras in the history of a repertoire and periods during which it displays growth and transformation. We need a descriptive mode that deals as comfortably with change as with stability.

Since Table 9-1 gives consolidated information from a survey carried out during a two-year period, it does not in itself set forth the extent to which those act-populations remain the same or are altered. The behavior table tells about the population of acts in a given time period. It is based on a single survey and is related to the biography of the repertoire in the same way that a single frame of a filmstrip is related to an entire motion picture. If a series of such photographs were taken in successive periods and then viewed apace, one might see the behavior table remaining unchanged, undergoing minor alterations here and there, or showing wholesale fluctuations in the types and numbers of acts. Some acts may flourish and swell in frequency with the passage of time. Others may decline. New types may appear while others dwindle and ultimately vanish. We stop the flow of action and print it in the behavior table like a snapshot in order to be able to study it. The transition matrices (9-3 and 9-4) lend themselves to depicting evolution, for they contain cells with zero probability. These imply logically possible combinations that were not observed. Since the matrix is prepared for what might take place as well as what does happen, it is a format for showing more than the events of any period. It is able to cope with possible future states of the social relationship.

Definitions and Measurements

A population is stable if its behavior categories and their probabilities remain the same over time. Change is the significant alteration of act categories or their probabilities over an extended interval. Neither stability nor change is the real property of an act-population merely punctuated by the other. The two are manifestations of the same existence.

Change is initially discernible by shifts in probabilities. A much-used act abates in its likelihood, or a rarely used act becomes more likely. Before a particular category disappears from a population, its probability diminishes. Additionally, an act with a low probability may have just appeared. Table 9-1 provides for common and rare events alike, so it is an instrument sensitive to change. Consider situation 26 (A patient smiles and his false tooth drops out). It is a rare event in the aide-patient repertoire; it takes place in only one of the hospitals. Can we make something from this small piece of information?

Once a procedure for studying behavior has been developed, one with clear-cut assumptions and classification techniques, we must be willing to honor all the evidence assembled by using that method. An act announces itself. It demands to be acknowledged, counted, and given accommodation in the scheme. If it does not fit well with other situations, it must be assigned its own niche. However rare, it can be given a probability in accordance with the procedures for estimating from a sample. Instead of a dismissal of situation 26 as an amusing novelty, its rare occurrence is plausible if it represents a new trend.

The practice of sophisticated and extensive renovation of the body is recent in human history. In our society it is increasingly common for people to falsify their appearance for health or for cosmetic purposes. They replace lost teeth, fill hollow bosoms, and wear glass eyes and artificial legs. Bald salesmen find that secretaries do not permit them entry into executive offices as readily as their hairy-headed competitors, so the practice of wearing hairpieces is growing among this occupational group. There is also a contemporary trend toward taking greater risks in sports. It will be accompanied by a higher proportion of the population having injuries that call for replacement of a limb or covering up of other defects in appearance. With a greater proportion of the citizenry concealing such flaws, the statistical likelihood of an accidental unmasking—a toupee dislodged, an artificial limb turned askew—will increase.

These sudden revelations are sorry moments. They bespeak falseness in one's presentation of self. The reaction of other persons, by laughing or by expressing sympathy, could have a strong effect on the person unmasked. If the person unmasked is a mental patient, the reaction of others bears on his therapy. It may well be that extended observation of the aide-patient repertoire would not glimpse this particular plight more than once or twice. It could be that rare. Situation 26 is more likely to happen in the private hospital. These spare parts are costly. Patients at the private hospital can secure them sooner because they come from a more affluent segment of society. It is more common to find patients in the state hospital who are gap-toothed. If other similar events followed by the same reactions took place, they might all be consolidated into a broader category of embarrassing situations.

Here are several reasons why situation 26 is a significant part of the aide repertoire. The first reason is that it happens. Its birthright cannot be denied. It is a fact revealed by a systematic method that gives us awareness of the behavioral universe. No action should be omitted or ignored if it was identified through use of the sample survey and the classification procedure. Second, because the situation involves the unmasking of a false front presented to others, it may be especially troubling to emotionally disturbed persons. It is therefore germane to the interaction between mental patients and psychiatric aides. Third, it will happen more often in the future. With increased technological ability to manufacture parts of the body to replace those damaged or worn out, and with spare parts made available to more people through government subsidies for medical care, situation 26 is likely to make its appearance at the state hospital too. Today's rarity in the repertoire may be a commonplace tomorrow.

The appearance of a new category, either of situation or reaction, is the most noticeable sign of change. The category may be an offshoot of a type already established in earlier classification, whose attributes have slowly altered until it becomes necessary either to broaden the existing class, with a resultant increase in internal variation, or to establish a new category.

Stability or change is a property of the whole population. For example, a reaction category not associated with a particular situation cannot make its appearance in that situation without pushing a quantity to change elsewhere. Its introduction forces revised probabilities. Such accommodation to change could simply be an internal instability, for it is a secondary realignment of numbers. If there are tides of readjustment, stable eras may be rare because of compensating changes propagated in this way.

We hear on one side that changes in the meanings of acts are more rapid than most of us are aware. On the other side, we are told that meanings exhibit a high degree of stability and are rather slow to change. Both impressions may be correct if they refer to different types of change. The saying that "the more things change the more they are the same" resembles the idea of symmetry transformation in particle physics in that certain parts of the system may undergo change without altering the character of the whole with respect to certain important qualities. It also resembles homeostasis in biological systems in that some material components of behavior may be substituted while the meaningful states of the system remain steady. Let us call this condition in interpersonal behavior *epistability*. It is the persistence of a meaningful pattern of behavior despite substitutions and probability shifts for reactions in the set. Some reactions may vanish from sets and others may make their appearance. Probabilities may alter so that some go up and others decline. Yet at the end of a period of reshuffling, all these exchanges may cancel out so that the connotations remain intact. For example, in describing and comparing the population of acts for aides in the two hospitals, I subsumed three reaction categories to identify the trait of aloofness in the repertoire: SHOWS NO OVERT CHANGE IN BEHAVIOR (d), LEAVES THEM TO THEMSELVES (e), and WITHDRAWS (r) (Table 11-1). A second sample survey might show that the probability of reaction e had declined significantly in its situations whereas the probability of reaction r had increased significantly, such that the gain in the latter offset the loss in the former. If the resulting degree of aloofness in the repertoire is the same as before, the repertoire is epistable.

The principle of epistability exposes the difference between behavioral change and meaningful change. Since changes in reactions may balance out, the persistence of a significant theme in a repertoire does not imply that it is being sustained by the original acts.

On the other hand, the connotations of acts do change. An act does not carry all its meanings in one era. Its connotation can be revised by replacing one of its likely alternatives. The meaning may transfer from one alternative to another.

A well-established tradition in the study of social change is the focus on moral meanings. What is the connection between repertoire change and moral change? Moral change is an alteration in one type of meaningful assessment of behavior. It deals with the ethical import of conduct or with the matter of approval and disapproval or with the act's implication for society's ultimate values. Moral change can provoke or follow behavioral change. As circumstances evolve, acts thought constructive and good may be downgraded while others once taken as repugnant may be reinterpreted as natural for humans. So, for example, because of new alternatives, the whites who used to bring baskets of food to poor black families on Thanksgiving are today considered not generous but condescending. The patriotic soldiers who used to destroy the enemy's crops and villages are in today's wars considered inhumane. Nude exposure on the stage, once judged indecent and limited to burlesque houses, is today a dramatic art form. Yesterday's evenhandedness toward criminal suspects is laxity today.

Alternativeness fits consequential meanings too. The matter of reward and punishment refers to an act's effect on the individual. "Thank you" is not rewarding to a bellboy who is used to money tips instead. On the other hand, a twenty-year prison sentence may be received joyfully by a convicted man if his more probable alternative was not freedom but execution. Consequential meanings may be revised as we improve our knowledge of the alternatives people have in mind. If we could teach them new alternatives, we could deliberately alter the meanings of rewards sought today.

Another topic that deserves study is the relation between meaning and the resistance to change. Romer's rule, cited by Hockett and Ascher, connects acceptance of change with epistable meaning. It implies that those behavioral changes which promise to do away with traditional meanings will be objected to most: "The initial survival value of a favorable innovation is conservative, in that it renders possible the maintenance of a traditional way of life in the face of changed circumstances." Should a novel reaction occur that undermines a major connotation of a particular act, people who rely on that connotation would be offended and threatened by the novelty. They would condemn it, resist it, and try to suppress it.

Because meanings vary according to the alternatives in repertoires, a disruption is felt more severely when cultural borders are crossed and a single reaction is forced upon a people or pried from them. The outsider does not appreciate how this implant or excision invalidates the meanings of the *other* alternatives in the set. No wonder people of a culture often resist piecemeal intrusions into their way of life and insulate the forcefully inserted ways of behaving with readjustments in alternative reactions.

Limits and Trends

The appearance and preservation of a novel reaction in a population is a sign of change. So is its counterpart, the suppression and disappearance of a category of conduct. Given that the settings for my case study are two mental hospitals, one may wonder why no category for physical violence toward patients by aides is listed in Figure 7-3. After all, the abuse of patients by aides has been part of many descriptions of life in mental institutions. Because the behavior table does not contain evidence for such conduct, I present here a list of the violent episodes I have been exposed to in such settings. This list reflects over a decade of research in eight institutions (including the two described in this book), large and small, federal and state and private, in three different states from 700 to 2000 miles apart from one another in the United States.

1. Patients attacking patients: In another hospital, some patients gathered in a deserted corridor after midnight to gamble with dice. When one patient argued against a particular outcome, a fight started and he was knocked out.

2. Patients attacking aides: In another hospital, an instance with obscure beginnings in which a patient broke an aide's jaw.

3. Aides attacking aides: In one of the two hospitals in the survey, an instance with obscure beginnings in which an aide leaped on the back of another aide and drove him to the ground.

4. Aides attacking patients: (a) In another hospital, an aide subjected a patient to severe verbal abuse when the patient consumed the aide's dish of ice cream while the aide was taking his turn in a game of billiards. (b) In another hospital, two aides seized a patient whom they believed was succumbing to a convulsive fit. (As an onlooker, I did not believe he was entering a seizure.) The patient began to struggle fearfully against their assault, and this spurred the aides to redouble their efforts to subdue him and bind him onto a stretcher. (c) In one of the two hospitals in this survey, an aide testified that he made a practice of overturning the bed and dumping the patient onto the floor if the latter did not respond to the aide's second call to get up in the morning (page 151).

What has happened to brutality in mental hospitals? It has not wholly disappeared, but since this list is based on thousands of hours of personal observation as well as on the sample survey data, it seems as if the once-violent wards have become much calmer. This is not to deny sporadic acts of physical mistreatment. But they are now far less characteristic of mental hospitals than is the beating of children in the repertoire of parents. Perhaps the vestiges of physical authoritarianism, which in its more severe forms was interpreted as brutality, are to be found in the repertoire today in the form of compulsion. If so, then a review of the use of reaction k (COMPELS TO STOP OR TO DO IT) should be made. I have done so in Chapter 11. If this summary is valid, then a change has occurred in which the physical abuse of patients has all but disappeared from the aides' repertoire. How come?

Since situations elicit reactions, one reason for this reform is *a change in the behavior of patients* in psychiatric hospitals. Many of the reports of maltreatment by aides refer to earlier times during which chaos prevailed on the wards. When I first became acquainted with mental hospital settings in the middle 1950s as part of my training, I witnessed the end of one era and the beginning of another. It was signaled by the widespread introduction of tranquilizing drugs into patients' regimes. This survey of the two hospitals was begun a half dozen years later. By then the drugs had altered the climate of violence in the institutions. Indeed, in the early stages of use these drugs made patients sluggish and sleepy. Somnolence replaced agitated pacing. Patients lounged in the day rooms, slouched in chairs, and barely gazed at the out-of-focus eye of the television set that hung from the ceiling at one end of the room. The so-called acutely disturbed wards, where patients used to butt their heads against corridor walls as they walked, where patients used to unscrew legs from tables and try to smash their way out, and where aides scrupulously avoided turning their backs to patients, had changed drastically. The risks of physical attack were markedly lower, and consequently the aides' reactions toward patients changed. They less often engaged in self-defensive behavior or abuse and made more efforts to rouse patients and get them involved in some recreation. Reaction j (SUGGESTS ENTERING ACTIVITY) may be a category that was much rarer in the earlier custodial times.

Also, certain categories of conduct can be kept less likely in a population of acts by the organization's practices of recruiting, promoting, or discharging persons who manifest those actions. One of the most powerful influences for stability in the aides' repertoire is the hospitals' scheme for applying behavioral criteria to decide whether to keep certain patients or to let them go. Since those individuals whose conduct becomes more normal are discharged and are replaced with others who show symptoms of disorder, the probabilities of psychiatric situations are kept from dwindling, and the probabilities of ordinary contact opportunities are kept from increasing. Perhaps no other reason accounts as much for the pattern of patients' influences upon the aide repertoire.

Similarly, aides who are unusually likely to use reactions *j* (SUGGESTS ENTERING ACTIVITY), *i* (PARTICIPATES FULLY), and *p* (TEACHES OR CORRECTS) are likely to be promoted to the recreational therapy department. This selective promotion and replacement of aides works against altering the probabilities of certain reactions in the repertoire.

As I suggested in the case of the loose bridgework, new rare categories are indicators of changing behavior populations. The type of situation or reaction is novel, and its probability in the population is low. It is sometimes said that there is simply a progressive accumulation of types of behavior, that social life continually builds up its inventory of acts and relationships. If this applies to repertoires, then it may be that they have not reached their limits, and we can wonder about their future.

How much can a population grow in size? It is implausible that the variety of reaction categories and the number of acts in a population could expand indefinitely. There are several checks to this type of increase. Each population shows self-regulation related to its scale of existence. Ceilings are imposed by the time required to consummate acts and by the density of persons in the various social positions in the setting. The diversity and frequency of acts must stay within those bounds.

If limits in variety of categories and numbers of acts will inevitably be reached, what is the relation between the cumulative occurrence of novel categories of conduct and a population's finite size?

At some point novel acts must compete with other members of the population. Incorporation of a novel category may come at the cost of reduced frequencies of one or more other categories. Or the success of preserving a novel category may force abandonment of another type of action. This denies the idea that behavioral variety can enlarge unendingly. As the limits to the population's size and heterogeneity are neared, acquiring new categories of reactions entails the diminution in frequency or full discarding of old ones.

It is not necessary that novel events occur one at a time and that each one's preservation or elimination be resolved by itself. Several novel acts may appear in the population nearly simultaneously, and their fates may be conjointly decided. For example, as the accumulation of novelty proceeds, a repertoire may undergo division, yielding two or more repertoires each having less variety than their common ancestor, although the total variety and number of acts in the repertoires taken together may be more than that of the original repertoire. The outcome of this competition is found in the progression from simpler to more complex forms in society, such as the division of labor. The major behavioral feature of the increase in specialization in social organizations is the combination of more social relationships and the appearance of fewer different situations and reactions within each one of them.

The prospect of being able to discern trends, both in the rate and in the direction of change, implies that future populations might be predicted by extrapolating formulas. This in turn seems to require an assumption of unilinear evolution—that all repertoires traverse the same succession of stages along their route of change. Anthropologists have searched for evidence of continuity in the histories of cultures. Although the debate persists, the profound changes happening with industrialization in rapidly developing nations today indicate that the doctrine of unilinear evolution must be abandoned. Different cultures differ in the details and form of their development, rates of change, and durations of trends. The same applies to individuals and to social relationships. Some stages of growth are condensed and others skipped entirely. Not everyone who reaches manhood has attended college or has worked while going to school or marries or has children. Not every social relationship entails the same shifts in its kinds of behavior. Stages of amenity, friendship, directiveness, dependence, hostility, and indifference do not follow one another inevitably or in a fixed sequence.

While we may not be able to plot the trend of future change from the qualitative details of a repertoire, we might be able to infer its trajectory from the following quantitative attributes: (1) the total number of acts in the population, (2) the variety of situations, (3) the variety of reactions, (4) the probabilities of situations, (5) the probabilities of reactions, and (6) the probabilities of given reactions to given situations. They lend themselves to extrapolation. Variety of situations in a repertoire should decrease if the relationship is becoming more specialized. If a specialization is coming to rely more on interpersonal skills, the variety of reactions in each situational set should increase. The number of different situations will increase if the repertoire is becoming more generalized. If it is becoming more flexible or innovative, there will be changes in the probabilities of reactions and new categories will appear. Such indices would help plot the evolution of a repertoire as well as comparative trends among several of them.

16

Action Universals

The information presented here for psychiatric aides is bound to generate comparative interest in other social relationships. To what extent is the conduct of this repertoire found in others?

Hume answered this question by saying that ". . . there is a great uniformity among the actions of men, in all nations and ages. . . . Mankind are so much the same, in all times and places, that history informs us of nothing new or strange in this particular. Its chief use is only to discover the constant and universal principles of human nature, by showing men in all varieties of circumstances and situations, and furnishing us with materials from which we may form our observations and become acquainted with the regular springs of human action and behavior." Such an assumption deserves to be tested empirically. The population of acts is an appropriate guide for investigating, describing, and comparing the particulars of all repertoires. The formats of the behavior table and transition matrices offer places for both common and rare events and make comparison between pairs of social positions as easy as the study of one relationship. For example, nurses and aides in the same hospital can be considered in the same situations, or psychiatrists with nurses, and so on.

Any repertoire shares most of its situations and reactions with other repertoires. The aide-patient relationship may be distinctive as a whole, but many of its component acts occur elsewhere as well. Two friends pass each other on the street (situation 2), a wife tells her husband about her cares (11), an employee gripes about the company to his foreman (12), a college student jokingly distracts others who are studying in the dorms (13), a child refuses to eat (17), a new neighbor moves in next door

(25). The roster of reactions also turns up in other relationships. While all situations do not occur in all human relationships and while some are found more widely than others, a few sample surveys will suggest their extent. For example, one might guess that situations 5 (A patient performs an unusual verbal act) or 21 (A patient performs a usually private gesture in public) occur solely in mental hospital repertoires. But children often perform similarly for their parents. It should not be a surprise to learn that a repertoire involved in resocialization has something in common with one centered on primary socialization. Indeed, it will be found that substantial portions of disparate social relationships are the same. Social positions called by different names have much in common. There are a smaller number of different situations experienced by humans than the different positions with which they are associated. Also, social positions repeat themselves in different organizations and institutions, and there are a smaller group of positions than the different settings in which they are found. The United States Department of Labor, for example, lists only eighteen thousand job descriptions but about fifty thousand job titles.

In the repertoire of psychiatric aides with mental patients, there are twenty-four reaction categories and twenty-six situational categories. The pattern of less reaction variety than situation variety is not an accident but a significant reflection of the structure of behavior. The realm of interpersonal acts can be summarized by a smaller group of reactions than situations because situations are made up of reactions plus contextual conditions.

If another observational study were conducted for a different relationship—say friend with friend, salesperson with customer, or worker with coworker—not only would there be overlap with the components of the aide repertoire, but fewer additional reaction categories would be identified than would additional situations. If a third relationship were studied, there would be substantial overlap with the other two. The third survey might fail to yield new reactions and perhaps produce only a handful of other situations. There may be no greater diversity among reactions—once a set of these has been developed through a series of empirical studies in different settings—than the number of phonemes in all spoken languages. If so, we would confirm what has long been proposed, that the richly varied social experience emerges from the ways in which a small number of elements are *combined*. Repertoires are not unique because they are altogether different from one another. They are distinctive organizations of common elements.

Attention to the overlap between populations and to the statistical disparities among reactions to a situation found in two or more repertoires enables one to study the degree to which one individual's social positions are harmonious or discordant in the behavior to be anticipated from him. We can appreciate that when a situation is commonly part of two relationships that are not socially congruent, potential strains lurk about. It may be difficult to select the reaction most appropriate to both relationships. An example of this predicament would be an accidental meeting between a boss and his employee as golfers at a golf course or as clients at a bar. The leading of multiple lives, internal conflicts, and a fractionalized image of one's self may be bred in the circumstances of too little overlap among one's repertoires. On the other hand, the amount of overlap among repertoires suggests a person's potential for having a unified psychological experience. There is also the matter of overlap and similarity in behavior found in different cultures. We acknowledge cultural relativity and uniqueness. But we recognize that behavioral characteristics are shared by different peoples. Although conduct in diverse societies may appear strikingly different, behavior can be analyzed into its components. There is little difference in their objective properties. Bakuto Congolese show the same motor behavior that Bakersfield Californians do. What is noteworthy is the richness of combinations in which the handfuls of simple behavior components are used. The variety of combinations and the differences in probabilities among alternatives in sets are the grounds for concluding that there is behavioral distinctiveness in diverse cultures.

There would be high promise in using my method for cross-cultural analysis if it were not for an unavoidable snag—the method of establishing categories to describe behavior. Social scientists have persistently lacked a standard set of categories, fit for all repertoires, that could adequately portray actions and permit them to be meaningfully compared. I may have achieved the beginnings of such a set for the society found in the United States, perhaps even for those of other English-speaking peoples. It is usable for summarizing conduct and comparative studies in those cultures. But vernacular descriptions of the actors figure importantly in establishing the reaction categories.

Descriptions of acts are rooted in the vocabulary of a given tongue. They cast a form upon events that may not be matched by the phrases of another language. If one relies in part upon the testimony of participants for the establishment of categories, as I did, one must then decide which categories from different languages are the same and which are different. The matter may be solved for lone qualitative categories such as ASKS ASSISTANCE (o) or FULFILLS REQUEST (a). It is more difficult where another language yields a category that appears intermediate to an ordered set. For example, another culture or subculture may produce a category that is intermediate to the reactions of CONVERSES (b) and BRIEFLY AGREES OR DISAGREES (m). It may have another category wedged somewhere between the reactions PARTICIPATES FULLY (i), PARTICIPATES PARTLY (v), and SHOWS NO OVERT CHANGE IN BEHAVIOR (d). In my classification such intermediate types were merged into one or the other of those flanking it. In another culture those particular distinctions may be specifically made rather than overlooked.

Psathas writes that "the ethnoscientist in studying one culture's classification system has no reason to expect that another culture's classification system will be the same." "Every language," echoes Greenberg, "is an organized system which must be described in its own terms without the imposition of the observer's ethnocentrically derived categories." Many have remarked on the trials of devising questions for cross-cultural use because of different linguistic structures. Given that the validity of my categories rests partly upon the frame of reference of the actors themselves, how shall I accommodate valid but incongruent categories from two cultures? The method faces a serious challenge in the task of translation between different languages, for the categories will surely affect the findings.

How can I compare repertoires across cultures if the method of classification begets two or more sets of categories that patently overlap one another? One possibility is to establish conventions for a way of shifting sets of categories so that the junctures between the categories of two sets line up. This calls for more juggling judgments. It does not cope at all with the problem of nonequivalence in translations between languages. Words used in a language are implicated in the same type of semantic network that was outlined in the analysis of the meaning of an act (pages 77–78, 194). They are culturally luscious. They do not simply name or indicate behavioral elements but are suffused with the users' values and connotations.

Similarly, if change occurs and if change is associated with altered meanings as well, how could behavior semantics be used to interpret past or future events? It may not be feasible to develop a coding system for events that happen now and to apply it elsewhere in time. None of man's spoken languages may be an appropriate descriptive mode for a science of behavior.

A Contentless Scheme for Universal Comparisons

To skirt the trap of linguistic relativism, I will try out a characterization that relies only on quantitative aspects of interpersonal behavior. I do not aim to purge qualitative accounts or to imply that one descriptive mode has primacy over the other. The two may be used in conjunction. The sketch I propose, however, may solve some of the difficulties that come from the bond between language and culture. The ideas that follow can be evaluated empirically. If they prove useful, additional variables may be added.

Every population, whatever the language base of its act categories, has the following quantitative attributes: (1) a number of different situations (for example, in Table 9-1 there are twenty-six for the private hospital and twenty-five for the state hospital), (2) specific probability of each situation, (3) a number of different reactions (twenty-four in both hospitals in the case of aides), (4) a number of different reactions for each situation, and (5) a specific probability for each reaction in each situation. Still other quantitative attributes can be identified, but these few will be enough to demonstrate significant comparisons. I have already suggested that descriptions of change in a repertoire could rest on quantitative indices, and here I will explore what qualities of repertoires may be so implied.

I begin with only the variety of situations and their relative frequencies per population. Whatever the classifying scheme employed, the collection of situations is the primary delineator of the boundaries of the social relationship, the criterion by which interpersonal behavior will be identified as belonging to a given repertoire. The content of acts aside, there is progressively greater diffuseness or scope in relationships as one moves from fewer to greater numbers of different situations in a population of acts. Diffuseness is also greater where situations are more equiprobable. I have ordered the following relationships according to my estimate of the increasing variety of situations found in the population of acts of persons in the first social position with those in the second position: tollbooth attendant with motorist, cashier with customer, salesclerk with customer, doctor with patient, mayor with constituent, administrator with subordinate, teacher with student, friend with friend, prison guard with inmate, and mother with child. The rank order reflects progressively more extensive involvement of the first person with the second. Thus the nature of the relationship is partly revealed by the number of different situations found in the population.

Probability of occurrence is a complementary variable to that of the number of different situations. The relative frequency of each situation is a fraction of all situations occurring in the population—its probability. Two equal probabilities do not imply equal frequencies across populations. A tollbooth attendant, for example, has many times more contacts with paying motorists than does a cashier with paying customers. But the probability of the two situations in the two populations may be the same. Converting frequency to probability is a normalizing procedure that permits comparisons of different-sized act-populations.

Comparisons among repertoires can be made using a two-dimensional coordinate system to represent these two variables. The x-axis will be an enumeration of different situations in act-populations. Using relative frequency of occurrence as a guide, x-axis entries should be made in the order of the most likely situation first, and so on from left to right. The y-axis will be a scale giving the probability of each situation's occurrence. A curve can now be plotted for any population, connecting the series of points that represent the probabilities of its situations.

I have drawn some curves in Figure 16-1 to represent hypothetically three common populations of acts: (1) tollbooth attendant with motorist, (2) teacher with student, and (3) mother with child. The curve for the tollbooth attendant shows one or two situations occurring so frequently that they constitute almost all of his dealings with motorists. The teacher is open to a greater variety of contact opportunities with students, including lectures, counseling hours, discussion sections, examinations, and encounters during visits to the library. The curve for mother with child shows a more diffuse relationship than either of the other two. Many different situations occur. While some are frequent (such as getting the child washed, dressed, and fed), others are relatively rare even though they are familiar (such as dealing with appeals for an indoor activity on a rainy day, ministering to cuts and bruises, and helping a teen-age daughter prepare for a date). If the curves for the act-populations of aides with patients were plotted from the data of Matrices 9-3 and 9-4, both would approximate the slope of the hypothetical curve in Figure 16-1 for the mother with child. In each hospital the highest probability for a situation is rather low, and the probabilities drop mildly and then level off and gradually decline. There is much equiprobability too.

305

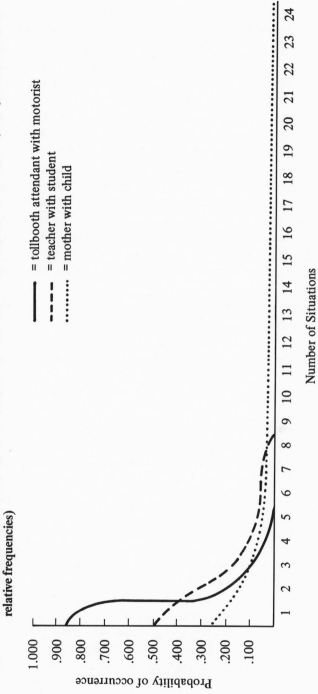

Figure 16–1. Three hypothetical curves representing repertoires having different degrees of diffuseness (variety of situations and relative frequencies)

—— = tollbooth attendant with motorist

- - - - = teacher with student

·········· = mother with child

Probability of occurrence

Number of Situations

All curves plotted in this way will subsume areas equal to 1.000, but their shapes will indicate basic differences in the relationships that their populations represent. They reflect the generality or specificity of the social relationship involved. The *specialist's* repertoire is constricted in its number of different situations. The toll collector is a specialist, for example. On the other hand, the repertoire of a parent with a child is that of a *generalist*.

In exploring this idea, I imagined that if a curve were drawn arbitrarily in a two-dimensional space (according to the conventions listed above) to depict the relationship between variety and likelihood of situations, I should be able to discern the degree to which the population it represented was generalist or specialized and perhaps even think of a repertoire that fitted the curve. A few tries quickly clarified some features of this quantitative description of interpersonal behavior. First, because it is numerical it does not depend upon a particular classification. As long as two researchers (who have not come into contact with each other and have not arrived at a taxonomic accord) are consistent in their own classifying performance, this descriptive abstraction permits comparisons to be made. It thereby provides a dimension of comparability across cultures. We can decide how similar in scope are two populations of acts even though two different sets of categories were established through independent classifications. This basic quality of repertoires might be called the degree of diffuse involvement in a relationship.

Second, there may be a family of curves that could be ordered along this dimension, representing the ensemble of repertoires in a society.

Third, it would not be a defect if some of the curves did not represent populations of acts presently discernible in a society. Perhaps they do not exist. Nonexistence of a population is not a flaw in the descriptive scheme for it is logical rather than empirical. It is a method to portray the possible as well as the observed. A form not currently extant may emerge some time in the future. Or it may have occurred in the past. The description would accommodate historical comparisons as well as those dealing with contemporaneous populations.

Fourth, the two-dimensional portrayal is a simple one. While not trivial it is gross, and additional variables could amplify the power of the description and comparisons.

I next took into consideration the sets of reactions per situation. The probability, which in the preceding scheme was allocated only among situations, is in this enlarged analysis further broken down within each situation and apportioned among its reactions. A graphical presentation is no longer adequate to depict the variables together. A matrix like that of 9-3 or 9-4 is more useful. Let the vertical axis be assigned to the different situations rank ordered from top to bottom by likelihood. The horizontal axis will now be used to indicate the reactions, rank ordered from left to right by overall probability.

Before turning to some applications, I will review what is being described and interpreted. The populations that represent repertoires are the foci of attention, not the behavior of an individual in the social position. Behavior for the repertoire may be wide-ranging while individuals in the social position may exhibit different narrow portions of the range. Although the format may be used to describe both, I deal here only with the populations for positions and not for individuals. The distinction is not always easy to make. For example, in a given setting for a given family there may be one mother and her several children. The population of acts for that position of mother in that familial setting will be the same as the population of acts for the individual in that position.

The distribution of probabilities across situations told us the extent to which a population of acts was generalist or specialist. For the specialist populations, the variety of reactions within situations may indicate the degree of interpersonal competence involved. To measure the variety, use one of the procedures I suggested earlier.

An *unskilled specialist* can be defined behaviorally as one who confronts others in only a few different situations and responds in standard fashion to those situations regardless of their frequency. The turnpike toll collector and the cashier in a retail store are examples. The events of cars driving into the gate area and of slowing down long enough to enable someone to reach and deliver a coin constrict the range of reactions the attendant may use.

On the other hand, specialization with expertise is exhibited in a population having a small number of situations for which a greater variety of reactions are employed. The *skillful specialist* varies his reactions in the few situations he encounters repeatedly. It may be that this stems from the ability to differentiate situations that look superficially the same. Even when confronted with ostensibly similar situations, the interpersonally skilled practitioner tends to assess them for dissimilarities and responds in more diverse ways. Table 16-2 denotes a hypothetical population of acts for a skilled specialist. The variety of situations and their probabilities are the same as that proposed in Figure 16-1 for the tollbooth attendant with motorists. The dispersion of reactions in Table 16-2 shows that in this population there is much variation in responding to the most common situation. If it is the conduct of a judge in court, his reactions may reveal selective concern about particular defendants coming before him and about the distinctiveness of each case, even though their legal predicament is one that he deals with frequently in his position. Tollbooth attendant and judge are both specialists, but one is interpersonally unskilled and the other is skilled. The difference is captured by the situation variety/reaction variety combination.

Table 16–2. Hypothetical probabilities of reactions of judge to defendants in court

| | | | | Reactions | | | | |
Situations	a	b	c	d	e	f	g	Σ
1	.017	.025	.010	.010	.007	.003	.001	.073
2	.012		.005					.017
3		.002	.006					.008
4			.001					.001
5					.001			.001
Σ	.029	.027	.022	.010	.008	.003	.001	1.000

I am not sure whether the skilled-unskilled distinction applies to generalists as well. There are alternative interpretations and I will mention them. Whether this engenders ambiguity and undermines the utility of this scheme cannot be decided in advance. It awaits empirical investigation. Moreover, the potential ambiguities of interpretation may be clarified by the introduction of additional quantitative variables.

The *skilled generalist* repertoire is one in which others are confronted in a variety of situations and in which a variety of reactions is used within each situation. Perhaps a gifted administrator displays this pattern.

Variety of reactions may also reveal which partners in a social relationship have more interpersonal power. Employing relatively more different reactions in a given situation implies more freedom and less submission to social control. This may indeed apply to the administrator and even to aides vis-à-vis patients. It is discernible in a social group as well. The leader and the peripheral members will employ a larger number of different reactions in a given situation and will deviate more from the norms of the group than will the central members who are not leaders.

An *unskilled generalist* would be manifested by a population of acts having many situations, in each of which there were only a few different reactions utilized. This may apply to the case of friends, reflected by rather few reactions following any given situation in their relationship. Close friends have settled upon highly gratifying modes of enjoying and helping one another. They tend to utilize those reactions repeatedly and do not search for alternative ways of responding. The element of social control may enter here too, for power does not have to be hierarchical, and good friends exert much control over one another.

I remarked earlier that behavior for a repertoire may be wide-ranging while individuals in the relevant social positions each use few reactions per situation. Such a pattern may occur in the populations that compose the repertoire of mother with children. Overall, a wide variety of reactions may be employed in the repertoire, but individual mothers differ a great deal from one another by selecting different narrow portions of the range of alternatives to situations. The average mother has no special competence derived from the consequences of her biological success in reproduction, and the skilled mother who is flexible in reacting to situations with her children is relatively rare.

Other populations of acts for other social positions may be similarly identified by being located at various points between the polar extremes of generalist and specialist, skilled and unskilled, equated with the variety and probabilities of situations and reactions. Some survey evidence would be required to investigate how promising these quantitative dimensions may be for systematic comparisons.

This form of description stimulates questions about the quantitative limits in populations of acts. One extreme would be a population in which only one situation occurs all the time, to which the same reaction inevitably follows. This limiting case would be exemplified by the repertoire of the conscientious hermit. Every time people approach him he avoids them. His one reaction ensures that no different situations will occur. In our society this limiting case is approached by the population of acts the telephone company's Information Operator uses with clients. She employs one reaction—selecting the appropriate item of information in response to a question about a telephone number—and limits the interaction to just that situation. When I was a boy I dialed Information and asked the operator, "How many nails in the Brooklyn Bridge?" After hesitating a moment she replied, "We don't give out that kind of information." Perhaps many other would-be repertoire-enlargers came after me, for the operator no longer greets me with "Information" but offers "Directory assistance" instead.

As social relationships endure, they tend to become more diffuse. At the same time, the individuals in the positions tend to settle upon a limited number of alternative responses that they employ in their oft-repeated contacts. Time thus works to enable a relationship to evolve toward the unskilled generalist from wherever else in the intersection of the various dimensions it began.

At a time when people lament the loss of universal symbols and the forfeiture of understanding, it is promising that the quantitative form of interpersonal behavior may be uncovered as a cache for meaning.

17

Concluding Remarks

We are all practiced in behavior, by ourselves and in the company of others. We never miss a day to rehearse our repertoires, and we do so without any reminders or special effort. My purpose in this essay was to describe, interpret, and explain that behavior as it happens and as it is understood.

I attended mainly to the outsides of acts. Instead of probing for internal states and hidden processes, I dealt with what could be noticed by all. In my descriptions I minimized inferences about what people think or feel as they do what they do. The interpersonal act is observable. It turns up as a rich packet of sensations when people come together. Sensations play a large role in conduct and in relationships. They are so connected with thinking and acting that if someone receives too little or too much sensation, or if stimuli from his own behavior are delayed in arriving at his receptors, he shows evidence of losing his mind. He becomes incapable of using language or of concentrating on solving problems by reasoning. Because this happens without damage to bodily structures, it shows that the mind exists in space and time. The Cartesian dualism—of a separate mind and body—perplexed us until we recognized that mind is a process that is partly composed of sensations from without. Accordingly, the minds of men merge whenever they are in one another's presence. A sizable portion of each one's conduct is in this way socially determined. That is, the actions of others nearby are part of one's mind, and those actions often dominate in deciding what one will do. This regulation of acts by acts occurs not only in occasional meetings but also where people interact repeatedly. In a hospital, for example, each staff member adjusts the scope

311

of his behavior to suit what his neighbors are doing. This practice accounts for a great deal of the particular division of labor.

There is a character of outsideness to the meaning of behavior, too. An act does not broadcast significance of itself. An event is observable, and *its outsides are the memories of similar events with other people at other times.* The act has centripetal force when it occurs. It induces the onlooker to draw together his knowledge of other reactions from other times, to treat them as possible alternatives, and to give this event meaning based on these considerations. One's understanding is refined by awareness of different probabilities among reactions. Numbers help shape the meaning. Thus even the reaction SHOWS NO OVERT CHANGE IN BEHAVIOR carries a message. The connotation of any act is formed in this way.

In making these claims, I do not reject what we know about inner urges, feelings, and qualitative understandings. Outsides by their nature imply insides. Choice of conduct derives from reason and emotion too. But the themes presented here deal with the must-not-be-overlooked empirical material of social life. When people come together they form a system. Acts are the system's units, and interpersonal acts can be explained and understood in their own terms.

The behavior table and transition matrices of Part Two are the result of my attempt to render the conception of behavior in measurement. My case study turned out to portray a modest number of acts, slightly more than 500 of them in two different settings. That was too few for investigating all the ideas in Part One. Those ideas that were studied are generally supported by the findings of Part Three. The findings also suggest useful revisions of the original notions. Overall, the case study leaves me satisfied with its accomplishment and with a whetted appetite for the possibilities of this approach. I have demonstrated a program of study and types of analyses that could be done.

When I first began this inquiry, I found myself backtracking, being skeptical and disputatious about many assumptions concerning acts that I came across in my review of the literature. The review lasted for several years. During it I carried on with uneasy doubt. Even while our field records were being made and when the classification had begun, I found myself rejecting popular assumptions that I could only employ by tilting the arrangement among the few premises that I did allow. I did not assume in advance the existence of social rules of conduct as a framework in which behavior occurs. I did not depend much on stated or implied expectations about what aides were supposed to do with patients before gathering information about their actions. Rules for conduct are held and used by people. So are attitudes about what is right and what ought to happen. I did not find it necessary to rely on such assumptions in order to describe what took place.

My experience in reporting these findings confirms that we cannot substitute expectations for direct knowledge about interpersonal behavior. On several occasions I talked about my research at conferences attended by leaders in the field of mental health. The audiences were composed of psychologists, social workers, psychiatrists, nurses, and supervisors of psychiatric aides. To kindle their interest, I distributed copies of the behavior table with the quantitative information omitted. I described the settings for my research and invited conference members to write in the probabilities of reactions to a few of the situations. When they committed themselves, I asked some of them to express their reasons for predicting that this act will happen so much and that one will not, and so on. My presentation was in this way a highly compressed research project in which the seekers, having generated predictions of conduct based on their knowledge of mental hospitals and theories about how people behave, could immediately review the outcomes of a survey whose data were relevant.

Although there were some impressively accurate forecasts, the majority of conference members declared for behavior patterns that were different from those we found. Specifically, they expected private hospital aides to show more variety in their behavior, to be more involved with patients, and to initiate more interaction with patients, while state hospital aides would be narrower and more aloof and more controlling. Conference members generally ascribed more authoritarianism to aides than was actually observed in either hospital. For example, reaction k (COMPELS TO STOP OR TO DO IT) was consistently assigned much higher probabilities than we observed. Psychiatrists, psychologists, and social workers, particularly, predicted inaccurately for the aides in the state hospital. But even supervisors from large state institutions tended to believe that private hospital aides were more involved with patients than were their own personnel. The conference members were then surprised at the findings I reported, muttering, "How strange" or "I don't understand it."

How can this discrepancy between the findings of a carefully designed survey and the testimony of experienced hospital personnel be explained? One possible reason is that my sample is not representative. It yielded, after all, information about only two hospitals. Need it apply to the conduct of psychiatric aides elsewhere? My knowledge of mental hospitals as well as experience in supervising students in such settings leads me to believe that these two hospitals are fairly representative of their classes of institutions in the United States. Perhaps this is a slanted exposure. The settings are a sample of institutions that were accessible to me. But the truth of the discrepancy was clinched by mistaken expectations on the part of supervisors from the very two hospitals we surveyed. For example, one nurse refused to accept my report and cited her own personal experience at a small private psychiatric institution as contrary to my findings. When she mentioned the institution's name, it turned out to be the private hospital represented in this study. On that occasion, as on all others, I did not identify the place. She remained unaware of it and persisted in declaring that the aides at her hospital acted in other ways. There is obviously a difference between what can be learned from experience when one is personally involved and what can be made known by creating a systematic ethnography based on a probability sampling design.

The discrepancy is also based on confusion between what people are supposed to do and what they actually do. Much of how people act is caused by an interplay of contemporary forces where each individual meets his social environment. The factors coming together there form a complex cause. It is harder to unravel than the simpler and more abstract values and opinions with which people are said to be imbued. Knowledge of value systems is not prophetic of actual conduct. Nor can one learn impartially about the connection between values and behavior unless he avoids presuming the extent of their congruence. A program of behavior research should distinguish between people's values and their actions, and the latter should be measured separately. We serve the question of the impact of norms and values and attitudes on conduct by providing independent evidence for actions.

The most telling experience that made me apprehensive about dwelling on norms and on role expectations was that I was startled by my findings. I worked to separate my predilections from my measurements so that the latter could be fair. Whatever separation was achieved still left me cognizant of the literature about mental hospitals. My wonderment gave way to private embarrassment as I realized how much I was conditioned by knowing the settings, what was expected of aides, and popular lore.

After such moments, when I ask myself where next to turn, the appeal of further surveys of behavior is strong. The lessons to be gotten from such study are far from exhausted. The habit of mind that keeps one impartially on the lookout for insights leads halfway to them. A descriptive venture is also justified by the impetus for public planning and application of social science. Theories are as useful as their fitness to how people act. Inaccurate descriptions undermine comprehension of social problems. Poor comprehension leads to misguided recommendations and monstrous policies. Sound descriptions themselves often point to solutions. That being so, I favor continuing the census of interpersonal acts. It would enlarge the store of information.

The first step in such a program could be fact-finding research on other repertoires. Researchers in different organizational, geographic, and national settings might cooperate to establish a pool of classified acts. Though it would entail massive and painstaking work, the findings for even a few more repertoires could help us deal with issues treated sparingly here. We would discover some repertoires in different settings that are more alike than believed. We would find more differences among populations of acts for the same repertoire than we now discern. There will be some eye-openers. When we finally study top managers without deciding in advance what is important, we will be surprised. So will the managers. More fascination will come from studies of child-rearing practices, of friends, perhaps even of turnpike tollbooth attendants. Actions speak louder than rules.

References

⟨⟨☙⟩⟩

[Bracketed dates following titles are original publication dates.
Page numbers in *italics* tell where reference is cited in this book.]

Abrahamson, Mark. "Some Comments on Awareness." *American Sociological Review* 30 (1965): 779–80. p. 779—*16*.

Allport, Floyd. *Theories of Perception and the Concept of Structure*. New York: Wiley, 1955. pp. 566–67—*288*.

Asch, Solomon E. *Social Psychology*. Englewood Cliffs, New Jersey: Prentice-Hall, 1952.—*6*.

Bales, Robert F., and Strodtbeck, Fred. "Phases in Group Problem-Solving." *Journal of Abnormal and Social Psychology* 46 (1951): 485–95—*221*.

Barker, Roger G. "The Stream of Behavior as an Empirical Problem." In *The Stream of Behavior*. Edited by R. Barker. New York: Appleton-Century-Crofts, 1963. pp. 1–22. p. 10—*105*.

Barker, Roger G., and Wright, Herbert F. *Midwest and Its Children*. New York: Harper and Row, 1955. pp. 14—*8-9;* 301—*55-56;* 214, 290–91—*97;* 397—*147*.

Bartlett, Frederick C. "Social Factors in Recall." In *Readings in Social Psychology*. Edited by T. M. Newcomb and E. L. Hartley, 1st ed. New York: Holt, Rinehart, and Winston, 1947. pp. 69–76—*84*.

Beers, Clifford. *A Mind That Found Itself*. [1908] New York: Doubleday, 1948. pp. 161–65—*92*.

Bell, Daniel. *The End of Ideology*. New York: Free Press, 1960. pp. 235–36 —*57*.

Bertalanffy, Ludwig von. *Problems of Life*. [1952] New York: Harper and Row (Torchbook #521), 1960. pp. 126–27—*281-82*.

Bexton, W. H.; Heron, W.; and Scott, T. H. "Effects of Decreased Variation in the Sensory Environment." *Canadian Journal of Psychology* 8 (1954): 70–76—*25*.

Birdwhistell, Ray L. *Introduction to Kinesics.* Louisville: University of Louisville Press, 1952.—*238.*

Birdwhistell, Ray L. "Kinesics Analysis in the Investigation of the Emotions." Paper presented at meeting of American Association for the Advancement of Science, 29–30 December 1960, New York.—*238.*

Blau, Peter M. *Exchange and Power in Social Life.* New York: Wiley, 1964. p. 13—*279.*

Borgatta, Edgar F., and Bales, Robert F. "Interaction of Individuals in Reconstituted Groups." *Sociometry* 16 (1953): 302–20. pp. 315—*221;* 309–10 —*259.*

Broadbent, D. E. "Information Processing in the Nervous System." *Science* 150 (October 22, 1965): 457–62. p. 458—*27.*

Byrd, Richard E. *Alone.* New York: Putnam, 1938.—*25; 38.*

Chase, R. A. et al. "Comparison of the Effect of Delayed Auditory Feedback on Speech and Key Tapping." *Science* 129 (April 3, 1959): 903–04—*40.*

Chomsky, Noam. *Language and Mind.* New York: Harcourt Brace and World, 1968. pp. 81—*48;* 11, 6—*49; 57.*

Claparède, E. "Expériences collectives sur le témoignage." [1906] Cited in *Historical Introduction to Modern Psychology.* Gardner Murphy. rev. ed. New York: Harcourt Brace, 1949. p. 245—*150.*

Collier, John. "Photography in Anthropology." *American Anthropologist* 59 (1957): 843–59—*117.*

Cooley, Charles H. *Human Nature and the Social Order.* [1902] New York: Schocken, 1964. p. 63—*288.*

Cottrell, Leonard S. "The Analysis of Situational Fields in Social Psychology." *American Sociological Review* 7 (1942): 370–82. p. 281—*185.*

Coutu, Walter. *Emergent Human Nature.* New York: Knopf, 1949. p. 13—*185.*

Croog, Sydney. "Interpersonal Relations in Medical Settings." In *Handbook of Medical Sociology.* Edited by H. Freeman, S. Levine, and G. Reader. Englewood Cliffs, New Jersey: Prentice-Hall, 1963. pp. 241–66; pp. 246–47 —*284–85.*

Darwin, Charles. *The Expression of the Emotions in Man and Animals.* [1872] New York: Philosophical Library, 1955. pp. 222, 228—*6.*

Darwin, Charles. *Origin of Species.* [1859] New York: Modern Library, 1936. —*4;* pp. 44–45—*106.*

Descartes, René, *Discourse on the Method of Rightly Conducting the Reason* [1637] pp. 51—*47;* 59–60, 77—*50, 51. Meditations on First Philosophy* [1641] pp. 98, 78—*47. Objections Against the Meditations and Replies* [1641] pp. 231, 115, 136—*47;* 209—*48.* All found in Great Books of the Western World. Vol. 31. Chicago: Encyclopedia Britannica, 1952.

Dewey, John. *Logic: The Theory of Inquiry.* [1938] New York: Holt, Rinehart, and Winston, 1966. p. 49—*194.*

Doyle, Arthur Conan. "Silver Blaze." In *Memoirs of Sherlock Holmes.* Reprinted in *The Complete Sherlock Holmes.* Vol. 1. Garden City, New York: Doubleday, 1930.—*200.*

Durkheim, Emile. *The Division of Labor in Society.* [1893] Translated by G. Simpson. New York: Macmillan, 1933. pp. 257, 267, 269, 262—*265; 275.*

Efron, David, and Foley, John P., Jr. "Gestural Behavior and Social Setting." [1937] In *Readings in Social Psychology.* Edited by T. M. Newcomb and E. L. Hartley. 1st ed. New York. Holt, Rinehart, and Winston, 1947. pp. 33–40—*20.*

Exline, R. V. "Explorations in the Process of Person Perception: Visual Interaction in Relation to Competition, Sex, and Need for Affiliation." *Journal of Personality* 31 (1963): 1–20—*239.*

Exline, R. V.; Gray, D.; and Schuette, D. "Visual Behavior in a Dyad as Affected by Interview Content and Sex of Respondent." *Journal of Personality and Social Psychology* 1 (1965): 201–09—*239.*

Festinger, Leon; Schachter, Stanley; and Back, Kurt. *Social Pressures in Informal Groups.* New York: Harper, 1950.—*20.*

First, Ruth. *117 Days.* New York: Stein and Day, 1965. pp. 70–71—*25.*

Freeman, G. L. *The Energetics of Human Behavior.* Ithaca, New York: Cornell University Press, 1948—*43.*

Freud, Sigmund. *Beyond the Pleasure Principle.* London: International Psycho-Analytical Press, 1922. p. 33—*46–47.*

Freud, Sigmund. *Inhibitions, Symptoms, and Anxiety.* [1926] Translated by A. Strachey. London: Hogarth, 1936. Ch. IX—*288.*

Goffman, Erving. *Encounters: Two Studies in the Sociology of Interaction.* Indianapolis: Bobbs-Merrill, 1961. pp. 79–81—*110–11.*

Goffman, Erving. *Stigma.* Englewood Cliffs, New Jersey: Prentice-Hall, 1963. p. 83—*4.*

Greenberg, Joseph H. "Language Universals: A Research Frontier." *Science* 166 (October 24, 1969): 473–78. p. 474—*302.*

Hall, Edward T. *The Hidden Dimension.* New York: Doubleday, 1966. pp. 40, 107—*238.*

Hall, Edward T. *The Silent Language.* [1959] New York: Fawcett [Premier #d117), 1961. pp. 149—*238; 164—238.*

Hall, Edward T. "A System for the Notation of Proxemic Behavior." *American Anthropologist* 65 (October 1963): pp. 1003–24—*238.*

Hardin, Garrett. "The Cybernetics of Competition: A Biologist's View of Society." [1963] In *Modern Systems Research for the Behavioral Scientist.* Edited by W. Buckley. Chicago: Aldine, 1968. pp. 449–59. p. 456—*252.*

Hartley, Eugene L. "Communication." In *A Dictionary of the Social Sciences.* Edited by J. Gould and W. L. Kolb. New York: Free Press, 1964. pp. 111–13. p. 112—*77.*

Hebb, D. O. "The Mammal and His Environment." In *Readings In Social Psychology.* Edited by E. Macoby et al. New York: Holt, Rinehart, and Winston, 1958. pp. 335–41. pp. 338–39—*48.*

Heisenberg, Werner. "The Uncertainty Principle." In *The World of Mathematics.* Edited by J. R. Newman, vol. 2. New York: Simon and Schuster, 1956. pp. 1051–55—*146.*

Herman, Robert, and Gardels, Keith. "Vehicular Traffic Flow." *Scientific American* 209 (December 1963): pp. 35–43. p. 42—*259*.

Heron, Woodburn. "Cognitive and Physiological Effects of Perceptual Isolation." In *Sensory Deprivation*. Edited by P. Solomon et al. Cambridge, Mass.: Harvard University Press, 1961. pp. 6–33. pp. 16—*26;* 13, 15—*49*.

Hockett, Charles F., and Ascher, Robert. "The Human Revolution." *Current Anthropology* 5 (1964): 135–47, 166–68. p. 137—*294*.

Hollingshead, A. B., and Redlich, F. C. *Social Class and Mental Illness*. New York: Wiley, 1958. p. 61—*244*.

Homans, George C. *Social Behavior: Its Elementary Forms*. New York: Harcourt Brace, 1961. p. 380—*279*.

Hughes, Everett C. *Men and Their Work*. New York: Free Press, 1958. p. 74 —*264*.

Huizinga, Johan. *Homo Ludens*. [1950] Boston: Beacon Press, 1955. p. 10 —*193*.

Hume, David. *An Enquiry Concerning Human Understanding*. [1748] In *The English Philosophers From Bacon to Mill*. Edited by E. A. Burtt. New York: Modern Library, 1939. pp. 585–689. p. 635—*299*.

Hutchinson, Ann. *Labanotation: The System for Recording Movement*. New York: New Directions. (P–106), 1954.—*238*.

Jacobson, Edmund. *Progressive Relaxation*. 2d ed. Chicago: University of Chicago Press, 1938. pp. 186–88. Cited in *Human Behavior*. Edited by B. Berelson and G. A. Steiner. New York: Harcourt Brace and World, 1964. pp. 169, 171—*43*.

Keller, Helen. *The Story of My Life*. [1902] New York: Dell, 1961. (Letter from Miss Sullivan, June 2, 1887—*38*.)

Langer, Susanne K. *Philosophy in a New Key*. [1942] New York: New American Library, 1948. p. 56—*71*.

Leacock, Stephen. "The Retroactive Existence of Mr. Juggins." In *Laugh With Leacock*. New York: Pocket Books, 1947. pp. 237–41. pp. 237—*1;* 241—*1*.

LeBon, Gustave. *The Crowd*. London: Unwin, 1896. pp. 36—*28;* 29—*53*.

Lee, Bernard S. "Artificial Stutter." *Journal of Speech and Hearing Disorders* 16 (March 1951): 53–55—*39*.

Lippitt, Ronald, and White, Ralph K. "An Experimental Study of Leadership and Group Life." In *Readings in Social Psychology*. Edited by E. Maccoby et al., 3d ed. New York: Holt, Rinehart, and Winston, 1958. pp. 496–511. p. 504—*265–66*.

Lowie, Robert. *Primitive Society*. [1920] New York: Harper and Row [Torchbook #TB–1056], 1961. Ch. 5—*20*.

Maine, Harold. *If A Man Be Mad*. New York: Doubleday, 1947. p. 267—*92*.

Matarazzo, J. D. et al. "Interviewer Influence on Duration of Interviewee Speech." *Journal of Verbal Learning and Verbal Behavior* 1 (1963): 451–58—*255*.

Matarazzo, Joseph D. et al. "Speech Durations of Astronaut and Ground Communicator." *Science* 143 (1964): 148–50—*255*.

Maurer, David W. *Whiz Mob: A Correlation of the Technical Argot of Pickpockets With Their Behavior Pattern.* New Haven, Conn.: College and University Press, 1964. pp. 58–75—*117.*

Mayo, Elton. *Human Problems of An Industrial Civilization.* [1933] New York: Viking [Compass #C67], 1960.—*57.*

Mead, George Herbert. "A Behavioristic Account of the Significant Symbol." *Journal of Philosophy* 19 (1922): 157–63. pp. 160–61—*207.*

Mead, George Herbert. *Mind, Self and Society.* Chicago: University of Chicago Press, 1934. pp. 67, 147, 172—*42;* 154—*62;* 71, 78—*72;* 80–81—*76;* 229—*279.*

Melbin, Murray. "The Action-Interaction Chart as a Research Tool." *Human Organization* 12 (1953): pp. 34–35—*117.*

Melbin, Murray. "Behavior Rhythms in Mental Hospitals." *American Journal of Sociology* 74 (May 1969): 650–65—*275.*

Merton, Robert K. *Social Theory and Social Structure.* 2d ed. New York: Free Press, 1957. p. 343—*23–24.*

Milgram, Stanley. "Some Conditions of Obedience and Disobedience to Authority." *Human Relations* 18 (1965): 57–75—*21–23;* p. 66—*23.*

Mommsen, Theodor. "Rectorial Address." [1874] In *The Varieties of History.* Edited by F. Stern. New York: World Publishing [Meridian #M37], 1956. pp. 192–96. p. 193—*81.*

Nagel, Ernest. *The Structure of Science.* New York: Harcourt Brace, 1961. pp. 552–54—*81–82.*

Peirce, Charles Sanders. "How to Make Our Ideas Clear." [1878] In *Philosophical Writings of Peirce.* Edited by J. Buchler. New York: Dover, 1955. pp. 23–41. pp. 30–31—*119–20.*

Plutarch. *The Lives of the Noble Grecians and Romans.* Translated by Dryden. New York: Modern Library. n.d. pp. 525–76—*82.*

Psathas, George. "Ethnomethods and Phenomenology." *Social Research* 35 (Autumn 1968): 500–20. p. 511–*302.*

Ray, Michael L., and Webb, Eugene J. "Speech Duration Effects in the Kennedy News Conferences." *Science* 153 (1966): 899–901—*255.*

Report of the National Advisory Commission on Civil Disorders. Otto Kerner, chairman. New York: Bantam Books, 1968. pp. 81, 88, 123—*31;* 66, 335, 372—*32;* 99–100—*32.*

Rock, Irwin, and Harris, Charles S. "Vision and Touch." *Scientific American* 216 (May 1967): 96–104—*27.*

Rosenthal, Robert. *Experimenter Effects in Psychological Research.* New York: Appleton-Century-Crofts, 1966.—*146.*

Rosenthal, Robert. "Covert Communication in the Psychological Experiment." *Psychological Bulletin* 67 (1967): 356–67. p. 359—*238–39.*

Rosenthal, Robert, and Jacobson, Lenore. "Self-Fulfilling Prophecies in the Classroom: Teachers' Expectations as Unintended Determinants of Pupil's Intellectual Competence." Paper presented at the meeting of the American Psychological Association, 4 September 1967, Washington, D.C.—*248.*

Rubin, Zick. "The Measurement of Romantic Love." Report based on "The Social Psychology of Romantic Love." Unpublished Ph.D. thesis, University of Michigan, 1969. pp. 11–12—*239*.

Russell, Bertrand. *Introduction to Mathematical Philosophy.* London: Unwin, 1919. p. 14—*120*.

Sapir, Edward A. *Language: An Introduction to the Study of Speech.* New York: Harcourt Brace, 1921. p. 20—*114*.

Shannon, Claude E., and Weaver, Warren. *The Mathematical Theory of Communication.* Urbana, Ill.: University of Illinois Press, 1949.—*179*.

Simmel, Georg. "The Number of Members as Determining the Sociological Form of the Group. I." *American Journal of Sociology* 8 (July 1902): 1–46. p. 45—*259–60*.

Simmel, Georg. *The Sociology of Georg Simmel.* Edited by K. Wolff. New York: Free Press, 1950. pp. 35, 227–28—*29;* 400—*74;* 9—*186;* 10, 40—*279*.

Smith, William M.; McCrary, John W.; and Smith, Karl U. "Delayed Visual Feedback and Behavior." *Science* 132 (October 14, 1960): 1013–14—*40*.

Strauss, Anselm et al. Cited in Buckley, Walter. "Society as a Complex Adaptive System." In *Modern Systems Research for the Behavioral Scientist.* Edited by W. Buckley. Chicago: Aldine, 1968. pp. 490–511. p. 504–505 —*265, 275*.

Taylor, Frederick W. *Principles of Scientific Management.* New York: Harper, 1911.—*56–57*.

Tiryakian, Edward A. "Typologies." In *International Encyclopedia of the Social Sciences,* Edited by D. Sills et al., vol. 16. New York: Macmillan and Free Press; 1968. pp. 177–85. p. 178—*137*.

Vogel, Ezra. *Japan's New Middle Class.* Berkeley, California: University of California Press, 1963. pp. 138–39, 197—*238*.

Watson, John B. *Behaviorism.* rev. ed. Chicago: University of Chicago Press [Phoenix #P23], 1930. pp. 225, 238–40—*288*.

Weber, Max. *The Theory of Social and Economic Organization.* Translated by A. M. Henderson and T. Parsons. Edited by T. Parsons. New York: Free Press, 1947. pp. 10—*137–38;* 331—*283*.

Whitehead, Alfred North. *Adventures of Ideas.* New York: Macmillan, 1933. p. 279—*33*.

Wiener, Norbert. *Cybernetics.* 2d ed. Cambridge, Mass.: M.I.T. Press, 1961. pp. 164, 163—*147*.

Wynne-Edwards, V. C. "Self-Regulating Systems in Populations of Animals." *Science* 147 (March 26, 1965): 1543–48. p. 1545—*279*.

Index